בס״ד

IN THE PATHS OF OUR FATHERS

INSIGHTS INTO *PIRKEI AVOS,* ADAPTED FROM THE WORKS OF THE LUBAVITCHER REBBE, RABBI MENACHEM M. SCHNEERSON שליט״א

By: Rabbi Eliyahu Touger

Published by:
Kehot Publication Society
770 Eastern Parkway
Brooklyn, New York 11213

5754 • 1994

IN THE PATH OF OUR FATHERS

Published and Copyrighted © by
KEHOT PUBLICATION SOCIETY
770 Eastern Parkway • Brooklyn, N.Y. 11213
Tel. (718) 774-4000 • (718) 778-5436 • (718) 778-0226

ISBN 0-8266-0535-4

5754 • 1994

TABLE OF CONTENTS

PUBLISHER'S FOREWORD

Pirkei Avos has always been treasured for its unique insights, which enhance our relationships with our fellowmen and with G-d. These insights acquire special flavor when seasoned with the teachings of *Chassidus*. For *Chassidus* adds a depth that enables us to penetrate to the core of these relationships.

The teachings included in this volume were collected from the works of the Rebbe *Shlita*. Each week at summer *farbrengens*, the Rebbe would devote some time to the chapter of *Pirkei Avos* being studied that week. After *Shabbos*, these insights were written down by a select group of scholars and circulated for in-house study. On certain occasions, the thoughts were further developed and, after being edited by the Rebbe *Shlita*, published in *Likkutei Sichos*, or in *Sefer HaSichos* 5748-5751. Moreover, the Rebbe often refers to *Pirkei Avos* in his other works, and several passages were taken from these. A large portion of these thoughts were published in Hebrew under the title, *Biurim LePirkei Avos*.[1]

It must be emphasized that this is not a comprehensive treatment of *Pirkei Avos*. There are many clauses of the *mishnayos* on which we were not able to find comments from the Rebbe, and others on which his remarks deal with non-literal interpretations, without focusing on the simple explanation. Moreover, there are many comments on *Pirkei Avos* by the Rebbe which we felt require a thorough familiarity with the language and style of *Talmudic* and *Kabbalistic* writings, and do not lend themselves to translation into English. But indeed, a comprehensive work on *Pirkei Avos* would fill several volumes. Our intent was to present a sampler of the Rebbe's unique

---

1. Kehot, N.Y., 5742, revised edition, 5750.

approach which would help readers as they dedicate themselves to the lifetime task of studying and applying *Pirkei Avos*.

When considering a presentation of these ideas in English,
the decision was made to adapt the Rebbe's talks rather than to
translate them literally. This involved omitting some points,
telescoping others, and at other times adding explanations from
different sources in order to bring the ideas involved closer to
our readers.

As the work began to take shape, we realized that we had
explanations for most, but not all, of the *mishnayos* in the tractate. To allow for a more complete work, we took the added
liberty of borrowing ideas which the Rebbe had related else-
where in regard to the general subjects mentioned in the *mishnayos*, but not in direct reference to the teachings of *Pirkei Avos*
themselves. In these instances, the connection to the *mishnayos*
in *Pirkei Avos* was made in the process of the adaptation. To
distinguish these comments, they have been marked with a
star.

In this context, the work contains several oft-repeated concepts which command attention. Among them:

a) that the teachings of *Pirkei Avos* are *mili dechassidusa*[2] —
guidelines for pious conduct beyond the measure of the law.
Every person who desires to live a Torah life commits himself
to the Law; a pious person commits himself to the *Law-Giver*.
His concern is not merely with the discharge of his own duty,
but with satisfying G-d's desire.

This is the thrust of *Pirkei Avos*. Even when the teachings
appear to be straightforward laws or points of fact, they contain
an inner meaning intended to propel us toward the all-encompassing commitment of piety.

b) the connection of the teachings to the divine service of
their authors. On the phrase from the *Haggadah*, *Chacham mahu
omar* (lit. "The wise son, what does he say?"), the Previous

---

2.   See *Bava Kama* 30a. See also the beginnings of the commentaries of R. Ovadiah
    of Bartenura and *Midrash Shmuel* to *Pirkei Avos*.

Rebbe offered a non-literal interpretation: "the wise son, what he is, he says." Similarly, with regard to the teachings of *Pirkei Avos*, each teaching reflects the nature of its author.[3]

c) that each *mishnah* has several different levels of interpretation. Our Sages[4] speak of the "seventy facets of Torah," and our Rabbis add[5] that every Jew has his own "letter in the Torah," i.e., a way of appreciating the Torah which reflects his unique spiritual potential. In this light, we must consider every teaching of the Torah — and particularly the teachings of *Avos* — as multi-dimensional.

* * *

Our Rabbis ordained[6] that *Pirkei Avos* be studied on the *Shabbasos* between Pesach and Shavuos in preparation for the giving of the Torah. For this reason, in addition to the *Mishnayic* tractate of *Avos*, which includes five chapters, a sixth chapter — a collection of *bereisos*[7] — was appended so that a chapter of *Avos* could be studied on each of the six *Shabbasos* between these two holidays.[8] One of the explanations for this custom is based on the adage,[9] *"Derech Eretz* (ethical conduct) takes precedence over the Torah." Before reliving our acceptance of the Torah on the holiday of Shavuos, we renew our commitment to its ethical standards through the study of *Pirkei Avos.*

In his text of the *Siddur*, the Alter Rebbe writes that there are those who study *Pirkei Avos* on all the *Shabbasos* throughout

3 .   See *Yoma* 83b, which states that "Rabbi Meir would derive lessons from names." Similarly, in this context, the author's name and more particularly, his approach to Divine service sheds light on his teachings. (See *Igros Kodesh* of the Rebbe *Shlita*, Vol. I, p. 288ff.)

4 .   *Bamidbar Rabbah* 13:16; *Zohar,* 47b.

5 .   *Megaleh Amukos*, sec. 186, based on *Zohar Chadash, Rus* 88d. See also *Sefer HaMaamarim 5689*, p. 69.

6 .   See the introduction to *Midrash Shmuel.*

7 .   This chapter, called *Kinyan Torah* ("On the Acquisition of the Torah"), is particularly appropriate for study on the *Shabbos* before Shavuos, because it is devoted entirely to praise of the Torah and its study.

8 .   See *Midrash Shmuel*, 6:1.

9 .   *Vayikra Rabbah* 9:13.

the summer. This is the present Lubavitch custom.[10] Among
the reasons given[11] is that during the summer, more attention
is paid to physical recreation and relaxation. To insure that the
"strengthening of the body" does not lead to a "weakening of
the soul,"[12] attention is directed to the eternally relevant truths
of *Avos*, which nurture balance and harmony between the
physical and the spiritual.

* * *

Pirkei Avos also encourages balance and harmony between
people. This principle found expression, not only in the content of this work, but in its very composition. Each contributor
brought a different perspective, and the patience and forbearance to consider that of his colleagues. Among those who
efforts contributed to this synthesis were: Rabbi Eliyahu
Touger, who adapted the texts from their Hebrew and Yiddish
originals; Gershom Gale, who edited the book; Rabbi Aharon
Leib Raskin who supplied many of the references, Yosef
Yitzchok Turner, who is responsible for the tasteful layout and
typography; and Rabbi Yonah Avtzon, Director of Sichos In
English, whose initiative fueled this project and encouraged it
at every phase.

And thankful acknowledgment must be made to Rabbi
Nissan Mangel, whose translation of *Pirkei Avos* in *Siddur Tehillat HaShem* served as the basis for our translation.

* * *

Our Sages state:[13] "A person who desires to be pious should
observe the teachings of *Nezikin* ('damages'), *Avos*, and *Berachos*

---

10. *Sichos Shabbos Parshas Mattos-Maasei*, 5747. On summer *Shabbasos* after the
    Minchah service, the Rebbe *Shlita* would regularly study *Pirkei Avos*, reading the
    chapter of the week together with the congregation. During the *Shabbos
    farbrengen*, he would explain one or more *mishnayos* from the chapter studied that
    week.
11. See the introduction of the *Midrash Shmuel* to *Pirkei Avos*.
12. See *Zohar* I, 180b, 140b.
13. *Bava Kama* 30a.

('blessings').'' This implies that the study of *Avos* shields us from damages, repairs them, and arouses Divine blessing.[14]

May the study of the Rebbe *Shlita's* insights into *Pirkei Avos* arouse blessings which will restore his health, and enable him to lead our people to *Eretz Yisrael* in the most immediate future.

The publication of this volume comes in connection with the Rebbe *Shlita's* 92nd birthday, *Yud-Alef* Nissan, 5754. The Baal Shem Tov taught[15] that every day, a person should recite the psalm in the Book of *Tehillim* that corresponds to the years of his life.

The Rebbe's 92nd birthday thus reflects the transition from psalm 92 to psalm 93. May he merit the blessings mentioned in the conclusion of psalm 92: "The righteous will flourish like a palm tree.... They shall blossom in the courtyards of our G-d. They shall be fruitful even in old age; they shall be full of sap and freshness." And may he lead our people and the world at large to the perfect state alluded to in the beginning of psalm 93: "G-d is King; He has garbed Himself with grandeur," i.e., the Era of the Redemption when G-d's Kingship will be revealed throughout all existence.

Sichos In English

11 Nissan, 5754 [March 23, 1994]
The 92nd Birthday of the Rebbe Shlita
לאורך ימים ושנים טובות

---

14 . *Sichos Shabbos Parshas Pinchas, 5745.*
15 . *Igros Kodesh* of the Rebbe Rayatz, Vol. I, p. 31, Vol. X, p. 53; *Sefer HaMaamarim* 5721, p. 231 and sources cited there.

כָּל יִשְׂרָאֵל יֵשׁ לָהֶם חֵלֶק לְעוֹלָם הַבָּא, שֶׁנֶּאֱמַר וְעַמֵּךְ כֻּלָּם צַדִּיקִים,
לְעוֹלָם יִירְשׁוּ אָרֶץ, נֵצֶר מַטָּעַי מַעֲשֵׂה יָדַי לְהִתְפָּאֵר:

ALL ISRAEL HAVE A SHARE IN THE WORLD TO COME, AS IT IS STATED:[1] "AND YOUR PEOPLE ARE ALL RIGHTEOUS; THEY SHALL INHERIT THE LAND FOREVER. [THEY ARE] THE BRANCH OF MY PLANTING, THE WORK OF MY HANDS IN WHICH TO TAKE PRIDE."[2]

ALL ISRAEL HAVE A SHARE IN THE WORLD TO COME — Within the Talmudic writings, there are two interpretations of the phrase "the World to Come":

a) *Gan Eden* — the spiritual realm of souls, the afterlife;

b) The Era of the Resurrection.

In this *mishnah*, the term obviously refers to the Era of the Resurrection,[3] for in its source,[2] the *mishnah* continues: "And these individuals do not have a portion in the World to Come. He who denies that the concept of the resurrection has a source in the Torah...."

Our Sages explain:[4] "He denied the resurrection of the dead; he therefore will not have a share in this resurrection — measure for measure."[5]

---

1. *Yeshayahu* 60:21.
2. *Sanhedrin* 10:1.
3. R. Ovadiah of Bartenura (and others) on *Sanhedrin, ibid., Midrash Shmuel,* beginning of *Pirkei Avos.*
4. *Sanhedrin, ibid.,* (90a).
5. See *Igros Kodesh* of the Rebbe *Shlita,* Vol. I, p. 148ff, which explains that the *mishnah's* statement that these individuals will not receive a portion in the World to Come refers only to their bodies; they will not be resurrected. Their souls,

Moreover, our Rabbis explain[6] that, with regard to this *mishnah*, no other interpretation is appropriate. Entry to *Gan Eden* — the spiritual world of the souls — is restricted, as it is written:[7] "Who may ascend the mount of the Lord? He who has clean hands and a pure heart."

For a person's position in the afterlife is a direct result of his conduct in this world; one who has not refined himself will not be found worthy of a portion in the afterlife.

Although the revelations of the Era of the Resurrection will be vastly superior to those of the afterlife, every Jew will receive a portion.

Why? Because the Jews are...

THE BRANCH OF MY PLANTING, THE WORK OF MY HANDS — Every Jew's soul is an actual part of G-d.[8] Therefore, in the Era of the Resurrection when the essential G-dliness that pervades every dimension of our existence will be revealed, this holiness — the fundamental vitality present in every Jew — will emerge.

The prooftext uses material entities — "the branch," "the work" — as analogies to highlight the fact that the Resurrection — the return of the body to this material plane — represents the ultimate reward.[9] For our material world will then be G-d's dwelling.[10] Just as a person reveals the innermost dimensions of his personality only in his own home, so too the essence of G-dliness — those dimensions of His Being that

---

however, will be resurrected and live in another body, for every soul is "an actual part of G-d" *(Tanya,* ch. 2), or to refer to the wording of this *mishnah,* "the branch of My planting, the work of My hands."

6 . See the discourse *Ki Yishalcha (Sefer HaMaamarim 5700* end of p. 44ff). See also *Chagigah* 15b which states that were it not for the prayers of R. Meir, Achar would not have entered *Gan Eden* (i.e., even the lower level of *Gan Eden*).

7 . *Tehillim* 24:3-4.

8 . *Tanya,* ch. 2.

9 . See *Ramban,* conclusion of *Shaar HaGemul, Likkutei Torah, Tzav* 15c.

10 . *Midrash Tanchuma, Parshas Bechukosai,* sec. 3; see *Tanya,* chs. 33 and 36.

transcend even spiritual existence — will be revealed in our material world.

(Maamar, Kol Yisrael Yesh La'hem Cheilek L'olam Habah, 5733;
Likkutei Sichos, Vol. XVII, p. 343ff.)

IN WHICH TO TAKE PRIDE — Since every Jew's soul is an actual part of G-d, each and every Jew — man, woman, and child — praises G-d by virtue of his very existence.[11] "Even the sinners of Israel are filled with *mitzvos* as a pomegranate is filled with seeds."[12]

This teaching serves as an introduction to each chapter of *Pirkei Avos* because *Pirkei Avos* focuses on ethical development and personal refinement. When one becomes aware of the essential G-dly core of every individual, one appreciates: a) the necessity to refine oneself so that this essential quality can be expressed, and b) that every individual, regardless of his present level of development, has the potential to achieve such refinement.[13]

(Sichos Shabbos Parshas Vayikra, 5750)

---

11 . See *Sichos Shabbos Mevorchim Nissan,* 5750.

12 . The conclusion of the Tractate of *Chagigah.*

13 . One of the reasons *Pirkei Avos* is studied is to prepare us to relive the experience of the giving of the Torah on the holiday of Shavuos. *Ahavas Yisrael* was a necessary prerequisite for the giving of the Torah, as *Rashi* comments on the verse *(Shmos* 19:2): "And Israel camped before the mountain," "as one man, with one heart." Similarly, every year, we must prepare for the giving of the Torah with an emphasis on *Ahavas Yisrael.* (See *Likkutei Sichos,* Vol. I, p. 262.)

CHAPTER ONE

CHAPTER ONE

א מֹשֶׁה קִבֵּל תּוֹרָה מִסִּינַי וּמְסָרָהּ לִיהוֹשֻׁעַ, וִיהוֹשֻׁעַ לִזְקֵנִים, וּזְקֵנִים
לִנְבִיאִים, וּנְבִיאִים מְסָרוּהָ לְאַנְשֵׁי כְנֶסֶת הַגְּדוֹלָה. הֵם אָמְרוּ שְׁלֹשָׁה
דְבָרִים: הֱווּ מְתוּנִים בַּדִּין, וְהַעֲמִידוּ תַלְמִידִים הַרְבֵּה, וַעֲשׂוּ סְיָג
לַתּוֹרָה.

1. MOSHE RECEIVED THE TORAH FROM SINAI AND PASSED IT ON TO YEHOSHUA; YEHOSHUA [PASSED IT ON] TO THE ELDERS; THE ELDERS TO THE PROPHETS; THE PROPHETS PASSED IT ON TO THE MEN OF THE GREAT ASSEMBLY.

THEY [THE MEN OF THE GREAT ASSEMBLY] MADE THREE STATEMENTS: "BE DELIBERATE IN JUDGMENT; RAISE UP MANY STUDENTS; AND MAKE A FENCE AROUND THE TORAH."

MOSHE RECEIVED THE TORAH FROM SINAI — Why does the *Mishnah* describe the chain of tradition only in *Pirkei Avos?* Would it not have been proper to do so earlier, at the very beginning of the *Mishnah?*

It can be explained that in the previous tractates there was no need to mention the chain of tradition. Those tractates deal with ritual obligations, which are obviously Divine in origin. *Pirkei Avos,* on the other hand, deals with ethics. It is extremely important to emphasize that the source of these teachings is also Divine revelation, and not mere human wisdom.[1]

---

1. See the commentary of R. Ovadiah of Bartenura.

RECEIVED — In regard to many matters, e.g., the holiday of Shavuos, emphasis is placed on the *giving* of the Torah. In regard to ethics, it is the *receiving* of the Torah — how the Torah is internalized in one's being — which is highlighted. For in this realm it is not abstract knowledge which is important, but rather how the Torah is applied in life.

(Sichos Yud Shvat, 5739)

FROM SINAI — Why does the *mishnah* state "from Sinai," instead of "from G-d"? Saying "Sinai" underscores two important character traits. On the one hand, Sinai is a mountain, reminding us to stand tall in the face of any and all challenges. Nevertheless, Mount Sinai is "lower than all the mountains,"[2] emphasizing that this pride must be tempered by humility.[3]

(Sichos Shabbos Parshas Shemini, 5731)

AND PASSED IT ON — Moshe realized that he was merely a steward of the knowledge he had been given, and therefore endeavored to share it with Yehoshua and, through him, with the entire Jewish people. Each of us must emulate Moshe's example and share the wisdom we have learned with others.

(Sichos Shabbos Parshas Naso, 5738)

MOSHE... YEHOSHUA... THE ELDERS... THE PROPHETS... THE MEN OF THE GREAT ASSEMBLY — If the *mishnah's* purpose was merely to describe the chain of tradition, a more detailed list would have been appropriate.[4] By mentioning only these five individuals or groups, the *mishnah* alludes to five traits that are essential in developing a relationship with the Torah.

---

2 . *Midrash Tehillim* 68:17.

3 . See the explanation of this concept in the essay entitled "The Revelation at Mt. Sinai," *Timeless Patterns in Time*, Vol. II, p. 109 (Kehot, N.Y., 5754).

4 . See the *Rambam's* Introduction to the *Mishneh Torah*, where he indeed provides a more detailed index.

"Moshe" represents a unique fusion of humility and pride. Although he was "more humble than any man on the face of the earth,"[5] he served as a firm leader of the people, confidently telling them: "It is I who stood between you and G-d."[6]

"Yehoshua" represents the epitome of dedicated devotion — "a youth who never left the tent."[7] Such dedication is also necessary if one is to make the Torah a part of one's thinking processes.

"The elders" represent the virtues of maturity and cultivated wisdom. The commitment of Yehoshua must be nurtured through disciplined study.

"The prophets" represent a drive to make one's thinking processes reflect one's spiritual values. This is necessary to ensure that the knowledge of the elders remains more than human wisdom, and reflects the G-dly source of the Torah.

In regard to "the Men of the Great Assembly," our Sages explain the name was given because they "restored the original glory."[8]

> Moshe referred to the Almighty as "the great, mighty and awesome G-d."[9]
>
> Yirmeyahu said: "Gentiles are celebrating in His palace; where is His awesomeness?" And when he referred to G-d,[10] he did not use the term "awesome."
>
> Daniel said: "Gentiles are subjugating His children; where is His might?" And he did not use the term "mighty."[11]
>
> They [the Men of the Great Assembly] arose and said: "On the contrary, this is His might; that He overcomes

---

5. *Bamidbar* 12:2.
6. *Devarim* 5:5.
7. *Shmos* 33:11.
8. *Yoma* 69b.
9. *Devarim* 10:17.
10. *Yirmeyahu* 32:18.
11. *Daniel* 9:4.

His natural tendency, and shows patience to the wicked. And this is His awesomeness; for were it not for His awesomeness, one nation could not endure among the many."[12]

The Men of the Great Assembly were able to see G-dliness even in the darkness of exile. This is the last quality which the *mishnah* chose to emphasize as a prerequisite for our study of the Torah; regardless of the situation in which we find ourselves, we must appreciate G-d's intent.

(Likkutei Sichos, Vol. IV, p. 1175ff)

RAISE UP MANY STUDENTS — Implied in the Hebrew term העמידו is the notion that one must instruct one's students until they are able to stand independently. A teacher's responsibility is not merely to impart knowledge, but rather to give his students a strong base of values and principles which will continue to give them strength.

(Sichos Shabbos Parshas Naso, 5740)

MANY STUDENTS — The word "many" does not imply a limit. No matter how many students a teacher has, he must always seek to add more.

(Sichos Shabbos Parshas Kedoshim, 5744)

ב שִׁמְעוֹן הַצַּדִּיק הָיָה מִשְׁיָרֵי כְנֶסֶת הַגְּדוֹלָה, הוּא הָיָה אוֹמֵר עַל שְׁלֹשָׁה דְבָרִים הָעוֹלָם עוֹמֵד: עַל הַתּוֹרָה, וְעַל הָעֲבוֹדָה, וְעַל גְּמִילוּת חֲסָדִים.

2. SHIMON THE RIGHTEOUS WAS ONE OF THE LAST OF THE MEN OF THE GREAT ASSEMBLY.

---

12 . Hence, in the daily prayers which they instituted we say "the great, mighty, and awesome G-d," as Moshe did.

HE USED TO SAY: "THE WORLD STANDS ON THREE
QUALITIES: ON [THE STUDY OF] TORAH, THE SERVICE
[OF G-D], AND DEEDS OF KINDNESS."

**SHIMON THE RIGHTEOUS WAS ONE OF THE LAST
OF THE MEN OF THE GREAT ASSEMBLY** — The Men of
the Great Assembly were a gathering of great Sages, each possessing different tendencies. Each Sage's influence balanced
and moderated the input of the others. With an emphasis on
harmony, this auspicious body charted the course of Jewish
observance.

As long as this body functioned, it was able to bring balance
to the different character traits possessed by people at large.
When, however, this assemblage ceased to exist, there was a
need to highlight the importance of equilibrium. Shimon the
Righteous, one of the last participants in this body, showed
how the three modes of divine service mentioned enable both
the individual's private world and the world outside to stand
with strength and stability.

(Sichos Shabbos Parshas Shemini, 5741)

THE WORLD STANDS ON THREE QUALITIES — This
expression implies that the world is above the Torah, divine
service, and deeds of kindness, for a support is always inferior
to the entity it is supporting. This is problematic, for the Torah
"preceded the world,"[13] and represents a higher plane than
material existence.

In resolution, it can be explained that this *mishnah* is concerned with the ultimate purpose of the world — that it serve
as a dwelling for G-d.[14] It focuses on the Torah, divine service,
and deeds of kindness as the means which will enable the
world to realize this purpose. Thus in this context, these three

---

13 . *Bereishis Rabbah* 8:2 *et al.*
14 . *Midrash Tanchuma, Parshas Bechukosai,* sec. 3; *Tanya,* chs. 33 and 36.

modes of religious expression are seen, not as goals in their own right, but as ways of bringing the world to fulfillment.

(Sichos Shabbos Parshas Chukas, 5744)

[THE STUDY OF] TORAH, THE SERVICE [OF G-D], AND DEEDS OF KINDNESS — The Torah shows a person how to conduct his life. Service (prayer) enables one to internalize the Torah's teachings, and deeds of kindness express these teachings in the world at large.

(Sichos Shabbos Parshas Shemini, 5741)

ג אַנְטִיגְנוֹס אִישׁ סוֹכוֹ קִבֵּל מִשִּׁמְעוֹן הַצַּדִּיק, הוּא הָיָה אוֹמֵר: אַל תִּהְיוּ כַּעֲבָדִים הַמְשַׁמְּשִׁין אֶת הָרַב עַל מְנָת לְקַבֵּל פְּרָס, אֶלָּא הֱווּ כַּעֲבָדִים הַמְשַׁמְּשִׁין אֶת הָרַב שֶׁלֹּא עַל מְנָת לְקַבֵּל פְּרָס, וִיהִי מוֹרָא שָׁמַיִם עֲלֵיכֶם.

3. ANTIGONUS OF SOCHO RECEIVED [THE ORAL TRADITION] FROM SHIMON THE RIGHTEOUS. HE USED TO SAY: "DO NOT BE LIKE SERVANTS WHO SERVE THEIR MASTER FOR THE SAKE OF RECEIVING A REWARD, BUT RATHER BE LIKE SERVANTS WHO SERVE THEIR MASTER WITHOUT THE INTENT OF RECEIVING A REWARD; AND LET THE FEAR OF HEAVEN BE UPON YOU."

DO NOT BE LIKE SERVANTS WHO SERVE THEIR MASTER FOR THE SAKE OF RECEIVING A REWARD — We find many verses in the Torah which promise rewards for observance of the *mitzvos*. For example, the Ten Commandments instruct us[15] to "Honor your father and your mother so that your days will be prolonged."

This *mishnah*, like so many of the teachings of *Pirkei Avos*, is an expression of *mili dechassidusa*,[16] pious conduct beyond the measure of the Law. In that vein, it teaches that although every *mitzvah* generates a reward, a person's focus should not be on the reward, but on the very fact that he has been found worthy to serve G-d.

The reward which the *mishnah* mentions can also be understood as referring to spiritual attainments such as the love and fear of G-d. Just as a person should not focus on the material rewards he will receive for observance, so too he should not have in mind the spiritual benefits it will bring him.

(Sichos Shabbos Parshas Pinchas, 5737)

RATHER BE LIKE SERVANTS WHO SERVE THEIR MASTER WITHOUT THE INTENT OF RECEIVING A REWARD — There are other versions of this *mishnah*[17] which read "be like servants who serve their master without receiving a reward."

What is the difference between these two versions? The version included by the Alter Rebbe in his *siddur* emphasizes that people will receive rewards for divine service, but that the reward should not be the focus of one's attention. The other version, by contrast, negates the very concept of reward. As the Alter Rebbe would say:[18] "I do not want Your *Gan Eden*, nor do I want Your World to Come. I want only You."

Although the Alter Rebbe himself was able to reach this rung, he realized that it was beyond the reach of most people. Therefore, when choosing the text of *Pirkei Avos* to be included

---

15 . *Shmos* 20:12.
16 . *Bava Kama* 30a.
17 . *Machzor Vitri, Rashi's* commentary to the Talmud (*Avodah Zarah* 19a); see *Hemshech VeKocha* 5637, ch. 15.
18 . Cited by the *Tzemach Tzedek* in *Derech Mitzvosecha*, p. 138a.

in the *siddur* — a text to be used by all people — he chose the former version.

(Sichos Shabbos Parshas Pinchas, 5737)

LET THE FEAR OF HEAVEN BE UPON YOU — Our Sages relate[19] that Antigonus of Socho had two talented students, Tzadok and Beitus. When Antigonus taught: "Do not be like servants who serve their master for the sake of receiving a reward," they turned away in disgust, commenting: "Is it proper for a worker to toil the entire day without receiving any recompense?"

They began splinter groups which coveted material wealth and rejected the core of Jewish practice.

On finding that they could not convince the majority of the people to reject the Torah, they claimed they were true to Torah, but that the only Torah that was G-dly in origin was the Written Law. The Oral Law, they maintained, was merely a human invention.[20]

Antigonus appreciated that his students' error stemmed from a dearth of *yiras shomayim*, fear of heaven. Therefore he felt it necessary to emphasize the importance of this quality.

(Sichos Shabbos Parshas Naso, 5742)

ד יוֹסֵי בֶּן יוֹעֶזֶר אִישׁ צְרֵדָה, וְיוֹסֵי בֶּן יוֹחָנָן אִישׁ יְרוּשָׁלַיִם קִבְּלוּ מֵהֶם, יוֹסֵי בֶּן יוֹעֶזֶר אִישׁ צְרֵדָה אוֹמֵר: יְהִי בֵיתְךָ בֵּית וַעַד לַחֲכָמִים, וֶהֱוֵי מִתְאַבֵּק בַּעֲפַר רַגְלֵיהֶם, וֶהֱוֵי שׁוֹתֶה בַצָּמָא אֶת דִּבְרֵיהֶם.

4. YOSAY BEN YOEZER OF TZREDAH AND YOSAY BEN YOCHANAN OF JERUSALEM RECEIVED [THE ORAL TRADITION] FROM THEM. YOSAY BEN YOEZER

---

19. *Avos d'Rabbi Nossan* 5:2
20. See the *Rambam's Commentary to the Mishnah, Avos* 1:3.

OF TZREDAH SAID: "LET YOUR HOUSE BE A MEETING
PLACE FOR SAGES; SIT IN THE DUST AT THEIR FEET,
AND DRINK IN THEIR WORDS THIRSTILY."

**LET YOUR HOUSE BE A MEETING PLACE FOR
SAGES** — One's dwelling should continually serve this function, to the extent that it defines the nature of the home. Then,
even when the Sages are not present, their influence will continue to affect the events that transpire within.

(Sichos Shabbos Parshas Acharei, 5722)

SIT IN THE DUST AT THEIR FEET — It is possible that
a person will become proud that sages frequent his home.
Therefore, the *mishnah* emphasizes the importance of conduct-
ing oneself with humility.

(Sichos Shabbos Parshas Acharei, 5722)

Alternatively, the term "dust at their feet" can be interpreted figuratively. "Feet" can refer to the sages' students, and
"dust" to negative attributes.

During the time of Yosay ben Yoezer, gaps appeared in the
chain of tradition and differences of opinion arose between the
Sages.[21] When this happens, it is natural for "dust to be stirred
up" by their students, as each tries to argue the virtues of his
own teacher's position. The *mishnah* teaches that one should
"Sit... at their feet," and "drink in their words," for by patiently
opening oneself to the teachings of the sages themselves, one
will offset any negative influence that might be generated by
the "dust" of their students.

(Sichos Motzoei Shabbos Parshas Matos-Masei, 5739)

---

21. See *Tosafos, Chagigah* 16a, the gloss of *Tosafos Yom Tov* to this *mishnah*.

ה יוֹסֵי בֶּן יוֹחָנָן אִישׁ יְרוּשָׁלַיִם אוֹמֵר: יְהִי בֵיתְךָ פָּתוּחַ לִרְוָחָה,
וְיִהְיוּ עֲנִיִּים בְּנֵי בֵיתֶךָ, וְאַל תַּרְבֶּה שִׂיחָה עִם הָאִשָּׁה, בְּאִשְׁתּוֹ אָמְרוּ,
קַל וָחֹמֶר בְּאֵשֶׁת חֲבֵרוֹ. מִכַּאן אָמְרוּ חֲכָמִים: כָּל הַמַּרְבֶּה שִׂיחָה עִם
הָאִשָּׁה, גּוֹרֵם רָעָה לְעַצְמוֹ, וּבוֹטֵל מִדִּבְרֵי תוֹרָה, וְסוֹפוֹ יוֹרֵשׁ
גֵּיהִנֹּם.

5. YOSAY BEN YOCHANAN OF JERUSALEM SAID: "LET YOUR HOUSE BE WIDE OPEN [FOR GUESTS]. TREAT THE POOR AS MEMBERS OF YOUR HOUSEHOLD, AND DO NOT INDULGE EXCESSIVELY IN CONVERSATION WITH THE WOMAN."

THIS WAS SAID CONCERNING ONE'S OWN WIFE; HOW MUCH MORE SO DOES IT APPLY TO THE WIFE OF ANOTHER! HENCE THE SAGES HAVE DECLARED: "ANYONE WHO INDULGES EXCESSIVELY IN CONVERSATION WITH A WOMAN CAUSES EVIL TO HIMSELF, NEGLECTS THE STUDY OF TORAH, AND WILL IN THE END INHERIT GEHINOM."

*TREAT THE POOR AS MEMBERS OF YOUR HOUSEHOLD — Our Sages state[22] that "poverty is becoming to the Jews," for it humbles a person and brings him closer to *teshuvah*. By opening one's home to the poor, one benefits from the humbling influence of poverty without being subjected to it oneself.

(Likkutei Sichos, Vol. XVII, p. 364)

*DO NOT INDULGE EXCESSIVELY IN CONVERSATION — In *chassidic* terminology, when mankind is contrasted with the animal and plant kingdoms, a human being is referred to as a מְדַבֵּר, "one who talks."

Why is speech singled out over intellect or emotion to define man's uniqueness? Because every other element of a person's character centers around himself, while speech gives him

---

22 . *Chagigah* 9b.

the ability to transcend his own being and relate to another person.[23]

In light of the uniqueness of this potential, our Sages proposed[24] that שיחה, "conversation," is the purpose of man's creation. Nevertheless, they reject this hypothesis and explain instead that the goal of man's creative efforts should be Torah study. For Torah study enables a person to establish a bond with G-d that transcends the natural limits of creation and endows a person and his environment with a new dimension of spiritual awareness.

(Likkutei Sichos, Vol. VI, pgs. 115-116; Vol. XV, p. 96ff)

ו יְהוֹשֻׁעַ בֶּן פְּרַחְיָה וְנִתַּאי הָאַרְבֵּלִי קִבְּלוּ מֵהֶם, יְהוֹשֻׁעַ בֶּן פְּרַחְיָה

אוֹמֵר: עֲשֵׂה לְךָ רַב, וּקְנֵה לְךָ חָבֵר, וֶהֱוֵי דָן אֶת כָּל הָאָדָם לְכַף

זְכוּת.

6. YEHOSHUA BEN PERACHYAH AND NITTAI OF ARBEL RECEIVED [THE ORAL TRADITION] FROM THEM. YEHOSHUA BEN PERACHYAH SAID: "PROVIDE YOURSELF WITH A MASTER; ACQUIRE FOR YOURSELF A FRIEND; AND JUDGE EVERY PERSON FAVORABLY."

PROVIDE YOURSELF WITH A MASTER — The intent is not merely to recommend getting a teacher who will enhance one's knowledge, but a guide whom one consults regarding one's conduct.

By nature, man is influenced by self-love. This natural bias makes it difficult to know whether we are making adequate efforts in our study of Torah, in our gifts to charity, and in other elements of our divine service.

---

23 . *Sefer HaMaamarim* 5628, p. 167.
24 . *Sanhedrin* 99b.

How can we know? By consulting another person who can look at our situation objectively. Every man, woman and child should consult a Torah personality whom he respects, and should accept that person's advice, not merely as friendly counsel, but as the directives of "a master."

Holding himself responsible for the evaluation of another individual will enable a person to make maximum use of the potential with which he has been endowed.

Even when a person is himself a teacher and capable of instructing others, he should seek a master for himself.[25] No matter how great his own wisdom, he can make greater progress when his conduct is scrutinized by the objective eyes of a person who wants to help him advance.

The Hebrew term עשה, translated as "provide," can also mean "force."[26] In this vein, the *mishnah* is teaching us to accept a master even if we must force ourselves to do so.

(Sichos Shabbos Parshas Devarim, 5746)

ACQUIRE FOR YOURSELF A FRIEND — The guidance of a master is not sufficient. A person also needs colleagues at his own level with whom to share the trials and triumphs of advancing in divine service.[27]

(Sichos Shabbos Parshas Matos-Masei, 5742)

JUDGE EVERY PERSON FAVORABLY — Even when a person's conduct does not seem worthy of favorable judgment, one should endeavor to find redeeming virtue within him.

---

25. This concept is reflected in the fact that the author of this teaching was Rabbi Yehoshua ben Perachyah, the *Nasi*, the Torah leader of the Jewish people. Even Rabbi Yehoshua appreciated the necessity of subjugating his conduct to the review of a colleague *(Sichos Shabbos Parshas Behaalos'cha, 5741)*.

26. See the notes of the *Beis Yosef* to the *Tur (Yoreh De'ah, sec.* 248). See also the commentary of the *Rambam* and R. Ovadiah of Bartenura to this *mishnah*.

27. See also Chapter 6, *Beraisa* 6, which teaches that one of the means through which "the Torah is acquired" is "close association with colleagues."

In this context, it is possible to cite a narrative from Rabbi Yehoshua's own life. Our Sages relate[28] that "that person" (a Talmudic term used to refer to J. of Nazareth) was one of Rabbi Yehoshua's students. Even after "that person" had forsaken Jewish observance, Rabbi Yehoshua tried to persuade him to repent.

"That person" refused, replying: "I received the following tradition from you: 'A person who sins and causes others to sin is not given the opportunity to repent.'"

Of course Rabbi Yehoshua knew this principle, but he also knew that if a person makes a sincere attempt, his repentance will be accepted regardless of his previous conduct.[29] Despite his former student's behavior, Rabbi Yehoshua judged him as capable of repenting sincerely enough to regain G-d's favor.

(Sichas Shabbos Parshas Behaalos'cha, 5741)

*Judging a person favorably involves an honest appreciation of the challenges which that person faces.[30] And this awareness should also lead to the understanding that G-d has surely given that person the ability to overcome these challenges.[31] This, in turn, should heighten the esteem with which we regard this individual, for he is a person to whom G-d has entrusted the formidable powers necessary to overcome severe challenges.

When the manner in which we relate to that person reflects such respect, this will inspire the individual to bring these potentials to the surface.

(Likkutei Sichos, Vol. XXVII, p. 164-165)

---

28. *Sanhedrin* 107b, according to *Chisronos HaShas.*
29. *Rambam, Mishneh Torah, Hilchos Teshuvah* 4:6; *Tanya*, ch. 25.
30. See *Tanya*, ch. 30, in explanation of *Pirkei Avos* 2:4, which explains that a person should not look down at a colleague who is involved in worldly affairs. Such a person faces greater challenges in his divine service than one who is involved in Torah study.
31. For as our Sages *(Bamidbar Rabbah* 12:3) state, G-d forces a person to confront only those challenges which he can overcome.

ז נִתַּאי הָאַרְבֵּלִי אוֹמֵר: הַרְחֵק מִשָּׁכֵן רָע, וְאַל תִּתְחַבֵּר לָרָשָׁע, וְאַל תִּתְיָאֵשׁ מִן הַפֻּרְעָנוּת.

7. NITTAI OF ARBEL SAID: "KEEP AWAY FROM A BAD NEIGHBOR; DO NOT FRATERNIZE WITH A WICKED MAN; AND DO NOT ABANDON BELIEF IN [DIVINE] RETRIBUTION."

KEEP AWAY FROM A BAD NEIGHBOR — The *mishnah* does not say: "Keep away from a wicked neighbor," for its intent is not that one should judge another's conduct. Instead, the intent is that a person should decide whether closeness to a particular individual is beneficial or detrimental to his own divine service. The neighbor may be above all reproach, but traveling a different path of divine service. Any attempt to identify with him might thus be "bad," i.e., create confusion and discord.

(Likkutei Sichos, Vol. IV, p. 1181ff)

DO NOT FRATERNIZE WITH A WICKED MAN — Here, the *mishnah* does not use the term "keep away," for the intent is not that one should sever contact with a person because his conduct is unworthy. אל תתחבר, translated as "do not fraternize," literally means "do not join to." One should not "join" a wicked person by accepting his standards. One should, however, reach out with warmth and love to all people, regardless of their conduct, and endeavor to inspire them to improve themselves.

(Ibid.)

DO NOT ABANDON BELIEF IN [DIVINE] RETRIBUTION — When a person lives in constant awareness of the possibility of Divine retribution, he will sincerely regret any misconduct. The discomfort this awareness brings will itself atone for his misdeeds, precluding the necessity for retribution from Heaven.

(Ibid.)

ח יְהוּדָה בֶּן טַבַּאי וְשִׁמְעוֹן בֶּן שָׁטַח קִבְּלוּ מֵהֶם. יְהוּדָה בֶּן טַבַּאי אוֹמֵר: אַל תַּעַשׂ עַצְמְךָ כְּעוֹרְכֵי הַדַּיָּנִין, וּכְשֶׁיִּהְיוּ בַּעֲלֵי הַדִּין עוֹמְדִים לְפָנֶיךָ, יִהְיוּ בְעֵינֶיךָ כִּרְשָׁעִים, וּכְשֶׁנִּפְטָרִים מִלְּפָנֶיךָ, יִהְיוּ בְעֵינֶיךָ כְּזַכָּאִין, כְּשֶׁקִּבְּלוּ עֲלֵיהֶם אֶת הַדִּין.

8. YEHUDAH BEN TABBAI AND SHIMON BEN SHATACH RECEIVED [THE ORAL TRADITION] FROM THEM. YEHUDAH BEN TABBAI SAID: "DO NOT ACT AS A COUNSELOR [WHEN SITTING AS A JUDGE]. WHEN THE LITIGANTS STAND BEFORE YOU, REGARD THEM BOTH AS GUILTY, BUT WHEN THEY LEAVE, HAVING ACCEPTED THE JUDGMENT, REGARD THEM BOTH AS GUILTLESS."

*REGARD THEM BOTH AS GUILTY — רשעים, translated as "guilty," also means "wicked." The very fact that two people are involved in a dispute severe enough to bring them before a judge appears to indicate that both possess a certain measure of wickedness. When two people cannot resolve their differences without arbitration, both need to increase their love for their fellow man.

(Likkutei Sichos, Vol. XXIV, p. 155)

ט שִׁמְעוֹן בֶּן שָׁטַח אוֹמֵר: הֱוֵי מַרְבֶּה לַחֲקוֹר אֶת הָעֵדִים, וֶהֱוֵי זָהִיר בִּדְבָרֶיךָ, שֶׁמָּא מִתּוֹכָם יִלְמְדוּ לְשַׁקֵּר.

9. SHIMON BEN SHATACH SAID: "EXAMINE THE WITNESSES THOROUGHLY; AND BE CAUTIOUS WITH YOUR WORDS, LEST THROUGH THEM THEY [THE WITNESSES OR THE LITIGANTS] LEARN TO SPEAK FALSEHOOD."

SHIMON BEN SHATACH SAID: "EXAMINE THE WITNESSES THOROUGHLY" — Our Rabbis[32] associate this teaching with a tragedy that occurred to Rabbi Shimon: his son was executed because of false testimony delivered in court.[33] Moreover, we find that Shimon ben Shatach reproved his colleague, Yehudah ben Tabbai, for executing a lying witness when Torah law did not require his death.[34] These two incidents intensified Rabbi Shimon's commitment to investigate testimony thoroughly before acting upon it.

There is also a homiletic dimension to this teaching. Our Sages say:[35] "The walls of a person's house testify regarding his [character]." On the most simple level, it is possible to "examine the witnesses" and determine a person's character by studying the walls of his house — which books, whose pictures, and which art do they feature.

(Sichos Motzoei Shabbos Parshas Shemini, 5739; Sichos Shabbos Parshas Kedoshim, 5741)

י שְׁמַעְיָה וְאַבְטַלְיוֹן קִבְּלוּ מֵהֶם. שְׁמַעְיָה אוֹמֵר: אֱהוֹב אֶת הַמְּלָאכָה, וּשְׂנָא אֶת הָרַבָּנוּת, וְאַל תִּתְוַדַּע לָרָשׁוּת.

10. SHEMAYAH AND AVTALYON RECEIVED [THE ORAL TRADITION] FROM THEM. SHEMAYAH

---

32 . *Midrash Shmuel*, quoting the *Rashbam*.
33 . *Rashi, Sanhedrin* 44b, based on *Yerushalmi, Sanhedrin* 6:6.
34 . *Makkos* 5b.
35 . *Taanis* 11a.

SAID: "LOVE WORK; ABHOR TAKING HIGH OFFICE; AND DO NOT SEEK INTIMACY WITH THE RULING POWER."

SHEMAYAH SAID — These three directives reflect Shemayah's humility.

LOVE WORK — Do not say: "It is beneath my dignity to perform common labor."[36]

ABHOR TAKING HIGH OFFICE — A person should not seek to place a crown on his own head.[37]

DO NOT SEEK INTIMACY WITH THE RULING POWER — Nor should he boast: "I am a friend of the ruler of the city!"[38]

Since Shemayah was the *Nasi* — the Torah leader of the Jewish people — he knew the importance of humility. For a leader's prominence comes as a result of his selflessness. Because he has no concern for himself, he is fit to serve as a medium to lead his people to an awareness of G-d's sovereignty.[39]

(Sichos Shabbos Parshas Shemini, 5728)

יא אַבְטַלְיוֹן אוֹמֵר: חֲכָמִים, הִזָּהֲרוּ בְדִבְרֵיכֶם, שֶׁמָּא תָחוֹבוּ חוֹבַת גָּלוּת וְתִגְלוּ לִמְקוֹם מַיִם הָרָעִים, וְיִשְׁתּוּ הַתַּלְמִידִים הַבָּאִים אַחֲרֵיכֶם וְיָמוּתוּ, וְנִמְצָא שֵׁם שָׁמַיִם מִתְחַלֵּל.

11. AVTALYON SAID: "SAGES, BE CAREFUL WITH YOUR WORDS, FOR YOU MAY INCUR THE PENALTY OF EXILE AND BE BANISHED TO A PLACE OF EVIL WATERS [HERESY], AND THE DISCIPLES WHO

---

36 . See *Rashi's* commentary.
37 . The interpretation of *Avos d'Rabbi Nossan* 11:2.
38 . *Ibid.*:3.
39 . See *Tzemech Tzedek, Derech Mitzvosecho, Mitzvas Minui Melech*, sec. 1.

FOLLOW YOU THERE WILL DRINK AND DIE
[SPIRITUALLY], AND CONSEQUENTLY THE NAME OF
HEAVEN WILL BE DESECRATED."

**THE DISCIPLES WHO FOLLOW YOU THERE WILL
DRINK AND DIE** — The *mishnah* does not express fear with
regard to the future of the teacher himself, since he is a mature
person, protected by the virtues of his Torah knowledge.[40] His
students, by contrast, are more vulnerable, since they have not
developed as thorough a knowledge of the Torah. Therefore
there is greater concern for their fate.

(Sichos Shabbos Parshas Shemini, 5728)

יב הִלֵּל וְשַׁמַּאי קִבְּלוּ מֵהֶם, הִלֵּל אוֹמֵר: הֱוֵי מִתַּלְמִידָיו שֶׁל אַהֲרֹן,
אוֹהֵב שָׁלוֹם, וְרוֹדֵף שָׁלוֹם, אוֹהֵב אֶת הַבְּרִיּוֹת, וּמְקָרְבָן לַתּוֹרָה.

12. HILLEL AND SHAMMAI RECEIVED [THE ORAL
TRADITION] FROM THEM. HILLEL SAID: "BE
OF THE DISCIPLES OF AHARON, LOVING PEACE AND
PURSUING PEACE, LOVING THE CREATED BEINGS, AND
BRINGING THEM NEAR TO THE TORAH."

**BE OF THE DISCIPLES OF AHARON... LOVING THE
CREATED BEINGS, AND BRINGING THEM NEAR TO
THE TORAH** — The use of the term "created beings" instead
of "people" implies that Aharon would reach out to individuals
whose only redeeming virtue was the fact that they were G-d's
creations.[41]

---

40 . See *Yoma* 38b.
41 . See *Tanya*, ch. 32.

Aharon's concern for his fellow man was all the more impressive because of his exalted position as High Priest. Leaving the Sanctuary where G-d's Presence was openly revealed, he would reach out to people who had no virtue other than their having been created by G-d.[42]

The order used in the *mishnah* is also significant. It implies that Aharon first concerned himself with establishing a relationship of love and trust, confidant that this would in turn enable him to draw them near to the Torah.[43]

Also significant is the phrase, "bringing them near to the Torah." Although Aharon reached out to these individuals and tried to accommodate them to the fullest degree possible, his efforts were centered on "bringing them near to the Torah," and not, חיו, bringing the Torah near to them.

His willingness to extend himself on behalf of others did not involve any compromise of Torah law.

(Sichos Shabbos Kedoshim, 5727; Sichos Acharon Shel Pesach, 5736; Sichos Matos-Masei, 5737)

יג הוּא הָיָה אוֹמֵר: נְגַד שְׁמָא אֲבַד שְׁמֵהּ, וּדְלָא מוֹסִיף יָסֵף, וּדְלָא יַלִּיף קְטָלָא חַיָּב, וּדְאִשְׁתַּמֵּשׁ בְּתַגָּא חֲלָף.

13. HE USED TO SAY: "HE WHO SEEKS RENOWN LOSES HIS REPUTATION; HE WHO DOES NOT INCREASE [HIS KNOWLEDGE OF THE TORAH]

---

42 . There is an added dimension of self-sacrifice to Aharon's conduct. While outside the Sanctuary dealing with people on this level, it is very possible that Aharon would contract ritual impurity and this would require him to remain outside the Sanctuary for an even longer period. Nevertheless, he was willing to take this risk to spread love and unity.

43 . *Shir HaShirim Rabbah* (ch. 2, second order, sec. 19) explains that G-d followed the same pattern. First He revealed miracles and wonders for the Jews while redeeming them from Egypt, despite their low spiritual level. Only afterwards did He give them the Torah on Mount Sinai.

DECREASES IT. HE WHO DOES NOT STUDY [THE
TORAH] DESERVES DEATH; AND HE WHO EXPLOITS
THE CROWN [OF THE TORAH FOR HIS OWN ENDS]
SHALL PERISH."

HE USED TO SAY — This *mishnah*, in contrast to the
majority of *Pirkei Avos*, is in Aramaic, the language used by the
common folk in Talmudic times. The rationale is that it follows the previous *mishnah*, which teaches that one must "be of
the disciples of Aharon... loving the created beings, and
bringing them near to the Torah." In this *mishnah*, Hillel
reaches out to people who do not understand *Lashon HaKodesh*,
the holy tongue of the *Mishnah*.

He explains that a person involved in outreach may feel
superior, and seek to be honored for his efforts. Therefore,
Hillel states...

HE WHO SEEKS RENOWN LOSES HIS REPUTATION,
— emphasizing that the opposite will happen. Such an approach will cause him to lose his reputation rather than amplify
it.

Moreover, by stating this teaching in Aramaic, Hillel
informs the person's students that granting their teacher the
honor he seeks will hurt his growth.

Since a person's efforts toward outreach may harm his progress, it is quite possible that he will think: "Why involve myself
in the first place? It is better to proceed without seeking new
frontiers." To this Hillel replies...

HE WHO DOES NOT INCREASE... DECREASES — To
quote an expression of the Mitteler Rebbe: "*A zibela zel fun dir
veren, uber chassidus zolstu chazzaren.*"[44] {The expression defies

---

44 . See *Sichos Kodesh* 5740, Vol. II, p. 216ff.

translation; this is our best attempt: Even if the pride a person feels when teaching others arouses negative effects so great that they cause him to become an onion, he should continue.} For a person must constantly open new frontiers, extending the Torah's teachings so that more people will be exposed to them.

With regard to material wealth, it is often explained that a rich man's affluence is granted to him so that he can serve as a trustee, spreading charity throughout the world. This concept is even more applicable with regard to knowledge. Whatever insights a person has been granted were endowed to him for the benefit of others as much as for himself.

(Sichos Shabbos Parshas Naso, 5734, 5743)

HE WHO EXPLOITS THE CROWN [OF THE TORAH]
— Our Sages explain[45] that "the crown of the Torah" refers to the study of *halachah,* the practical application of Torah law. Thus there is an obvious connection with Hillel's exhortation to spread Torah. For as one comes in contact with people on the fringes of Jewish observance, one must teach them Torah law. Also, the new situations which one confronts require new applications of *halachah.*

(Sichos Shabbos Parshas Shemini, 5745)

יד הוּא הָיָה אוֹמֵר: אִם אֵין אֲנִי לִי, מִי לִי, וּכְשֶׁאֲנִי לְעַצְמִי, מָה אֲנִי, וְאִם לֹא עַכְשָׁו, אֵימָתָי.

14. HE USED TO SAY: "IF I AM NOT FOR MYSELF, WHO IS FOR ME? AND IF I AM ONLY FOR MYSELF, WHAT AM I? AND IF NOT NOW, WHEN?"

---

45 ، *Megillah* 28b, explained in *Iggeres HaKodesh,* Epistle 29.

This teaching can be interpreted within the context of the charge to reach out to others *(mishnah 12)*.

IF I AM NOT FOR MYSELF — I.e., if I do not take an active role in these efforts...

WHO IS FOR ME? — What merit will I have? Whether or not a person involves himself, the task he was required to fulfill will be accomplished, for the good destined to be achieved in our world will not be decreased. Nevertheless, when a person does not shoulder the task destined for him, he will lack the merit he was fated to acquire.

(Sichos Shabbos Parshas Shemini, 5737)

AND IF I AM ONLY FOR MYSELF — A person may be willing to apply himself to the task before him, but "only for himself," without seeking advice or help from others. And then...

WHAT — not who

AM I? — i.e., he falls beneath the level of humanity.

(Ibid.)

AND IF NOT NOW, WHEN? — He must be conscious of the urgency involved, and not postpone his efforts.

(Ibid.)

טו שַׁמַּאי אוֹמֵר: עֲשֵׂה תוֹרָתְךָ קֶבַע, אֱמוֹר מְעַט וַעֲשֵׂה הַרְבֵּה, וֶהֱוֵי מְקַבֵּל אֶת כָּל הָאָדָם בְּסֵבֶר פָּנִים יָפוֹת.

15. SHAMMAI SAID: "SET A FIXED TIME FOR YOUR STUDY OF TORAH; SAY LITTLE AND DO

MUCH; AND RECEIVE EVERY PERSON WITH A
CHEERFUL COUNTENANCE."

SET A FIXED TIME FOR YOUR STUDY OF TORAH
— The Alter Rebbe explains[46] that Torah study must be fixed
not only in time, but also in its position in the soul, serving as
the foundation of a person's life. Even if a person's talents lie
along another path of divine service, e.g., prayer or deeds of
kindness, the foundation on which his effort rests must be the
study of Torah.

(Likkutei Sichos, Vol. XXVII, p. 347ff)

SAY LITTLE AND DO MUCH — On a simple level, this
clause is teaching us to minimize the commitments we make,
and fulfill them in excess of our promises.[47] Nevertheless, from
a deeper perspective, this clause can be seen as an extension of
the directive to make Torah study the foundation of our lives.

In that context, "say little" can be interpreted to mean: Do
not be overly concerned with making statements of Torah law.
Instead, a person should immerse himself in Torah study for
the sake of the Torah itself, above all other considerations.
This approach may cause him to retreat from involvement in
worldly things, so the *mishnah* continues:

DO MUCH — Perform an abundance of *mitzvos*. Moreover,
it emphasizes...

**RECEIVE EVERY PERSON WITH A CHEERFUL
COUNTENANCE** — Do not let your involvement in Torah
study prevent you from developing relationships with others.
More specifically, the *mishnah* states that one must extend oneself to "every person," i.e., not only to those dedicated to the

---

46 . *Likkutei Dibburim*, Vol. I, p. 13 (English translation).
47 . R. Ovadiah of Bartenura and others.

study of Torah, but to all others, regardless of their level of religious commitment.

(Ibid.)

Alternatively, "every person" can be interpreted to include even gentiles.[48] This raises a question: There is a well-known narrative[49] which relates that a gentile came to Shammai and demanded: "Teach me the entire Torah while I stand on one foot." Shammai drove him away. Hillel, by contrast, received him with gentle forbearance and told him: "What is distasteful to you, do not do to a colleague. This is the entire Torah; the rest is merely explanation."

Shammai's conduct seems to conflict with his own directive to "receive every person with a cheerful countenance."

It can be explained that the above narrative reflects Shammai's natural tendencies. Nevertheless, after Shammai heard Hillel's teaching — "Be of the students of Aharon" — he changed his nature and taught his students to "receive every person with a cheerful countenance."[50]

(Op. cit., p. 114-115)

טז רַבָּן גַּמְלִיאֵל הָיָה אוֹמֵר, עֲשֵׂה לְךָ רַב, וְהִסְתַּלֵּק מִן הַסָּפֵק, וְאַל תַּרְבֶּה לְעַשֵּׂר אֻמָּדוֹת.

16. RABBAN GAMLIEL SAID: "PROVIDE YOURSELF WITH A MASTER AND FREE

---

48 . See *Tosafos* (*Yevamos* 61a).
49 . *Shabbos* 31a.
50 . This explains why in this instance, Hillel's teachings are mentioned before those of Shammai although generally Shammai's teachings are given precedence. See *Tosafos, Chagigah* 16a.

YOURSELF OF DOUBT. AND DO NOT TITHE BY
ESTIMATION, EVEN IF GIVING IN EXCESS OF THE
REQUIRED AMOUNT."

PROVIDE YOURSELF WITH A MASTER — This direc-
tive was mentioned previously in this chapter.[51] Why is it necessary to repeat it?

The answer depends on the rationale — "and free yourself
of doubt" — appended by Rabban Gamliel. After Hillel and
Shammai died, their students perpetuated the differences in
approach which had characterized their masters, causing the
Talmudic academy to be split among the School of Shammai
and the School of Hillel. In Rabban Gamliel's age, unanimity
did not exist with regard to many questions of Torah law. Thus
it was necessary for a person to find a Torah guide to direct him
in areas where doubt might arise. This relates to Rabban Gamliel's second directive...

**DO NOT TITHE BY ESTIMATION, EVEN GIVING IN
EXCESS OF THE REQUIRED AMOUNT** — Because of
doubt as to the precise requirements of his religious obligations, a person might decide to always act more stringently, as
in the case of tithes when, instead of measuring exactly, he
gives more than the necessary amount.

The *mishnah* emphasizes that this is not a proper approach.
One should find a master who can instruct him with regard to
the course of conduct which is particularly appropriate to his
nature and character, and follow that master's directives,
whether lenient or stringent.[52]

(Sichos Shabbos Parshas Shemini, 5747)

---

51 . 1:6.
52 . See also the *Midrash Shmuel*, which explains that when a person has several
teachers, their different perspectives may confuse him. But when he has a single
teacher, he will have a straightforward path charted out for him.

יז שִׁמְעוֹן בְּנוֹ אוֹמֵר: כָּל יָמַי גָּדַלְתִּי בֵּין הַחֲכָמִים, וְלֹא מָצָאתִי
לַגּוּף, טוֹב מִשְּׁתִיקָה, וְלֹא הַמִּדְרָשׁ עִקָּר אֶלָּא הַמַּעֲשֶׂה, וְכָל הַמַּרְבֶּה
דְּבָרִים מֵבִיא חֵטְא.

17. SHIMON HIS SON SAID: "ALL MY DAYS I GREW UP AMONG THE SAGES AND DID NOT FIND ANYTHING BETTER FOR ONE'S PERSON THAN SILENCE.

"STUDY IS NOT THE ESSENTIAL THING, PRACTICE IS; AND WHOEVER ENGAGES IN EXCESSIVE TALK BRINGS ON SIN."

SHIMON HIS SON — Although the following *mishnah* refers to him by the title Rabban Shimon, this *mishnah* refers to this Sage merely as "Shimon his son." As will be explained, the fundamental purpose of this *mishnah* is to teach humility.

(Sichos Shabbos Parshas Matos, 5741)

ALL MY DAYS I GREW UP — An important lesson can be derived from this introductory phrase. Rabbi Shimon never ceased growing as a person; he was constantly expanding his horizons. And the *mishnah* explains that this is because he lived...

AMONG THE SAGES — Their company and example pushed him toward continued advancement.

(Ibid.)

I... DID NOT FIND ANYTHING BETTER FOR ONE'S PERSON THAN SILENCE — Silence refers to the qualities of humility and selflessness. לגוף, translated as "one's person," literally means "his body." The most effective means of refining the body is by studying the Torah with humility and selflessness. For the Torah is transcendent, G-dly truth.

Thus rather than "breaking" the body[53] as other approaches might, studying Torah with humility enables one to transform it into a vehicle for holiness.

(Ibid., Likkutei Sichos, Vol. I, p. 70ff)

STUDY IS NOT THE ESSENTIAL THING, PRACTICE IS — Since the purpose of creation as a whole is to give G-d a dwelling in the lower worlds,[54] living the Torah in deed and action — and not merely in thought and speech — is of fundamental priority.[55]

(Likkutei Sichos, Vol. IV, p. 1186)

WHOEVER ENGAGES IN EXCESSIVE TALK BRINGS ON SIN — Pride and self-consciousness — the opposites of humility — are often characterized by excessive talk. The *mishnah* points out that adopting this manner may therefore lead to sin. Moreover, חטא can also be interpreted as meaning "a lack."[56] Surely a tendency to excessive talk implies a lack of awareness of the true nature of the Torah.

Alternatively, this clause can be considered as a directive to teachers. Our Sages state[57] that a person should always instruct his students in short, concise phrases. "Excessive talk" could create confusion and cause a student to misinterpret the teacher's instructions. At the very least, it could lead to a lack as mentioned above.

(Sichos Shabbos Parshas Matos, 5741)

---

53 . See *HaYom Yom*, entry 28 Shvat.
54 . *Midrash Tanchuma, Parshas Bechukosai*, sec. 3; see *Tanya*, chs. 33 and 36.
55 . See *Likkutei Sichos*, Vol. VIII, p. 108.
56 . *Likkutei Torah, Matos* 82a, based on *I Melachim* 1:21; and *Rashi's* commentary.
57 . *Pesachim* 3b.

יח רַבָּן שִׁמְעוֹן בֶּן גַּמְלִיאֵל אוֹמֵר, עַל שְׁלשָׁה דְבָרִים הָעוֹלָם קַיָּם:
עַל הַדִּין, וְעַל הָאֱמֶת, וְעַל הַשָּׁלוֹם, שֶׁנֶּאֱמַר: אֱמֶת וּמִשְׁפַּט שָׁלוֹם
שִׁפְטוּ בְּשַׁעֲרֵיכֶם:

18. RABBAN SHIMON BEN GAMLIEL SAID: "THE
WORLD ENDURES BY VIRTUE OF THREE
QUALITIES — JUSTICE, TRUTH, AND PEACE — AS IT IS
STATED:[58] 'ADMINISTER TRUTH AND THE JUDGMENT
OF PEACE IN YOUR GATES.'"

**THE WORLD ENDURES BY VIRTUE OF THREE
QUALITIES** — This *mishnah* does not run contrary to the second *mishnah* of this chapter, which states that "The world
stands on three qualities," yet mentions three different qualities. As R. Ovadiah of Bartenura explains, the phrase "the
world stands" refers to the very existence of the world, while
the phrase "the world endures" refers to the successful development of society.

The world may exist because of the Torah study, prayer,
and kind deeds of certain individuals. For society to flourish,
however, mankind as a whole must come to appreciate the importance of justice, truth, and peace, and conduct itself accord-
ingly.

(Sichos Shabbos Parshas Pinchas, 5739)

---

58 . *Zechariah* 8:16.

CHAPTER TWO

CHAPTER TWO

א רַבִּי אוֹמֵר: אֵיזוֹ הִיא דֶרֶךְ יְשָׁרָה שֶׁיָּבוֹר לוֹ הָאָדָם, כָּל שֶׁהִיא תִּפְאֶרֶת לְעֹשֶׂיהָ וְתִפְאֶרֶת לוֹ מִן הָאָדָם, וֶהֱוֵי זָהִיר בְּמִצְוָה קַלָּה כְּבַחֲמוּרָה, שֶׁאֵין אַתָּה יוֹדֵעַ מַתַּן שְׂכָרָן שֶׁל מִצְוֹת, וֶהֱוֵי מְחַשֵּׁב הֶפְסֵד מִצְוָה כְּנֶגֶד שְׂכָרָה, וּשְׂכַר עֲבֵרָה כְּנֶגֶד הֶפְסֵדָהּ. הִסְתַּכֵּל בִּשְׁלֹשָׁה דְבָרִים, וְאֵין אַתָּה בָא לִידֵי עֲבֵרָה, דַּע מַה לְמַעְלָה מִמְּךָ, עַיִן רוֹאָה וְאֹזֶן שׁוֹמַעַת, וְכָל מַעֲשֶׂיךָ בְּסֵפֶר נִכְתָּבִים.

1. REBBI WOULD SAY: "WHICH IS THE RIGHT PATH THAT A MAN SHOULD CHOOSE FOR HIMSELF? THAT WHICH IS HONORABLE TO HIMSELF AND BRINGS HIM HONOR FROM MAN.

"BE AS CAREFUL IN [THE PERFORMANCE OF A SEEMINGLY] MINOR *MITZVAH* AS OF A MAJOR ONE, FOR YOU DO NOT KNOW THE REWARD GIVEN FOR THE *MITZVOS*.

"CONSIDER THE LOSS [THAT MIGHT BE INCURRED WHILE PERFORMING] A *MITZVAH* AGAINST THE REWARD [EARNED BY ITS OBSERVANCE], AND THE GAIN [DERIVED] FROM [COMMITTING] A SIN AGAINST THE LOSS.

"REFLECT UPON THREE THINGS AND YOU WILL NEVER COME TO SIN: KNOW WHAT IS ABOVE YOU — AN EYE THAT SEES, AN EAR THAT HEARS, AND A BOOK IN WHICH ALL YOUR DEEDS ARE RECORDED."

REBBI WOULD SAY: "WHICH IS THE RIGHT PATH THAT A MAN SHOULD CHOOSE FOR HIMSELF?" — This opening clause presents several difficulties. Among them:

a) The very question: "Which is the right path that a man should choose for himself?" is problematic. There is only one proper path of conduct for a Jew — the Torah's way. Furthermore, we are obligated to fulfill the Torah; the matter is not a question of choice.

b) There are four Hebrew terms for "man" — *adam, ish, gevar,* and *enosh.*[1] The *mishnah* uses the term *adam,* which refers to man at the highest level — one who has developed his intellectual capacities. Yet the need to follow "the right path" applies even to a person on the lowest level.

c) What is the relationship of this teaching to its author? Furthermore, why does the *mishnah* refer to him as simply Rebbi? On the surface, it would have been appropriate to refer to him using his name and title, Rabbi Yehudah *HaNasi.* Indeed, the next *mishnah* refers to him in this manner.

These difficulties can be resolved as follows: In this *mishnah,* Rebbi is instructing a person who has reached the level of *adam.* For other people, the right path to follow is obvious; one must adhere to the directives of the Torah and its *mitzvos.* When, however, a person already fulfills the Torah and its *mitzvos* in a complete manner and has internalized them, thus meriting the title, *adam,* there is room to ask: Which path should he follow now?

G-d, the Torah, and the Jewish people are all infinite. Therefore a person must realize that at all times he has both the potential and the responsibility to advance in divine service. There are, however, many paths which grant such an opportunity. Which should the person take? This is the question which Rebbi addresses.

---

1. See *Zohar* III, 48a, which discusses the significance of each of these four names, and see the explanations of these concepts in *Likkutei Torah, Shir HaShirim,* 25a, *Sefer HoArochim-Chabad,* Vol. I, p. 148ff.

THAT WHICH IS HONORABLE TO HIMSELF AND BRINGS HIM HONOR FROM MAN — "That which is honorable to himself" points to the potential of human beings to unite with G-d without intermediaries. After a person has thoroughly developed his required connection to G-d through the Torah, he should also seek to develop an intimate, private relationship with G-d.

Nevertheless, the connection with G-d a person establishes must also "bring him honor from man." Coming close to G-d must not take one away from worldly life.[2] A person's conduct should be "good to the heavens, and good to the creations,"[3] i.e., the good one performs should be appreciated by others. While striving for the spiritual heights, a man must find favor in the eyes of his fellowmen, Jews and gentiles alike.

To explain this concept in terms of the *mitzvah* of *Kiddush HaShem*, the Sanctification of G-d's Name: On one hand, *Kiddush HaShem* represents the deepest possible bond between man and G-d.[4] Nevertheless, when communicating this *mitzvah*, the Torah uses the expression:[5] "I will be sanctified among the children of Israel," i.e., one's sanctification of G-d must also find favor "among the children of Israel." In this vein, our Sages explain[6] that this *mitzvah* involves making G-d's name beloved. One's conduct should make others exclaim: "How fortunate is he for having studied the Torah!"

This level of service is possible because one is already an *adam*. I.e., the name *adam* relates to the word *adamah* as in the phrase,[7] *adamah l'elyon* — "I resemble the One above." Just as G-d can combine and resolve opposite tendencies, a person should seek to rise above the limits of worldliness while at the same time remaining involved with his surroundings. Moreover, his efforts to relate to his environment should reflect his

2 .   See *Rambam, Mishneh Torah, Hilchos De'os* 3:1.
3 .   *Kiddushin* 40a.
4 .   See *Rambam, Mishneh Torah, Hilchos Yesodei HaTorah* 5:4.
5 .   *Vayikra* 22:32.
6 .   *Yoma* 86a, quoted by the *Rambam*, loc. cit.:11.
7 .   *Yeshayahu* 14:14; *Shaloh* 3a, 20b.

connection to G-d and his appreciation of G-d's desire for "a dwelling in this world."[8]

The *mishnah* communicates this teaching in the name of Rebbi. In this context, Rebbi is not a name (as used in the following *mishnah*), but rather a title meaning "teacher." In composing the *Mishnah*, Rebbi served as a teacher to the entire Jewish people; this title describes the essence of his existence.

To emphasize this point, the *mishnah* refers to him as Rebbi instead of using his name, Rebbi Yehudah *HaNasi*. The title *Nasi*, "leader," reflects a connection with the entire people. Nevertheless, it also means "uplifted," indicating that the leader is on a much higher rung than the people at large.

The term Rebbi, i.e., teacher of Israel, indicates the point at which all Jews are united — the level at which "Israel and the Holy One, blessed be He, are one." Rebbi relates to the Jewish people on this level, and teaches them how to achieve this inner and outer harmony.

These concepts are particularly relevant in the present age, when we anticipate *Mashiach*'s coming. For it was concerning Rebbi that our Sages said:[9] "If *Mashiach* is among those alive today, he is surely our holy teacher [Rebbi]."

Rebbi speaks about an *adam* — a person who like himself has reached a level of personal fulfillment, and yet is forced to suffer the pains of exile. At present, this is relevant to all of us. Since mankind as a whole has fulfilled all the divine service required of us, we have, to borrow an expression of the Previous Rebbe,[10] "polished the buttons"; as a collective, we are on the level of *adam*.

Having completed everything required of us, we must know what is the right path — the most direct and effective

---

8.   See *Midrash Tanchuma, Bechukosai,* sec. 3; *Tanya,* chs. 33 and 36.
9.   *Sanhedrin* 98b.
10. *Sichos Simchas Torah,* 5689.

means to bring about the actual coming of *Mashiach* and the raising of the world to a higher plane of divine service.

(Sefer HaSichos 5750, Vol. II, p. 420ff; 5751, Vol. II, p. 497ff.)

BE AS CAREFUL — The Hebrew word *zahir*, translated as "careful" also means "shine." All the *mitzvos* share a fundamental quality; each of them enables one's soul to shine forth.[11]

(Likkutei Sichos, Vol. IV, p. 1191ff)

BE AS CAREFUL IN [THE PERFORMANCE OF A SEEMINGLY] MINOR *MITZVAH* AS OF A MAJOR ONE, FOR YOU DO NOT KNOW THE REWARD GIVEN FOR THE *MITZVOS* — In his *Commentary to the Mishnah*, the *Rambam* points out that there is no statement in the Torah detailing the relative severity of the positive commandments. Therefore, one should be careful in the observance of all of them.

Nevertheless, the *Rambam* continues, there is an indirect means of appreciating the relative severity of positive commandments. The severity of each negative commandment is reflected in the severity of the punishment for its violation. Certain positive commandments are paralleled by negative ones — e.g., there are both positive and negative commandments to observe the Sabbath. By comparing the positive commandment to the negative commandment that parallels it, one can appreciate its relative importance.

In that vein, the *Rambam* interprets the subsequent clause of the *mishnah* as follows: "Calculate the loss incurred by [the violation of] a *mitzvah* [in order] to know the reward [for its fulfillment]"; i.e., appreciate the severity of a negative commandment and from it, assess the importance of the parallel positive commandment.

The *Rambam*'s statements raise a question: Since it is possible to appreciate the relative severity of some positive com-

---

11. See *Tzavoas HaRivosh*, sec. 1.

mandments, how can a person be expected to be equally committed to the performance of all *mitzvos?*

It can be explained that there are two dimensions to each *mitzvah*: a) the particular effect it has in refining the person performing it and the world at large; b) the strengthening of a transcendent bond with G-d.

With regard to the first dimension, there is a difference between one *mitzvah* and another, for each *mitzvah* is intended to refine a different element of our personality and of the world at large. And yet, such differences do not apply with regard to the second dimension; every *mitzvah* serves equally to strengthen our connection with the Infinite.

Similar concepts apply in regard to the reward brought about by the observance of *mitzvos*. On one hand, the reward for a *mitzvah* depends on the extent of its effects, and thus there are differences between the reward for one *mitzvah* and another. On the other hand, the ultimate reward for performing a *mitzvah* is the *mitzvah* itself,[12] i.e., the *tzavsa*, or "bond,"[13] with G-d that is established by its performance. The realization that such a connection is possible should motivate a person to "Be as careful of [the performance of a seemingly] minor *mitzvah* as of a major one."

(Likkutei Sichos, Vol. IV, p. 1191ff; Sichos Shabbos Parshas Matos-Masei, 5747)

CONSIDER THE LOSS [THAT MIGHT BE INCURRED WHILE PERFORMING] A *MITZVAH* AGAINST THE REWARD [EARNED BY ITS OBSERVANCE], AND THE GAIN [DERIVED] FROM [COMMITTING] A SIN AGAINST THE LOSS — R. Ovadiah of Bartenura teaches that this clause instructs a person to focus on the endless spiritual advantage he will gain from the observance of a *mitzvah*, rather than on the momentary material loss he might suffer. Similarly,

---

12 . *Pirkei Avos* 4:2.
13 . *Likkutei Torah, Bechukosai* 45c.

committing a sin may provide a temporary material gratification, but also involves an eternal spiritual loss.

This concept raises a question: We are taught that *teshuvah*, repentance, has the potential to wipe away all a person's sins. How then, can sin be considered as an eternal loss?

This difficulty can be resolved as follows: In *Tanya*, ch. 29, the Alter Rebbe explains that when a person turns to G-d in complete *teshuvah*, he renews his relationship with Him, and it is as if he had never sinned. Nevertheless, the sin is not wiped away entirely, since "there are many levels and dimensions within our hearts." As a person advances in his divine service and experiences deeper dimensions of love for G-d, the sins he committed previously create a block, making it necessary for him to rise to an even more complete level of *teshuvah*.

So even though *teshuvah* is effective at every level, the effect of sin is lasting.

(Likkutei Sichos, Vol. IV, p. 1196)

KNOW WHAT IS ABOVE YOU — The Maggid of Mezritch would say:[14] "Know that everything above" — all that transpires in the spiritual realms — is "from you" — dependent on your conduct. Each of us has the potential to influence the most elevated spiritual realms.

(Likkutei Sichos, Vol. XX, p. 331)

ב רַבָּן גַּמְלִיאֵל בְּנוֹ שֶׁל רַבִּי יְהוּדָה הַנָּשִׂיא אוֹמֵר: יָפֶה תַלְמוּד תּוֹרָה עִם דֶּרֶךְ אֶרֶץ, שֶׁיְּגִיעַת שְׁנֵיהֶם מַשְׁכַּחַת עָוֹן, וְכָל תּוֹרָה שֶׁאֵין עִמָּהּ מְלָאכָה סוֹפָהּ בְּטֵלָה וְגוֹרֶרֶת עָוֹן, וְכָל הָעוֹסְקִים עִם הַצִּבּוּר, יִהְיוּ עוֹסְקִים עִמָּהֶם לְשֵׁם שָׁמַיִם, שֶׁזְּכוּת אֲבוֹתָם מְסַיַּעְתָּם, וְצִדְקָתָם עוֹמֶדֶת לָעַד, וְאַתֶּם, מַעֲלֶה אֲנִי עֲלֵיכֶם שָׂכָר הַרְבֵּה כְּאִלּוּ עֲשִׂיתֶם.

14 . Cited in *Or HaTorah al Aggados Chazal*, p. 112b.

2. RABBAN GAMLIEL, SON OF RABBI YEHUDAH
HANASI, SAID: "IT IS GOOD [TO COMBINE] THE
STUDY OF TORAH WITH AN OCCUPATION, FOR THE
EFFORT REQUIRED BY THEM BOTH KEEPS SIN OUT OF
MIND; WHILE ALL TORAH STUDY THAT IS NOT
COMBINED WITH WORK WILL ULTIMATELY CEASE
AND WILL LEAD TO SIN.

"ALL WHO OCCUPY THEMSELVES WITH THE AFFAIRS
OF THE COMMUNITY SHOULD BE ENGAGED WITH
THEM FOR THE SAKE OF HEAVEN, FOR THE MERIT OF
THEIR FATHERS ASSISTS THEM, AND THEIR
RIGHTEOUSNESS ENDURES FOREVER. AND UPON YOU
[SAYS G-D] I WILL BESTOW GREAT REWARD, AS
THOUGH YOU HAD ACCOMPLISHED IT [ALL BY
YOURSELVES]."

**ALL TORAH STUDY NOT COMBINED WITH WORK
WILL CEASE IN THE END AND LEAD TO SIN** — Although the obvious meaning of the term "work" is actual labor,
there is the possibility of an extended interpretation. The Previous Rebbe relates[15] that R. Levi Yitzchak of Berditchev
would quote the Baal Shem Tov as explaining that in this context, "work" refers to *ahavas Yisrael* — our efforts to establish
bonds of love with other Jews. For Torah study to be perpetuated, it must be coupled with *ahavas Yisrael.*

R. Levi Yitzchak explained that this teaching brought
about a fundamental change in his life, motivating him to dedicate himself to the welfare of his fellow Jews.

Why does the *mishnah* refer to *ahavas Yisrael* as "work"? To
teach us that we must strain to extend our *ahavas Yisrael* to
include even those whom we have no inclination to love. And
we must use every means possible to reach out to others.

(Likkutei Sichos, Vol. I, p. 260-261)

---

15 . *Sefer HaSichos Kayitz* 5700, p. 115.

ג הֱווּ זְהִירִין בָּרָשׁוּת, שֶׁאֵין מְקָרְבִין לוֹ לְאָדָם, אֶלָּא לְצֹרֶךְ עַצְמָן, נִרְאִין כְּאוֹהֲבִין בְּשַׁעַת הַנָּאָתָן, וְאֵין עוֹמְדִין לוֹ לְאָדָם בְּשַׁעַת דָּחֳקוֹ.

3. BE WARY OF THOSE IN POWER, FOR THEY BEFRIEND A PERSON ONLY FOR THEIR OWN BENEFIT; THEY SEEM TO BE FRIENDS WHEN IT IS TO THEIR ADVANTAGE, BUT DO NOT STAND BY A MAN IN HIS HOUR OF NEED.

BE WARY OF THOSE IN POWER — Here also, a non-literal interpretation provides an important lesson in our divine service. "Those in power" can refer to our conscious egos, thoughts and feelings. Although we must rely on these powers to control the functioning of our lives, we must be aware of their fundamental self-interest, that they are concerned only for their own benefit. Our essential selves, by contrast, are pointed towards self-transcendence. And it is through such self-transcendence that a person achieves what is truly to his benefit — a good far higher than can be perceived by intellect.

(Sichos Shabbos Parshas Tazria-Metzora, 5739)

ד הוּא הָיָה אוֹמֵר: עֲשֵׂה רְצוֹנוֹ כִּרְצוֹנְךָ, כְּדֵי שֶׁיַּעֲשֶׂה רְצוֹנְךָ כִּרְצוֹנוֹ, בַּטֵּל רְצוֹנְךָ מִפְּנֵי רְצוֹנוֹ כְּדֵי שֶׁיְּבַטֵּל רְצוֹן אֲחֵרִים מִפְּנֵי רְצוֹנֶךָ. הִלֵּל אוֹמֵר: אַל תִּפְרוֹשׁ מִן הַצִּבּוּר, וְאַל תַּאֲמִין בְּעַצְמְךָ עַד יוֹם מוֹתָךְ, וְאַל תָּדִין אֶת חֲבֵרְךָ עַד שֶׁתַּגִּיעַ לִמְקוֹמוֹ, וְאַל תֹּאמַר דָּבָר שֶׁאִי אֶפְשָׁר לִשְׁמוֹעַ שֶׁסּוֹפוֹ לְהִשָּׁמַע, וְאַל תֹּאמַר לִכְשֶׁאֶפָּנֶה אֶשְׁנֶה, שֶׁמָּא לֹא תִפָּנֶה.

4. HE USED TO SAY: "MAKE HIS WILL YOUR WILL, SO THAT HE MAY FULFILL YOUR WILL AS

THOUGH IT WERE HIS WILL. SET ASIDE YOUR WILL
BECAUSE OF HIS WILL, SO THAT HE MAY SET ASIDE
THE WILL OF OTHERS BEFORE YOUR WILL."

HILLEL SAID: "DO NOT SEPARATE YOURSELF FROM
THE COMMUNITY. DO NOT BE SURE OF YOURSELF
UNTIL THE DAY YOU DIE. DO NOT CONDEMN YOUR
FELLOWMAN UNTIL YOU HAVE STOOD IN HIS PLACE.

"DO NOT MAKE A STATEMENT WHICH IS NOT READILY
UNDERSTOOD [IN THE HOPE] THAT IT WILL UL-
TIMATELY BE UNDERSTOOD. AND DO NOT SAY,
'WHEN I WILL HAVE FREE TIME I WILL STUDY,' FOR
PERHAPS YOU WILL NEVER HAVE FREE TIME."

MAKE HIS WILL — This teaching conveys a fundamental lesson: Each of us has the ability to remake G-d's will, as it
were, to arouse a new desire on His part.

To apply this principle: A person might think that since it
is G-d's will that we are in exile, we should resign ourselves to
the situation. Nothing is further from the truth. G-d is anxiously waiting for us to arouse a new will on His part. He is
waiting for us to motivate Him to bring the Redemption.

(Sichos Shabbos Parshas Masei, 5744)

MAKE HIS WILL YOUR OWN WILL — Jewish law requires us to fulfill G-d's will as expressed by the Torah and its
mitzvos. Pirkei Avos teaches us to go beyond mere observance of
the law and remake our characters, molding them to mirror the
intent of the commandments.

The letter of the law tells us which deeds to perform and
which to avoid. *Pirkei Avos* teaches that fulfilling G-d's will
should not be a burden we must discharge, but a reflection of
our own innermost selves.

When a person makes this commitment..., **G-D WILL
FULFILL YOUR WILL AS IF IT WERE HIS WILL** — that

person's will as though it were His will. G-d will modify a person's environment, granting him blessings of health and well-being so that he will be able to express this commitment in his daily life.[16]

SET ASIDE YOUR WILL BECAUSE OF HIS WILL, SO THAT HE MAY SET ASIDE THE WILL OF OTHERS — A person's commitment to the Torah must extend beyond his own individual tendencies. When it becomes necessary to set aside his personal will because of His will, he seeks to transform his nature to reflect G-d's desire. This in turn causes G-d to set aside the will of others before that person's will.

The commentaries[17] explain that in addition to its simple meaning, "others" can be understood as a subtle reference to G-d. Even when there is a Divine decree against a person, that person can abrogate it by serving G-d beyond the limits of his nature.

(Sichos Shabbos Parshas Tazria-Metzora, 5747)

*DO NOT BE SURE OF YOURSELF — It is only the constant assistance of G-d which enables a person to proceed in his divine service, so his apparent achievements are no indication of his true standing. Thus, without detracting from his overall positive self-image, he must guard against over-confidence.

(Likkutei Sichos, Vol. XVI, p. 361)

*DO NOT CONDEMN YOUR FELLOWMAN UNTIL YOU HAVE STOOD IN HIS PLACE — A person should never criticize his fellowman until he establishes a commonalty with him. Even when a person's conduct seems worthy of reproof, one should not talk to him with a condescending attitude. By focusing instead on the essential connection which all

---

16 . See *Rambam, Mishneh Torah, Hilchos Teshuvah* 9:1.
17 . R. Ovadiah of Bartenura.

men share, we can nurture the positive qualities in others and
enable them to surface.

(Sichos Shabbos Parshas Vayakhel, 5752)

ה הוּא הָיָה אוֹמֵר: אֵין בּוּר יְרֵא חֵטְא, וְלֹא עַם הָאָרֶץ חָסִיד, וְלֹא
הַבַּיְשָׁן לָמֵד, וְלֹא הַקַּפְּדָן מְלַמֵּד, וְלֹא כָל הַמַּרְבֶּה בִסְחוֹרָה מַחְכִּים
וּבְמָקוֹם שֶׁאֵין אֲנָשִׁים, הִשְׁתַּדֵּל לִהְיוֹת אִישׁ.

5. HE USED TO SAY: "A BOOR CANNOT BE SIN-
FEARING, NOR CAN AN IGNORAMUS BE PIOUS. A
BASHFUL PERSON WILL NOT LEARN, NEITHER CAN
THE SHORT-TEMPERED TEACH; NOR CAN ANYONE
WHO IS OVER-OCCUPIED IN TRADE BECOME A
SCHOLAR. IN A PLACE WHERE THERE ARE NO MEN,
STRIVE TO BE A MAN."

*A BOOR CANNOT BE SIN-FEARING — "Sin-fearing"
does not refer to a fear of the punishment to be received for
sinning, but to the fear of sin itself, the fear that one will do
something that is against G-d's will. A boor — a person who has
not cultivated and developed his personality — is not capable
of such feelings.

(Likkutei Sichos, Vol. XVIII, p. 61)

ו אַף הוּא רָאָה גֻּלְגֹּלֶת אַחַת שֶׁצָּפָה עַל פְּנֵי הַמָּיִם, אָמַר לָהּ: עַל
דְּאַטֵּפְתְּ אַטְּפוּךְ, וְסוֹף מְטַיְפָיִךְ יְטוּפוּן.

6. HE ALSO SAW A SKULL FLOATING ON THE
WATER. HE SAID TO IT: "BECAUSE YOU

DROWNED OTHERS, THEY DROWNED YOU; AND
ULTIMATELY THOSE WHO DROWNED YOU WILL
THEMSELVES BE DROWNED."

HE ALSO SAW A SKULL FLOATING ON THE WATER
— Our Rabbis[18] explain that this refers to the skull of Pharaoh,
who was drowned in punishment for having Jewish boys
drowned in the Nile. When Hillel saw Pharaoh's skull, he realized that this was an extraordinary phenomenon, and contem-
plated the matter, gaining this insight.

Why did G-d cause this to happen? The fact that Hillel
learned a lesson from the skull and shared it with others
enabled the skull to come to eternal rest after thousands of
years of drifting on the waters. This is the intent of the phrase
"he said to it." Hillel made his statement for the skull's benefit. Once the skull had communicated its lesson, it had fulfilled
its purpose and could rest.

(Sichos Shabbos Parshas Emor, 5744)

ז הוּא הָיָה אוֹמֵר: מַרְבֶּה בָשָׂר מַרְבֶּה רִמָּה, מַרְבֶּה נְכָסִים מַרְבֶּה
דְאָגָה, מַרְבֶּה נָשִׁים מַרְבֶּה כְשָׁפִים, מַרְבֶּה שְׁפָחוֹת מַרְבֶּה זִמָּה,
מַרְבֶּה עֲבָדִים מַרְבֶּה גָזֵל. מַרְבֶּה תוֹרָה מַרְבֶּה חַיִּים, מַרְבֶּה יְשִׁיבָה
מַרְבֶּה חָכְמָה, מַרְבֶּה עֵצָה מַרְבֶּה תְבוּנָה, מַרְבֶּה צְדָקָה מַרְבֶּה
שָׁלוֹם. קָנָה שֵׁם טוֹב קָנָה לְעַצְמוֹ, קָנָה לוֹ דִבְרֵי תוֹרָה קָנָה לוֹ חַיֵּי
הָעוֹלָם הַבָּא.

7. HE USED TO SAY: "INCREASING FLESH IN-
CREASES WORMS [IN THE GRAVE]; INCREASING
POSSESSIONS INCREASES WORRY; INCREASING [THE
NUMBER OF] WIVES INCREASES SORCERY; INCREASING

---

18 . The *AriZal (Shaar Mamaarei Razal)* and Rav David *HaNaggid*, the *Rambam*'s
grandson *(Midrash David)*.

MAIDSERVANTS INCREASES LEWDNESS; INCREASING MANSERVANTS INCREASES THIEVERY.

"[BUT] INCREASING TORAH INCREASES LIFE; INCREASING ASSIDUOUS STUDY INCREASES WISDOM; INCREASING COUNSEL INCREASES UNDERSTANDING; INCREASING CHARITY INCREASES PEACE.

"ONE WHO HAS ACQUIRED A GOOD NAME HAS ACQUIRED IT FOR HIMSELF; ONE WHO HAS ACQUIRED FOR HIMSELF TORAH KNOWLEDGE HAS ACQUIRED FOR HIMSELF LIFE IN THE WORLD TO COME."

*ONE WHO HAS ACQUIRED FOR HIMSELF TORAH KNOWLEDGE HAS ACQUIRED FOR HIMSELF LIFE IN THE WORLD TO COME — The World to Come refers to the Resurrection, the zenith of the Era of the Redemption. At that time, as the *Rambam* writes:[19] "The occupation of the entire world will be solely to know G-d. For the world will be filled with the knowledge of G-d as the waters cover the ocean bed."[20]

Just as fish in the sea depend on their watery environment for life itself, in the Era of the Redemption, each being will realize that its existence depends on the knowledge of G-d, which encompasses it.

A person's connection to the life of the World to Come — the outpouring of Divine knowledge in that future era — depends on the acquisition of Torah knowledge in the present time. As implied by our Sages' statement:[21] "Happy is he who comes here having attained knowledge."

---

19. *Mishneh Torah, Hilchos Melachim* 12:5.
20. *Yeshayahu* 11:9.
21. *Pesachim* 50a. This statement is interpreted *(Likkutei Torah, Vaes'chanan* 6c) to apply to the soul's reward in *Gan Eden*, i.e., through the study of Torah in our material world, the soul attains the knowledge of *pnimiyus HaTorah* in the spiritual realms. Nevertheless, the same motif applies with regard to the teachings of the *Mashiach*, as implied by *(Likkutei Torah, Shir HaShirim* 22d and)

The knowledge we have attained in the present age influences our appreciation of the teachings to be revealed by *Mashiach*.

(Sichos Shabbos Tazria-Metzora, 5742; Likkutei Sichos, Vol. XXIV, p. 470)

ח רַבָּן יוֹחָנָן בֶּן זַכַּאי קִבֵּל מֵהִלֵּל וּמִשַּׁמַּאי, הוּא הָיָה אוֹמֵר: אִם לָמַדְתָּ תוֹרָה הַרְבֵּה, אַל תַּחֲזִיק טוֹבָה לְעַצְמָךָ, כִּי לְכָךְ נוֹצָרְתָּ.

8. RABBAN YOCHANAN BEN ZAKKAI RECEIVED [THE ORAL TRADITION] FROM HILLEL AND SHAMMAI. HE USED TO SAY: "IF YOU HAVE STUDIED MUCH TORAH, DO NOT CLAIM SPECIAL CREDIT FOR YOURSELF; FOR THIS VERY PURPOSE WERE YOU CREATED."

IF YOU HAVE STUDIED MUCH TORAH — A person should constantly seek to study "much Torah," i.e., he should always be extending himself further, to greater achievements. Since the Torah is in essence unlimited, a person should never restrict his efforts to attain it. Instead, he must constantly strive to increase his attainments.

(Sichos Shabbos Parshas Matos-Masei, 5737)

DO NOT CLAIM SPECIAL CREDIT FOR YOURSELF — In essence, a person who studies the Torah has just reason to be proud: through his study, he becomes united with G-d — a bond that transcends all worldly heights.[22] Nevertheless, since this privilege is endowed by the Torah itself, and is thus

---

Tanya, ch. 37, which states that all the revelations of the Era of the Redemption are dependent on our service in the present time.

22 . See *Tanya*, ch. 5.

not a result of his own efforts, the *mishnah* advises him to remain humble.

(Ibid.)

FOR THIS VERY PURPOSE WERE YOU CREATED — Creation is an ongoing process. As the Alter Rebbe writes in *Tanya*,[23] at each moment all existence is renewed. By emphasizing the connection between Torah study and creation, the *mishnah* underscores the concept that a person can never "rest on his laurels." Instead, at every moment, he must move forward, thus constantly fulfilling the purpose of his creation.

(Ibid.)

ט חֲמִשָּׁה תַלְמִידִים הָיוּ לוֹ לְרַבָּן יוֹחָנָן בֶּן זַכַּאי, וְאֵלּוּ הֵן: רַבִּי אֱלִיעֶזֶר בֶּן הוֹרְקְנוֹס, וְרַבִּי יְהוֹשֻׁעַ בֶּן חֲנַנְיָא, וְרַבִּי יוֹסֵי הַכֹּהֵן, וְרַבִּי שִׁמְעוֹן בֶּן נְתַנְאֵל, וְרַבִּי אֶלְעָזָר בֶּן עֲרָךְ. הוּא הָיָה מוֹנֶה שְׁבָחָם, רַבִּי אֱלִיעֶזֶר בֶּן הוֹרְקְנוֹס בּוֹר סוּד שֶׁאֵינוֹ מְאַבֵּד טִפָּה, רַבִּי יְהוֹשֻׁעַ בֶּן חֲנַנְיָא אַשְׁרֵי יוֹלַדְתּוֹ, רַבִּי יוֹסֵי הַכֹּהֵן חָסִיד, רַבִּי שִׁמְעוֹן בֶּן נְתַנְאֵל יְרֵא חֵטְא וְרַבִּי אֶלְעָזָר בֶּן עֲרָךְ כְּמַעְיָן הַמִּתְגַּבֵּר. הוּא הָיָה אוֹמֵר: אִם יִהְיוּ כָל חַכְמֵי יִשְׂרָאֵל בְּכַף מֹאזְנַיִם, וֶאֱלִיעֶזֶר בֶּן הוֹרְקְנוֹס בְּכַף שְׁנִיָּה, מַכְרִיעַ אֶת כֻּלָּם. אַבָּא שָׁאוּל אוֹמֵר מִשְּׁמוֹ, אִם יִהְיוּ כָל חַכְמֵי יִשְׂרָאֵל בְּכַף מֹאזְנַיִם וֶאֱלִיעֶזֶר בֶּן הוֹרְקְנוֹס אַף עִמָּהֶם, וְאֶלְעָזָר בֶּן עֲרָךְ בְּכַף שְׁנִיָּה, מַכְרִיעַ אֶת כֻּלָּם.

9. RABBAN YOCHANAN BEN ZAKKAI HAD FIVE [OUTSTANDING] DISCIPLES. THEY WERE: RABBI ELIEZER BEN HORKENUS, RABBI YEHOSHUA BEN CHANANYA, RABBI YOSAY THE KOHEN, RABBI SHIMON BEN NESANEL, AND RABBI ELAZAR BEN ARACH.

---

23 . *Shaar HaYichud VehaEmunah*, ch. 1.

HE USED TO ENUMERATE THEIR PRAISEWORTHY
QUALITIES: "RABBI ELIEZER BEN HORKENUS — A
CEMENTED CISTERN WHICH DOES NOT LOSE A DROP;
RABBI YEHOSHUA BEN CHANANYA — HAPPY IS SHE
WHO BORE HIM; RABBI YOSAY THE PRIEST — A
CHASSID; RABBI SHIMON BEN NESANEL — SIN-
FEARING; AND RABBI ELAZAR BEN ARACH — LIKE A
SPRING WHICH FLOWS WITH EVER-INCREASING
STRENGTH."

HE USED TO SAY: "IF ALL THE SAGES OF ISRAEL WERE
ON ONE SIDE OF THE SCALE, AND ELIEZER BEN
HORKENUS WERE ON THE OTHER, HE WOULD
OUTWEIGH THEM ALL."

ABBA SHAUL SAID IN HIS NAME: "IF ALL THE SAGES OF
ISRAEL, INCLUDING EVEN ELIEZER BEN HORKENUS,
WERE ON ONE SIDE OF THE SCALE, AND ELAZAR BEN
ARACH WERE ON THE OTHER, HE WOULD OUTWEIGH
THEM ALL."

**HE USED TO ENUMERATE THEIR PRAISEWORTHY
QUALITIES** — Each of these students possessed a quality in
which he surpassed all others. As a teacher, Rabbi Yochanan
did not push them all in a single direction. Instead, he appreciated their uniqueness and endeavored to give each the opportunity to develop his own potential.

This concept can be applied on a larger scale. Each person
possesses a particular virtue in which he surpasses all others,
even the leaders of the generation. He (and those who help
him in his growth and development) should not seek universal
conformity, but should strive to cultivate this unique gift.

(Sichos Shabbos Parshas Matos-Masei, 5743)

**RABBI YEHOSHUA BEN CHANANYA — HAPPY IS
SHE WHO BORE HIM** — Why does the *mishnah* ascribe happiness to Rabbi Yehoshua's mother? Because she was to a large

degree responsible for his greatness. When Rabbi Yehoshua
was an infant, she would hang his cradle in the House of Study
so that he would become accustomed to the sweet singsong of
Torah study.[24] As he matured, the influence of his formative
years played a large part in shaping his sagelike character.

This message is relevant to Jewish women today, for they
bear the brunt of the responsibility for shaping the environment of their children. A child is always learning from his surroundings; whatever he sees or hears makes an impression.[25]
When the home in which a child lives — and more particularly,
his individual room — is filled with Torah teachings, when a
pushkah is proudly displayed and a *siddur* is always handy, the
values of study, kindness, and prayer will permeate his character.

(Likkutei Sichos, Vol. XXIII, p. 258; Sichos Shabbos Parshas Kedoshim, 5736)

RABBI SHIMON BEN NESANEL — SIN-FEARING —
The intent is not to say that he feared the punishment he
would receive; he feared the sin itself.[26] The Hebrew word for
sin — חטא — also has the meaning "lack."[27] Rabbi Shimon
feared the loss which sin would cause to his relationship with
G-d.

(Likkutei Sichos, Vol. IV, p. 1200)

IF ALL THE SAGES OF ISRAEL WERE ON ONE SIDE OF THE SCALE, AND ELIEZER BEN HORKENUS WERE ON THE OTHER, HE WOULD OUTWEIGH THEM ALL —
Both Rabbi Eliezer ben Horkenus and Rabbi Elazar ben Arach
represent paradigms of excellence to which all students should
aspire. They each, however, had a different approach to study.

---

24 . *Jerusalem Talmud, Yevamos* 1:6; R. Ovadiah of Bartenura.
25 . And this applies from the earliest age. From birth (and even from conception)
onward, a child is learning.
26 . See *Likkutei Torah, Matos* 82a.
27 . See the commentary of *Rashi* and *Metzudos* to *I Melachim* 1:21.

Rabbi Eliezer, the "cemented cistern," represents the epitome of concentrated effort to absorb his teachers' wisdom. No other Sage matched his capacity for retention.

Not only during the time he studied under his masters did he diligently strive to soak up their teachings, but even after he became an independent authority, he saw himself as no more than a repository for their wisdom. Although "his two arms were like the two staves of a Torah scroll,"[28] he never mentioned an original concept; "never did he relate a teaching that he had not heard from his teachers."[29]

Nevertheless, Abba Shaul said: "If all the Sages of Israel, including even Eliezer ben Horkenus, were on one side of the scale, and Elazar ben Arach were on the other, he would outweigh them all." Rabbi Elazar ben Arach had a different approach to study. His thrust did not center on preserving his teachers' wisdom, but rather on extending it. "Like a spring which flows with ever-increasing strength," he constantly surged towards new frontiers of knowledge, building on the teachings he received as he proceeded into new domains.

Although this approach required the development of independent ideas and ways of thinking, Rabbi Elazar was still considered a student of Rabbi Yochanan ben Zakkai. For it was Rabbi Yochanan who nurtured his conceptual development until he was able to make these independent strides. Moreover, even his original ideas reflected the teachings he had received from Rabbi Yochanan.[30]

Each of these approaches possesses an advantage over the other. Rabbi Eliezer enjoyed a more direct bond to the guiding light of his master's teachings. Rabbi Elazar, by contrast, by tapping the potential for personal initiative, showed how the

---

28. *Sanhedrin* 68a.
29. *Sukkah* 27b.
30. A similar concept can be derived from the verse (*Mishlei* 22:6): "Educate a child according to his way; even when he grows older he will not depart from it." The path which a child follows will remain with him as he matures. He will follow this path through new and different frontiers, but the fundamental thrust will be the same.

fundamental truth of the Torah can be revealed in new and different settings.[31]

These concepts are relevant to our response to the challenge of exile. One approach is to preserve the teachings of the past, to cling to them so that nothing is lost. An alternative is to use these teachings as a springboard to the future — to show how they can permeate the thought patterns which Jews are forced to adopt in exile. Since the Torah is eternally relevant, it must be applicable in all settings and frames of reference.

And as the Torah is taken into these new settings, it remakes them and infuses them with a greater purpose. As these settings become transformed, a dwelling for G-d is established in mortal realms.[32] For worldliness has not been rejected, but neither has it been accepted on its own terms. Instead, it is revealed that while the world exists within its own conception, it constantly gives expression to the essential G-dly truth which the Torah conveys. And this heralds the coming of the era when the awareness of G-dliness will permeate existence — when "the world will be filled with the knowledge of G-d as the waters cover the ocean bed."[33]

(Likkutei Sichos, Vol. V, p. 460ff; Vol. X, p. 82-83)

י אָמַר לָהֶם: צְאוּ וּרְאוּ אֵיזוֹ הִיא דֶרֶךְ טוֹבָה שֶׁיִּדְבַּק בָּהּ הָאָדָם, רַבִּי אֱלִיעֶזֶר אוֹמֵר: עַיִן טוֹבָה. רַבִּי יְהוֹשֻׁעַ אוֹמֵר: חָבֵר טוֹב, רַבִּי יוֹסֵי אוֹמֵר: שָׁכֵן טוֹב. רַבִּי שִׁמְעוֹן אוֹמֵר: הָרוֹאֶה אֶת הַנּוֹלָד. רַבִּי אֶלְעָזָר אוֹמֵר, לֵב טוֹב. אָמַר לָהֶם: רוֹאֶה אֲנִי אֶת דִּבְרֵי אֶלְעָזָר בֶּן עֲרָךְ

---

31. It must be emphasized that Rabbi Eliezer did not merely retain his masters' teachings; he integrated them into his own thinking processes (see our notes to ch. 6, *beraisa* 6). Nevertheless, the desire to extend these teachings into new frames of reference was indicative of Rabbi Elazar's unique thrust, and not that of Rabbi Eliezer's.

32. Cf. *Midrash Tanchuma, Parshas Bechukosai*, sec. 3.

33. *Yeshayahu* 11:9.

מִדִּבְרֵיכֶם, שֶׁבִּכְלָל דְּבָרָיו דִּבְרֵיכֶם. אָמַר לָהֶם: צְאוּ וּרְאוּ אֵיזוֹ הִיא
דֶּרֶךְ רָעָה שֶׁיִּתְרַחֵק מִמֶּנָּה הָאָדָם, רַבִּי אֱלִיעֶזֶר אוֹמֵר: עַיִן רָעָה. רַבִּי
יְהוֹשֻׁעַ אוֹמֵר: חָבֵר רָע. רַבִּי יוֹסֵי אוֹמֵר: שָׁכֵן רָע. רַבִּי שִׁמְעוֹן
אוֹמֵר: הַלֹּוֶה וְאֵינוֹ מְשַׁלֵּם. אֶחָד הַלֹּוֶה מִן הָאָדָם כְּלֹוֶה מִן הַמָּקוֹם,
שֶׁנֶּאֱמַר לֹוֶה רָשָׁע וְלֹא יְשַׁלֵּם, וְצַדִּיק חוֹנֵן וְנוֹתֵן. רַבִּי אֶלְעָזָר אוֹמֵר:
לֵב רָע. אָמַר לָהֶם: רוֹאֶה אֲנִי אֶת דִּבְרֵי אֶלְעָזָר בֶּן עֲרָךְ מִדִּבְרֵיכֶם,
שֶׁבִּכְלָל דְּבָרָיו דִּבְרֵיכֶם. הֵם אָמְרוּ שְׁלֹשָׁה דְבָרִים, רַבִּי אֱלִיעֶזֶר
אוֹמֵר: יְהִי כְבוֹד חֲבֵרָךְ חָבִיב עָלֶיךָ כְּשֶׁלָּךְ, וְאַל תְּהִי נוֹחַ לִכְעוֹס.
וְשׁוּב יוֹם אֶחָד לִפְנֵי מִיתָתָךְ. וֶהֱוֵי מִתְחַמֵּם כְּנֶגֶד אוּרָן שֶׁל חֲכָמִים
וֶהֱוֵי זָהִיר בְּגַחַלְתָּן שֶׁלֹּא תִכָּוֶה שֶׁנְּשִׁיכָתָן נְשִׁיכַת שׁוּעָל, וַעֲקִיצָתָן
עֲקִיצַת עַקְרָב, וּלְחִישָׁתָן לְחִישַׁת שָׂרָף, וְכָל דִּבְרֵיהֶם כְּגַחֲלֵי אֵשׁ.

10. HE SAID TO THEM: "GO AND SEE WHICH IS
THE GOOD WAY TO WHICH A MAN SHOULD
CLEAVE."

RABBI ELIEZER SAID: "A GOOD EYE"; RABBI
YEHOSHUA SAID: "A GOOD FRIEND"; RABBI YOSAY
SAID: "A GOOD NEIGHBOR"; RABBI SHIMON SAID:
"ONE WHO SEES THE CONSEQUENCES [OF HIS
ACTIONS]"; RABBI ELAZAR SAID: "A GOOD HEART."

[RABBAN YOCHANAN BEN ZAKKAI] SAID TO THEM: "I
PREFER THE WORDS OF ELAZAR BEN ARACH TO ALL
OF YOURS, FOR IN HIS WORDS YOURS ARE INCLUDED."

HE SAID TO THEM: "GO AND SEE WHICH IS THE EVIL
PATH FROM WHICH A MAN SHOULD KEEP FAR AWAY."

RABBI ELIEZER SAID: "AN EVIL EYE"; RABBI
YEHOSHUA SAID: "A WICKED FRIEND"; RABBI YOSAY
SAID: "A WICKED NEIGHBOR"; RABBI SHIMON SAID:
"HE WHO BORROWS AND DOES NOT REPAY, SINCE ONE
WHO BORROWS FROM MAN IS AS ONE WHO BORROWS
FROM G-D, AS IT IS STATED:[34] 'THE WICKED ONE
BORROWS AND DOES NOT REPAY, BUT THE RIGHTEOUS

---

34 . *Tehillim* 37:21.

ACTS GRACIOUSLY AND GIVES.'" RABBI ELAZAR SAID:
"A WICKED HEART."

[RABBAN YOCHANAN BEN ZAKKAI] SAID TO THEM: "I
PREFER THE WORDS OF ELAZAR BEN ARACH TO ALL
OF YOURS, FOR IN HIS WORDS YOURS ARE INCLUDED."

THEY [EACH] SAID THREE THINGS. RABBI ELIEZER
SAID: "CHERISH THE HONOR OF YOUR COLLEAGUE AS
YOUR OWN, AND DO NOT BE EASILY ANGERED.
REPENT ONE DAY BEFORE YOUR DEATH.

"WARM YOURSELF BY THE FIRE OF THE SAGES, BUT
BEWARE OF THEIR GLOWING EMBERS LEST YOU BE
BURNT, FOR THEIR BITE IS THE BITE OF A FOX, THEIR
STING IS THE STING OF A SCORPION, THEIR HISS IS
THE HISS OF A SERPENT, AND ALL THEIR WORDS ARE
LIKE FIERY COALS."

RABBI SHIMON SAID: "ONE WHO SEES THE CONSEQUENCES [OF HIS ACTIONS]" — This statement relates to Rabbi Yochanan's description of Rabbi Shimon as sin-fearing. Because he saw the consequences of his actions, he was not vulnerable to the temptations of his *yetzer hora*. He realized that sin would weaken his bond with G-d, and therefore was willing to forego the immediate benefits of indulgence in order to safeguard the lasting virtue of that bond.

One might ask, however, why Rabbi Shimon used the expression "sees the consequences." Why didn't he say "comprehends the consequences"? The answer is that the lures of the *yetzer hora* are very attractive, and sometimes appetite is more powerful than intellect. Moreover, the *yetzer hora* is crafty,[35] and offers rationalizations that enable a person to feel he is doing the right thing although he sins. A person whose awareness of the consequences of sin is merely intellectual may be swayed by such rationalizations. When, however, a person "sees" the consequences, i.e., when his conception is so power-

---

35 . *Shabbos* 100b.

ful that it is as if he sees the consequences with his eyes, he will refuse to allow his connection with G-d to be weakened at any time.

(Likkutei Sichos, Vol. IV, p. 1198ff)

RABBI ELIEZER SAID: "CHERISH THE HONOR OF YOUR COLLEAGUE AS YOUR OWN" — Rabbi Eliezer possessed far greater knowledge than his colleagues. Indeed, his colleagues would refer to him as Rabbi Eliezer the Great and as "Sinai,"[36] indicating their recognition of him as the repository of our Torah heritage. Despite his greatness, he appreciated the need to cherish the honor of others.

(Sefer HaSichos 5748, Vol. II, p. 563)

יא רַבִּי יְהוֹשֻׁעַ אוֹמֵר: עַיִן הָרָע, וְיֵצֶר הָרָע, וְשִׂנְאַת הַבְּרִיּוֹת, מוֹצִיאִין אֶת הָאָדָם מִן הָעוֹלָם.

11. RABBI YEHOSHUA SAID: "THE EVIL EYE, THE EVIL INCLINATION, AND HATRED OF ONE'S FELLOW DRIVE A MAN FROM THE WORLD."

THE EVIL INCLINATION... DRIVE[S] A MAN FROM THE WORLD — Our Rabbis often use the expression, "Happy is a person whose portion is..." For each person is given a particular portion of the world, and the potentials and tendencies necessary to connect that portion to G-d. The evil inclination stands in the way of a person developing this portion, thus driv[ing him] from the world. Although it tempts a person in many ways, its primary thrust is to thwart the fulfillment of this individual mission.

(Likkutei Sichos, Vol. III, p. 779; Vol. XVI, p. 553)

---

36 . See *Shir HaShirim Rabbah* 1:3 (1).

יב רַבִּי יוֹסֵי אוֹמֵר: יְהִי מָמוֹן חֲבֵרְךָ חָבִיב עָלֶיךָ כְּשֶׁלָּךְ. וְהַתְקֵן
עַצְמְךָ לִלְמוֹד תּוֹרָה, שֶׁאֵינָהּ יְרֻשָּׁה לָךְ, וְכָל מַעֲשֶׂיךָ יִהְיוּ לְשֵׁם
שָׁמָיִם.

12. RABBI YOSSE SAID: "LET THE MONEY OF YOUR FELLOWMAN BE AS DEAR TO YOU AS YOUR OWN. PREPARE YOURSELF FOR THE STUDY OF TORAH, FOR IT DOES NOT COME TO YOU THROUGH INHERITANCE; AND LET ALL YOUR DEEDS BE FOR THE SAKE OF HEAVEN."

LET THE MONEY OF YOUR FELLOWMAN BE AS DEAR TO YOU AS YOUR OWN — Everything in the world contains sparks of G-dliness which are concealed by the material nature of our existence. Mankind has been given the task of revealing matter's innate G-dliness. Every individual is destined to elevate certain sparks, and this divine service is necessary for his personal growth. If these G-dly energies are not elevated, that individual's soul remains incomplete.

The Baal Shem Tov expounded this concept in his interpretation[37] of the verse,[38] "Hungry and thirsty, their soul longs within." The Baal Shem Tov asks: "Why are they hungry and thirsty? Because 'their soul longs within.' Their souls seek a bond with the G-dly energy contained in food and drink."

On this basis, we can appreciate our Sages' statement,[39] "With regard to the righteous: Their money is more dear to them than their lives." For they desire to fulfill the spiritual purpose associated with these tokens of seemingly material wealth.

These concepts apply to all Jews, for "Your nation are all righteous."[40] Therefore we should each hold our wealth dear. And just as we hold our own wealth dear, we should hold dear

---

37. *Kesser Shem Tov*, sec. 194, p. 25c; see also *Likkutei Sichos*, Vol. I, p. 177.
38. *Tehillim* 107:5.
39. *Chulin* 91b.
40. *Sanhedrin* 10:1. This *mishnah* is quoted at the beginning of the recitation of *Pirkei Avos* every week.

the wealth of others. Torah law prohibits damaging a colleague's property, and obligates us to undertake any measures necessary to save it. The approach of *mili dechassidusa* teaches us to go further, and regard the other person's property as dearly as our own.

(Sichos Shabbos Parshas Matos-Masei, 5740)

PREPARE YOURSELF FOR THE STUDY OF TORAH, FOR IT DOES NOT COME TO YOU THROUGH INHERITANCE — There are two dimensions to a Jew's connection to Torah: a) an essential connection shared by all Jews regardless of their personal development, as it is written:[41] "The Torah which Moshe commanded us is the heritage of the congregation of Yaakov," and b) a conscious bond, the development of which is dependent on each person's efforts. This is the focus of our *mishnah*.

The essential connection reflects the fundamental G-dly core of the Torah that transcends mortal wisdom. There is, nevertheless, an advantage to the connection established through our own efforts. This bond with the Torah transforms our thinking processes and enables us to develop an internalized link with G-d.

(Ibid., Likkutei Sichos, Vol. IV, p. 1135)

LET ALL YOUR DEEDS BE FOR THE SAKE OF HEAVEN — Our Rabbis[42] identify this directive with the verse, "Know Him in all your ways."[43] But it is possible to distinguish between the two.

Performing a deed "for the sake of Heaven" implies that although it is performed with G-dly intent, the deed itself is mundane. To "know G-d in all your ways" implies a deeper bond — one which plays a part in every worldly activity.

---

41 . *Devarim* 33:5. See *Likkutei Torah, Berachah* 94d.
42 . *Avos d'Rabbi Nossan* 17:7, *Rambam* (*Shemoneh Perakim*, the conclusion of ch. 5), and the *Meiri*.
43 . *Mishlei* 3:6.

To cite an example: When one eats a meal with the intent of using the energy generated from the food to serve G-d, one's eating remains a mundane act. In contrast, when one eats on *Shabbos*, or when one partakes of sacrificial offerings, the eating itself is considered a *mitzvah*, an act of connection to G-d.

In a larger sense, this difference reflects two approaches with regard to the oneness of G-d. In the first, our material world serves as a means by which to establish a bond with G-d. This implies, however, that its actual material substance remains separate from G-d. The second approach maintains that even material existence can become unified with Him.

(Likkutei Sichos, Vol. III, p. 907; Vol. X, p. 104)

יג רַבִּי שִׁמְעוֹן אוֹמֵר: הֱוֵי זָהִיר בִּקְרִיאַת שְׁמַע וּבִתְפִלָּה, וּכְשֶׁאַתָּה מִתְפַּלֵּל, אַל תַּעַשׂ תְּפִלָּתְךָ קֶבַע, אֶלָּא רַחֲמִים וְתַחֲנוּנִים לִפְנֵי הַמָּקוֹם, שֶׁנֶּאֱמַר: כִּי חַנּוּן וְרַחוּם הוּא, אֶרֶךְ אַפַּיִם וְרַב חֶסֶד, וְנִחָם עַל הָרָעָה, וְאַל תְּהִי רָשָׁע בִּפְנֵי עַצְמֶךָ.

13. RABBI SHIMON SAID: "BE METICULOUS IN READING THE *SHEMA* AND IN PRAYER. WHEN YOU PRAY, DO NOT MAKE YOUR PRAYER ROUTINE, BUT RATHER [ENTREATY FOR] MERCY AND SUPPLICATION BEFORE G-D, AS IT IS STATED:[44] 'FOR HE IS GRACIOUS AND COMPASSIONATE, SLOW TO ANGER AND ABOUNDING IN LOVING KINDNESS, AND RELENTING OF THE EVIL DECREE.' AND DO NOT CONSIDER YOURSELF WICKED IN YOUR SELF-ESTIMATION."

---

44 . *Yoel* 2:13.

RABBI SHIMON SAID — Rabbi Shimon ben Nesanel shared a commonalty with Rabbi Shimon bar Yochai; about both it could be said: "his occupation was Torah study."[45]

When a person involves himself in the study of Torah in such an all-encompassing manner, he is freed from the obligation of reciting the *Shema* each day.[46] Therefore Rabbi Shimon instructs his students to be meticulous in reading the *Shema* and in prayer. Although he himself would not recite the *Shema* daily, he advised his students not to follow his example, since they were not on his level.

Similarly, Rabbi Shimon did not pray daily; he and all others whose "occupation was Torah study" would pray from time to time.[47] Therefore he tells his colleagues — those who, like himself, would pray from time to time — When you do pray, "do not make your prayer routine." Do not view prayer as a burden, but rather as "entreaty for mercy and supplication before G-d."

(Likkutei Sichos, Vol. XVII, p. 356)

---

45. An allusion to this is found in the fact that the *mishnah* refers to Rabbi Shimon ben Nesanel without mentioning his father's name. Generally, when the name Rabbi Shimon is mentioned without any further elucidation, the reference is to Rabbi Shimon bar Yochai (see *Rashi, Shavuos* 2b). By referring to Rabbi Shimon ben Nesanel in this manner, the *mishnah* points to a connection with Rabbi Shimon bar Yochai. Moreover, we find interpretations *(Seder HaDoros, Midrash David)* which indeed attribute this teaching to Rabbi Shimon bar Yochai.

46. This follows the ruling of the *Jerusalem Talmud (Berachos* 1:2). The *Babylonian Talmud (Shabbos* 11a*)*, by contrast, maintains that even a person who studies the Torah with total dedication should interrupt his studies to recite the *Shema*.

   It is possible to resolve the difference between the two rulings. The *Babylonian Talmud* speaks of a person on the level of Rabbi Shimon bar Yochai before he underwent his 13-year ordeal, hiding from the Romans in a cave. The *Jerusalem Talmud*, by contrast, speaks of a person whose commitment to Torah study is as all-encompassing as was Rabbi Shimon's after that experience.

47. Rabbeinu Yonah (in his notes to the *Rif, Berachos* 8a) states that Rabbi Shimon bar Yochai would pray once every year. See also the conclusion of the tractate of *Rosh HaShanah* with regard to Rabbi Yehudah's manner of prayer.

יד רַבִּי אֶלְעָזָר אוֹמֵר: הֱוֵי שָׁקוּד לִלְמוֹד תּוֹרָה, וְדַע מַה שֶׁתָּשִׁיב
לְאֶפִּיקוֹרוֹס. וְדַע לִפְנֵי מִי אַתָּה עָמֵל, וּמִי הוּא בַּעַל מְלַאכְתֶּךָ
שֶׁיְּשַׁלֶּם לָךְ שְׂכַר פְּעֻלָּתֶךָ.

14. RABBI ELAZAR SAID: "BE DILIGENT IN THE STUDY OF TORAH; KNOW WHAT TO ANSWER AN UNBELIEVER. KNOW BEFORE WHOM YOU TOIL, WHO YOUR EMPLOYER IS, AND WHO WILL PAY YOU THE REWARD OF YOUR LABOR."

RABBI ELAZAR SAID: "BE DILIGENT IN THE STUDY OF TORAH" — Rabbi Elazar's teaching reflected his nature — that of "a spring which flows with ever-increasing strength,"[48] constantly surging towards new frontiers. Rabbi Elazar emphasizes that the desire to cross new thresholds of experience should be tempered with diligent review of previous study.

An example can be brought from Rabbi Elazar's personal history. The *Talmud* relates[49] that Rabbi Elazar ben Arach went to the lands of Progissa and Diomisis, the wines and waters of which were pleasant. Indulging himself in these delights, he ignored his Torah studies. When he was called to read from the Torah the verse *Hachodesh hazeh lechem* ("This month shall be for you"), he read instead *Hacheresh hoyeh libem* ("Their hearts have become dumb"). His colleagues, seeing the depths to which he had fallen, prayed on his behalf, and his knowledge was restored.

(Sichos Shabbos Parshas Kedoshim, 5746)

KNOW BEFORE WHOM YOU TOIL — As explained in *Tanya*,[50] knowledge refers to an inner bond. Every person has the potential to develop such an inner bond with G-d. Al-

---

48. Above *mishnah* 9.
49. *Shabbos* 147b.
50. The conclusion of ch. 3.

though he labors for Him as a servant, there is nothing preventing him from establishing a deeper connection.

This also affects the nature of a person's relationship with G-d with regard to reward and punishment. Although there are many intermediaries by which G-d dispenses the reward granted for observance, a person must know "who his Employer is, and who will pay him the reward of his labor," and realize that the source for the reward is always G-d Himself, and not the intermediaries.

(Ibid.)

טו רַבִּי טַרְפוֹן אוֹמֵר: הַיּוֹם קָצֵר, וְהַמְּלָאכָה מְרֻבָּה, וְהַפּוֹעֲלִים עֲצֵלִים, וְהַשָּׂכָר הַרְבֵּה, וּבַעַל הַבַּיִת דּוֹחֵק.

15. RABBI TARFON SAID: "THE DAY IS SHORT, THE WORK IS MUCH, THE WORKMEN ARE LAZY, THE REWARD IS GREAT, AND THE MASTER IS PRESSING."

THE DAY IS SHORT — When a person realizes the nature of the task before him — to conduct his entire life in service of G-d, and to do so in a manner of *mili dechassidusa*, beyond the measure of the law, he will realize that one lifetime (the "day" allotted for these efforts) is brief indeed. Moreover, the work is even greater than can be conceived by our mortal minds.

(Sichos Shabbos Parshas Masei, 5741)

טז הוּא הָיָה אוֹמֵר: לֹא עָלֶיךָ הַמְּלָאכָה לִגְמוֹר, וְלֹא אַתָּה בֶן חוֹרִין
לְהִבָּטֵל מִמֶּנָּה, אִם לָמַדְתָּ תּוֹרָה הַרְבֵּה, נוֹתְנִין לְךָ שָׂכָר הַרְבֵּה,
וְנֶאֱמָן הוּא בַּעַל מְלַאכְתֶּךָ שֶׁיְּשַׁלֶּם לְךָ שְׂכַר פְּעֻלָּתֶךָ, וְדַע שֶׁמַּתַּן
שְׂכָרָן שֶׁל צַדִּיקִים לֶעָתִיד לָבוֹא:

16. HE USED TO SAY: "IT IS NOT INCUMBENT UPON YOU TO COMPLETE THE WORK, YET YOU ARE NOT FREE TO DESIST FROM IT; IF YOU HAVE STUDIED MUCH TORAH, MUCH REWARD WILL BE GIVEN TO YOU, AND YOUR EMPLOYER IS TRUST-WORTHY TO PAY YOU THE REWARD FOR YOUR LABOR. BUT KNOW THAT THE GIVING OF THE REWARD TO THE RIGHTEOUS WILL BE IN THE WORLD TO COME."

The realization of the immensity of the task before us should not lead people to despair, because...

IT IS NOT INCUMBENT UPON US TO COMPLETE THE WORK — A person is never required to do more than he can.[51] On the contrary, G-d gives each person a mission which he can fulfill without having to face challenges which he is unable to overcome.

Even if at times a person feels daunted by the task facing him, he must know that...

HE IS NOT FREE TO DESIST FROM IT — and must persist with *kabbalas ol.* Even when he does not naturally feel joy in his Torah service, he should persevere; such full-hearted dedication will lead to personal fulfillment.

(Ibid.)

---

51 . *Avodah Zarah* 3a.

CHAPTER THREE

CHAPTER THREE

א עֲקַבְיָא בֶּן מַהֲלַלְאֵל אוֹמֵר: הִסְתַּכֵּל בִּשְׁלֹשָׁה דְבָרִים, וְאֵין אַתָּה
בָא לִידֵי עֲבֵרָה. דַּע מֵאַיִן בָּאתָ, וּלְאָן אַתָּה הוֹלֵךְ, וְלִפְנֵי מִי אַתָּה
עָתִיד לִתֵּן דִּין וְחֶשְׁבּוֹן. מֵאַיִן בָּאתָ: מִטִּפָּה סְרוּחָה, וּלְאָן אַתָּה
הוֹלֵךְ: לִמְקוֹם עָפָר רִמָּה וְתוֹלֵעָה, וְלִפְנֵי מִי אַתָּה עָתִיד לִתֵּן דִּין
וְחֶשְׁבּוֹן: לִפְנֵי מֶלֶךְ מַלְכֵי הַמְּלָכִים הַקָּדוֹשׁ, בָּרוּךְ הוּא.

1. AKAVYA BEN MAHALEL WOULD SAY: "REFLECT UPON THREE THINGS AND YOU WILL NEVER COME TO SIN: KNOW FROM WHERE YOU CAME, TO WHERE YOU ARE GOING, AND BEFORE WHOM YOU ARE DESTINED TO GIVE AN ACCOUNTING.

"'FROM WHERE YOU CAME' — FROM A PUTRID DROP; 'TO WHERE YOU ARE GOING' — TO A PLACE OF DUST, MAGGOTS, AND WORMS; 'AND BEFORE WHOM YOU ARE DESTINED TO GIVE AN ACCOUNTING' — BEFORE THE KING OF KINGS, THE HOLY ONE, BLESSED BE HE."

REFLECT UPON THREE THINGS — Seemingly, the *mishnah* could have begun: "Know from where you came, and to where you are going...." Why does it mention the need to "reflect on three things"?

Herein lies an allusion to a concept of much greater scope. In addition to the obvious reference to the three concepts that follow, the *mishnah* teaches that a person must always have three things in mind, and promises that when he does so, he "will never come to sin."

Generally, a person thinks about two entities, himself and G-d, for "I was created solely to serve my Creator."[1] This *mishnah* comes to teach us that each of us must also be aware of a third entity — the world at large.

A person should always remember that the ultimate goal of his divine service is not merely a two-way relationship between him and G-d. He must broaden his scope, and endeavor to have his service encompass a third entity, the world.

Our involvement with worldly entities with the intent of transforming them into vessels for G-dliness fulfills G-d's ultimate intent in creation. For our world — and every individual creation — was brought into being for the purpose of fashioning a dwelling for G-d on the material plane.[2]

Ultimately, this outward thrust benefits the soul as well, though the soul is "an actual part of G-d,"[3] and is not in need of refinement. Its descent to a physical body is intended to refine the world at large, not itself. Nevertheless, by carrying out this task, the soul establishes a connection to G-d's essence which it could not have appreciated before its entry into this world.

(Sefer HaSichos 5751, Vol. II, p. 507ff)

KNOW FROM WHERE YOU CAME — מאין, the Hebrew for "from where," can also be rendered as "from nothingness."[4] Thus the phrase can be interpreted "Know that you came from nothingness," i.e., the source of the soul is transcendent G-dliness — above the limits of our mortal conception. Moreover, this source exerts a constant influence on the soul as it exists in our world, propelling it to selfless conduct. A person's awareness of this fact heightens the effectiveness of this influence, and takes the person further from sin.

(Likkutei Sichos, Vol. IV, p. 1202)

---

1. *Kiddushin* 28a.
2. *Midrash Tanchuma, Parshas Bechukosai*, sec. 3; *Tanya*, chs. 33 and 36.
3. *Tanya*, ch. 2.
4. See *Likkutei Torah, Parshas Bechukosai* 50d.

ב רַבִּי חֲנִינָא סְגַן הַכֹּהֲנִים אוֹמֵר: הֱוֵי מִתְפַּלֵּל בִּשְׁלוֹמָהּ שֶׁל מַלְכוּת, שֶׁאִלְמָלֵא מוֹרָאָהּ, אִישׁ אֶת רֵעֵהוּ חַיִּים בְּלָעוּ. רַבִּי חֲנִינָא בֶּן תְּרַדְיוֹן אוֹמֵר: שְׁנַיִם שֶׁיּוֹשְׁבִין וְאֵין בֵּינֵיהֶם דִּבְרֵי תוֹרָה, הֲרֵי זֶה מוֹשַׁב לֵצִים, שֶׁנֶּאֱמַר: וּבְמוֹשַׁב לֵצִים לֹא יָשָׁב. אֲבָל שְׁנַיִם שֶׁיּוֹשְׁבִין וְיֵשׁ בֵּינֵיהֶם דִּבְרֵי תוֹרָה, שְׁכִינָה שְׁרוּיָה בֵינֵיהֶם, שֶׁנֶּאֱמַר: אָז נִדְבְּרוּ יִרְאֵי י-י אִישׁ אֶל רֵעֵהוּ, וַיַּקְשֵׁב י-י וַיִּשְׁמָע, וַיִּכָּתֵב סֵפֶר זִכָּרוֹן לְפָנָיו, לְיִרְאֵי י-י וּלְחֹשְׁבֵי שְׁמוֹ. אֵין לִי אֶלָּא שְׁנַיִם, מִנַּיִן אֲפִילוּ אֶחָד, שֶׁיּוֹשֵׁב וְעוֹסֵק בַּתּוֹרָה שֶׁהַקָּדוֹשׁ בָּרוּךְ הוּא קוֹבֵעַ לוֹ שָׂכָר, שֶׁנֶּאֱמַר: יֵשֵׁב בָּדָד וְיִדֹּם כִּי נָטַל עָלָיו.

2. RABBI CHANINA, THE DEPUTY HIGH PRIEST, WOULD SAY: "PRAY FOR THE WELFARE OF THE [RULING] KINGDOM, FOR WERE IT NOT FOR THE FEAR OF IT, MEN WOULD SWALLOW ONE ANOTHER ALIVE."

RABBI CHANINA BEN TRADYON WOULD SAY: "IF TWO SIT TOGETHER AND NO WORDS OF TORAH ARE EXCHANGED BETWEEN THEM, IT IS A COMPANY OF MOCKERS, AS IT IS STATED:[5] 'HE DOES NOT SIT AMONG THE COMPANY OF MOCKERS.' BUT IF TWO SIT TOGETHER AND EXCHANGE WORDS OF TORAH, THE DIVINE PRESENCE RESTS BETWEEN THEM, AS IT IS WRITTEN:[6] 'THEN THE G-D-FEARING CONVERSED WITH ONE ANOTHER, AND G-D LISTENED AND HEARD, AND A BOOK OF REMEMBRANCE WAS WRITTEN BEFORE HIM FOR THOSE WHO FEAR G-D AND MEDITATE UPON HIS NAME.'"

"[FROM THIS VERSE, WE LEARN] ONLY THAT THE ABOVE APPLIES WITH REGARD TO TWO PEOPLE. WHICH SOURCE TEACHES THAT EVEN WHEN ONE PERSON SITS AND OCCUPIES HIMSELF WITH THE TORAH, THE HOLY ONE, BLESSED BE HE, ALLOTS A REWARD FOR HIM? THE VERSE:[7] 'HE SITS ALONE AND

5 . *Tehillim* 1:1.
6 . *Malachi* 2:16.
7 . *Eichah* 3:28.

[STUDIES] IN STILLNESS; HE TAKES [THE REWARD]
UNTO HIMSELF.' "

**PRAY FOR THE WELFARE OF THE [RULING]
KINGDOM... MEN WOULD SWALLOW ONE ANOTHER
ALIVE** — *Pirkei Avos* is not wont to speak in metaphors. If the
intent is merely to say that people would wantonly kill each
other were it not for the rule of law, the *mishnah* would have
said just that. Moreover, the purpose of *Pirkei Avos* is to teach
pious behavior, i.e., conduct beyond the measure of the law.[8]
Seemingly, Rabbi Chanina's advice and the situation it wishes
to forestall are basic matters — relevant to people at even a
rudimentary spiritual level.

So we should look for a much deeper message.
"Swallow[ing] one another alive" implies the subsuming of another person within one's own desires. The other person is
alive — he thinks and feels — but one has "swallowed" him
within one's self; i.e., one thinks of him only inasmuch as he
can further one's own purposes. Instead of appreciating who
that person is, what he wants and needs, one thinks only of
one's own self and the benefit the other person will bring him.

On this basis, we can appreciate the connection between
this teaching and the one which follows:[9]

**IF TWO SIT TOGETHER AND... EXCHANGE WORDS
OF TORAH** — This teaching emphasizes the importance of
communication, of two people sitting together as equals and
sharing words of Torah.

(Likkutei Sichos, Vol. XVII, p. 365ff)

---

8 . *Bava Kama* 30a.
9 . On the surface, the connection between the two statements is questionable. And
      yet, were there no connection, the two concepts would not have been included in
      a single *mishnah*. (See *Shaar HaKollel*, ch. 30, sec. 3, which states that one of the
      reasons the Alter Rebbe included *Pirkei Avos* in his text of the *Siddur* was to
      emphasize the proper division of the *mishnayos*.)

**THE DIVINE PRESENCE RESTS BETWEEN THEM...
ALLOTS A REWARD FOR HIM** — When two individuals study together, the Divine Presence — a level of revelation beyond the grasp of mortals — is drawn down. In contrast, when an individual studies alone, he receives a reward, for he has done a worthy act, but the reward is limited.

What is the difference? When a person communicates with others, he extends himself beyond his individual limits. Therefore, study in such a setting evokes a transcendent revelation of G-dliness. When, by contrast, a person studies alone, his understanding cannot grow beyond the limits of his own thought. Therefore, the reward he receives is also limited.

(Sichos Shabbos Parshas Devarim, 5741)

HE SITS ALONE AND [STUDIES] IN STILLNESS — This verse is a quote from *Eichah*, the book which laments the destruction of the *Beis HaMikdash*. The fact that a Jew must sit *alone* and study Torah is itself a sign of the exile. For in regard to the Era of the Redemption, it is written:[10] "The occupation of *the entire world* will be solely to know G-d."

(Ibid.)

ג רַבִּי שִׁמְעוֹן אוֹמֵר: שְׁלֹשָׁה שֶׁאָכְלוּ עַל שֻׁלְחָן אֶחָד, וְלֹא אָמְרוּ עָלָיו דִּבְרֵי תוֹרָה, כְּאִלּוּ אָכְלוּ מִזִּבְחֵי מֵתִים, שֶׁנֶּאֱמַר: כִּי כָּל שֻׁלְחָנוֹת מָלְאוּ קִיא צוֹאָה בְּלִי מָקוֹם. אֲבָל שְׁלֹשָׁה שֶׁאָכְלוּ עַל שֻׁלְחָן אֶחָד וְאָמְרוּ עָלָיו דִּבְרֵי תוֹרָה, כְּאִלּוּ אָכְלוּ מִשֻּׁלְחָנוֹ שֶׁל מָקוֹם, שֶׁנֶּאֱמַר: וַיְדַבֵּר אֵלַי, זֶה הַשֻּׁלְחָן אֲשֶׁר לִפְנֵי יי.

3. RABBI SHIMON WOULD SAY: "WHEN THREE EAT AT ONE TABLE WITHOUT SPEAKING WORDS OF

---

10 . *Rambam, Mishneh Torah, Hilchos Melachim* 12:5.

TORAH THERE, IT IS AS IF THEY ATE OF SACRIFICES
TO THE DEAD,[11] FOR IT IS WRITTEN: 'FOR ALL TABLES
ARE FULL OF FILTHY VOMIT WHEN THERE IS NO
[MENTION OF THE] OMNIPRESENT.'

"WHEN, BY CONTRAST, THREE SIT AT ONE TABLE
AND SPEAK WORDS OF TORAH, IT IS AS IF THEY HAD
EATEN FROM THE TABLE OF THE OMNIPRESENT, FOR
IT IS WRITTEN:[12] 'AND HE SAID TO ME: THIS IS THE
TABLE BEFORE G-D.'"

**RABBI SHIMON WOULD SAY:... "WHEN... THREE
SIT AT ONE TABLE AND SPEAK WORDS OF TORAH"** —
When three people discuss Torah while eating, the table becomes infused with the spiritual unity of the Torah. This concept shares a particular connection with Rabbi Shimon, for
Rabbi Shimon understood Torah study as all-encompassing[13]
— possessing the power to influence every aspect of our lives,
even our material concerns.[14] To demonstrate this, the *Zohar*[15]
relates that once *Eretz Yisrael* suffered a severe drought and the
Jews appealed to Rabbi Shimon for help. When he recited a
discourse on the verse:[16] "How good and how sweet it is for
brothers to sit together," it began to rain.

The connection with Rabbi Shimon also explains the emphasis on "three who ate at one table." Rabbi Shimon spent 13
years in a cave together with his son, hiding from Roman perse-

---

11. The commentaries interpret this as a reference to idol worship.
12. *Yechezkel* 41:22.
13. See the essay entitled "A Bond of Oneness," *Timeless Patterns in Time*, Vol. II, p. 83 (Kehot, N.Y., 1994).
14. This concept is also alluded to by referring to G-d with the name "the Omnipresent." This name highlights G-d's presence in every dimension of existence, even the most mundane.
15. III, 59b. There are several stories in the *Talmud* concerning Sages who prayed for rain and had their prayers answered (see *Taanis* 23a, 25b). What is unique about the story cited above is that rainfall came about, not as a response to prayer, but as a physical expression of the spiritual energies aroused through Torah study. See *Sefer HaMaamarim* 5679, p. 130ff.
16. *Tehillim* 133:1.

cution, absorbed in Torah study.[17] During this period, there was no third person to join them. Moreover, they were not able to study "at one table." They studied Torah without any involvement in material affairs. After this experience, Rabbi Shimon was able to appreciate the importance of "three [who] sit at one table and speak words of Torah."

(Sichos Shabbos Parshas Devarim, 5740)

ד רַבִּי חֲנִינָא בֶּן חֲכִינָאִי אוֹמֵר: הַנֵּעוֹר בַּלַּיְלָה, וְהַמְהַלֵּךְ בַּדֶּרֶךְ יְחִידִי, וּמְפַנֶּה לִבּוֹ לְבַטָּלָה, הֲרֵי זֶה מִתְחַיֵּב בְּנַפְשׁוֹ.

4. RABBI CHANINA BEN CHACHINA'I SAID: "WHEN A PERSON IS AWAKE AT NIGHT OR TRAVELS ALONE ON THE ROAD, AND TURNS HIS HEART TO IDLENESS, HE IS LIABLE TO LOSE HIS LIFE."

RABBI CHANINA BEN CHACHINA'I SAID: "WHEN A PERSON... TRAVELS ALONE ON THE ROAD, AND TURNS HIS HEART TO IDLENESS" — A person who travels alone, in contrast to one who travels with others, must pay attention to the road, lest he become lost or endanger himself. Therefore, there is reason to think that he should minimize the attention he pays to Torah study.[18] Nevertheless, Rabbi Chanina teaches that pious conduct — the approach taught by *Pirkei Avos* — requires that a person devote himself to the study of Torah even in such a situation. Indeed, the merit of Torah study will ward off danger.[19]

This teaching shares a connection to Rabbi Chanina's path of divine service, for he was totally devoted to the study of the

---

17 . *Shabbos* 33b.
18 . See *Taanis* 10b.
19 . See the commentary of R. Ovadiah of Bartenura.

Torah; "The Torah was his occupation,"[20] his sole concern in
life.

(Sichos Shabbos Parshas Vaes'chanan, 5751)

ה רַבִּי נְחוּנְיָא בֶּן הַקָּנָה אוֹמֵר: כָּל הַמְקַבֵּל עָלָיו עוֹל תּוֹרָה,
מַעֲבִירִין מִמֶּנּוּ עוֹל מַלְכוּת וְעוֹל דֶּרֶךְ אֶרֶץ, וְכָל הַפּוֹרֵק מִמֶּנּוּ עוֹל
תּוֹרָה, נוֹתְנִין עָלָיו עוֹל מַלְכוּת וְעוֹל דֶּרֶךְ אֶרֶץ.

5. RABBI NECHUNYA BEN HAKANAH SAID:
"WHENEVER A PERSON TAKES UPON HIMSELF
THE YOKE OF TORAH, THE YOKE OF GOVERNMENT
AND THE YOKE OF WORLDLY AFFAIRS ARE REMOVED
FROM HIM. WHENEVER, BY CONTRAST, A PERSON
CASTS OFF THE YOKE OF TORAH, THE YOKE OF
GOVERNMENT AND THE YOKE OF WORLDLY AFFAIRS
ARE IMPOSED UPON HIM."

THE YOKE OF TORAH — This expression is problematic, for the study of the Torah is a self-rewarding process, as
implied by the verse:[21] "I rejoice in Your statements like one
who has found a great treasure." Why then is Torah study considered a yoke?

It can, however, be explained that this *mishnah* is referring
to a person whose involvement in worldly affairs prevents him
from experiencing the satisfaction and pleasure of Torah study.
Instead, Torah study is a yoke, an obligation which he must
fulfill.

The *mishnah* teaches us that if the person perseveres in the
study of Torah despite his involvement in worldly affairs, he

---

20. See *Vayikra Rabbah* 21:3, which establishes a connection between Rabbi Chanina
   and Rabbi Shimon bar Yochai. See also *Kesubos* 62b.
21. *Tehillim* 119:162.

will be freed from these preoccupations; the yoke of government and the yoke of worldly affairs will be removed from him. As the *Rambam* explains:[22]

> We are promised by the Torah that if we fulfill it with joy and good spirit... G-d will remove all the obstacles that prevent us from maintaining it....
>
> He will grant us all the good that will reinforce our observance... so that we will not be preoccupied... by matters required by the body, and [thus have the opportunity to] study wisdom and perform *mitzvos*.

When, however, a person endeavors to reduce the tensions he faces by casting off the yoke of the Torah, the yoke of government and the yoke of worldly affairs are imposed upon him. The challenges he faces in the world at large will increase, rather than decrease.

(Sichos Shabbos Parshas Behar, 5719)

Alternatively, the "yoke of Torah" can refer to a person who experiences satisfaction and pleasure in the study of Torah, but dedicates himself to study above and beyond the point of satisfaction.

Every person has certain subjects which interest him and afford him pleasure. The *mishnah* is teaching us that a person must go beyond these natural tendencies. It promises that if a person succeeds in doing so, G-d will reward him by lifting him above the natural limits of the world and removing "the yoke of government and the yoke of worldly affairs" from him.

(Sichos Shabbos Parshas Vaes'chanan, 5745)

---

22 . *Mishnah Torah, Hilchos Teshuvah* 9:1.

ו רַבִּי חֲלַפְתָּא בֶּן דּוֹסָא אִישׁ כְּפַר חֲנַנְיָא אוֹמֵר: עֲשָׂרָה שֶׁיּוֹשְׁבִין
וְעוֹסְקִין בַּתּוֹרָה, שְׁכִינָה שְׁרוּיָה בֵּינֵיהֶם, שֶׁנֶּאֱמַר: אֱלֹהִי-ם נִצָּב
בַּעֲדַת אֵ-ל. וּמִנַּיִן אֲפִילוּ חֲמִשָּׁה, שֶׁנֶּאֱמַר: וַאֲגֻדָּתוֹ עַל אֶרֶץ יְסָדָהּ.
וּמִנַּיִן אֲפִילוּ שְׁלֹשָׁה, שֶׁנֶּאֱמַר: בְּקֶרֶב אֱלֹהִי-ם יִשְׁפֹּט. וּמִנַּיִן אֲפִילוּ
שְׁנַיִם, שֶׁנֶּאֱמַר: אָז נִדְבְּרוּ יִרְאֵי י-י אִישׁ אֶל רֵעֵהוּ, וַיַּקְשֵׁב י-י
וַיִּשְׁמָע. וּמִנַּיִן אֲפִילוּ אֶחָד, שֶׁנֶּאֱמַר: בְּכָל הַמָּקוֹם אֲשֶׁר אַזְכִּיר אֶת
שְׁמִי, אָבֹא אֵלֶיךָ וּבֵרַכְתִּיךָ.

6. RABBI CHALAFTA BEN DOSA OF KFAR CHANANYA SAID: "IF TEN PEOPLE SIT TOGETHER AND OCCUPY THEMSELVES WITH TORAH, THE DIVINE PRESENCE RESTS AMONG THEM, AS IT IS SAID:[23] 'G-D STANDS IN THE ASSEMBLY OF THE L-RD.'

"WHICH SOURCE TEACHES THAT THE SAME IS TRUE EVEN OF FIVE? IT IS SAID:[24] 'HE HAS FOUNDED HIS BAND UPON THE EARTH.'

"WHICH SOURCE TEACHES THAT THE SAME IS TRUE EVEN OF THREE? IT IS SAID:[25] 'AMONG THE JUDGES HE RENDERS JUDGMENT.'

"WHICH SOURCE TEACHES THAT THE SAME IS TRUE EVEN OF TWO? IT IS STATED:[26] 'THEN THE G-D-FEARING CONVERSED WITH ONE ANOTHER, AND THE L-RD HEARKENED AND HEARD.'

"WHICH SOURCE TEACHES THAT THE SAME IS TRUE EVEN OF ONE? IT IS SAID:[27] 'IN EVERY PLACE WHERE I HAVE MY NAME MENTIONED I WILL COME TO YOU AND BLESS YOU.' "

IF TEN PEOPLE — Whenever ten people congregate, regardless of the nature of the gathering, the Divine Presence

---

23 . *Tehillim* 82:1.
24 . *Amos* 9:6.
25 . *Tehillim* 82:1.
26 . *Malachi* 3:16.
27 . *Shmos* 20:21.

rests among them.[28] Their approach to each other and the nature of their activities amplify its influence on them.

SIT TOGETHER — Two positive dimensions are implied by this term:

a) Balance and permanence, for the Hebrew ישב ("sit") relates to the term התיישבות which has these implications.

b) Unity. Not only are the people located in the same place, they are joined together.

AND OCCUPY THEMSELVES — The Hebrew word עוסק, translated as "occupy themselves," implies concentrated attention and sustained effort.[29] We are referring to ten individuals who are able to make such a commitment, and to do so with feelings of unity and cooperation.

WITH TORAH — Although the union of different individuals in a project is always of value, a much higher level is reached when these individuals devote their combined energies to Torah study.

THE DIVINE PRESENCE RESTS AMONG THEM — Because of all the advantages mentioned, the level of the Divine Presence which rests upon such a gathering is higher than the level mentioned in the clauses that follow.

(Sichos Shabbos Parshas Shelach, 5746)

"IN EVERY PLACE WHERE I HAVE MY NAME MENTIONED I WILL COME TO YOU AND BLESS YOU" — Although the positive influences brought about when many

---

28 . *Sanhedrin* 39a, see *Tanya, Iggeres HaKodesh*, Epistle 23.
29 . See our notes to chapter 6, *mishnah* 1.

join in Torah study are greater, we must appreciate how important the efforts of one individual can be. As the prooftext indicates, G-d diverts His attention from all other matters, as it
were, and comes to bless him.

(Sefer HaSichos 5748, Vol. II, p. 582)

ז רַבִּי אֶלְעָזָר אִישׁ בַּרְתוֹתָא אוֹמֵר: תֶּן לוֹ מִשֶּׁלּוֹ, שֶׁאַתָּה וְשֶׁלָּךְ שֶׁלּוֹ.
וְכֵן בְּדָוִד, הוּא אוֹמֵר: כִּי מִמְּךָ הַכֹּל וּמִיָּדְךָ נָתַנּוּ לָךְ. רַבִּי יַעֲקֹב
אוֹמֵר: הַמְהַלֵּךְ בַּדֶּרֶךְ וְשׁוֹנֶה, וּמַפְסִיק מִמִּשְׁנָתוֹ וְאוֹמֵר: מַה נָּאֶה
אִילָן זֶה מַה נָּאֶה נִיר זֶה, מַעֲלֶה עָלָיו הַכָּתוּב כְּאִלּוּ מִתְחַיֵּב בְּנַפְשׁוֹ.

7. RABBI ELAZAR OF BARTOTA SAID: "GIVE TO
HIM OF THAT WHICH IS HIS, FOR YOU AND
WHATEVER IS YOURS ARE HIS. AND SO IT IS SAID BY
DAVID: 'FOR ALL THINGS ARE FROM YOU, AND FROM
YOUR OWN WE HAVE GIVEN YOU.'"[30]

RABBI YAAKOV SAID: "WHEN A PERSON WALKS ON A
JOURNEY REVIEWING [A PASSAGE OF THE TORAH],
AND INTERRUPTS HIS STUDY TO REMARK: 'HOW
BEAUTIFUL IS THIS TREE! HOW BEAUTIFUL IS THIS
PLOWED FIELD!' [THE TORAH] CONSIDERS IT AS IF HE
WERE GUILTY OF A MORTAL SIN."

**GIVE TO HIM OF THAT WHICH IS HIS, FOR YOU
AND WHATEVER IS YOURS ARE HIS** — This teaching
urges us to dedicate ourselves and our resources to G-d's service with an all-encompassing commitment. In many instances,
although a person is willing to fulfill the obligations the Torah
places upon him, it is natural for him to attach a certain degree
of self-importance to his deeds.

---

30. *I Chronicles* 29:14.

Take for example the *mitzvah* of giving *tzedakah*. We are obligated to tithe.[31] Most people feel proud when they choose to give their money away for such a purpose.

Our *mishnah* teaches us to perform such deeds with humility, for the very opportunity to possess property is granted by G-d. Therefore we should perform deeds of charity as a matter of course, without attaching great importance to them.

As proof, the *mishnah* cites a prooftext — "from Your own we have given You," which speaks of the donations given to construct the *Beis HaMikdash*, the ultimate expression of human activity, the building of a dwelling for G-d. Yet even these donations were given in a spirit of humility.[32]

(Sichos Shabbos Parshas Shelach, 5736)

RABBI YAAKOV SAID — There are versions of the *mishnah* which attribute this teaching to Rabbi Shimon bar Yochai, of whom it is said: "The Torah was his occupation."[33] The choice of the present version emphasizes that even a person who has not made such an all-encompassing commitment to the study of Torah can appreciate that, as an expression of *mili dechassidusa*, it is improper to cease studying in the instance mentioned.

(Sichos Shabbos Parshas Vaes'chanan, 5741)

ONE WHO WALKS ON THE ROAD REVIEWING [A PASSAGE OF THE TORAH] — Our Sages explained[34] that while traveling, a person should not involve himself in intense study, but should instead review straightforward laws which he has already learned. Nevertheless, he should not interrupt his study to say such things as "How beautiful is this tree!"

---

31 . See *Shulchan Aruch, Yoreh De'ah*, sec. 248.
32 . It is all the more significant that the statement was made by David, king of the Jewish people. Despite his exalted position, he was humble, and was able to inspire others with this feeling.
33 . *Shabbos* 11a.
34 . *Taanis, loc. cit.*

Though appreciation of the greatness of G-d's creative powers is itself an aspect of our divine service,[35] its importance does not compare with that of the study of Torah.

(Sichos Shabbos Parshas Shelach, 5736)

ח רַבִּי דוֹסְתָּאִי בְּרַבִּי יַנַּאי מִשּׁוּם רַבִּי מֵאִיר אוֹמֵר: כָּל הַשּׁוֹכֵחַ דָּבָר אֶחָד מִמִּשְׁנָתוֹ, מַעֲלֶה עָלָיו הַכָּתוּב כְּאִלּוּ מִתְחַיֵּב בְּנַפְשׁוֹ, שֶׁנֶּאֱמַר: רַק הִשָּׁמֶר לְךָ וּשְׁמֹר נַפְשְׁךָ מְאֹד פֶּן תִּשְׁכַּח אֶת הַדְּבָרִים אֲשֶׁר רָאוּ עֵינֶיךָ. יָכוֹל אֲפִילוּ תָּקְפָה עָלָיו מִשְׁנָתוֹ, תַּלְמוּד לוֹמַר וּפֶן יָסוּרוּ מִלְּבָבְךָ כֹּל יְמֵי חַיֶּיךָ, הָא אֵינוֹ מִתְחַיֵּב בְּנַפְשׁוֹ, עַד שֶׁיֵּשֵׁב וִיסִירֵם מִלִּבּוֹ.

8. RABBI DOSTA'EY BAR YANNAI SAID IN THE NAME OF RABBI MEIR: "WHENEVER ANYONE FORGETS ANY OF HIS TORAH KNOWLEDGE, THE TORAH CONSIDERS IT AS IF HE WERE GUILTY OF A MORTAL SIN, FOR IT IS SAID:[36] 'BUT BEWARE AND GUARD YOUR SOUL SCRUPULOUSLY, LEST YOU FORGET THE THINGS WHICH YOUR EYES HAVE SEEN.'

"ONE MIGHT THINK THAT THIS APPLIES EVEN IF THE SUBJECT MATTER WAS TOO DIFFICULT FOR HIM [AND THEREFORE HE FORGOT], HENCE THE TORAH ADDS:[37] 'AND LEST THEY BE REMOVED FROM YOUR HEART ALL THE DAYS OF YOUR LIFE.' ONE IS NOT GUILTY OF A MORTAL SIN UNTIL HE SITS AND CAUSES THEM TO BE REMOVED FROM HIS HEART."

---

35. As indicated by our Sages' institution of the blessing *shekachah lo beolamo* when a person sees beautiful creations or pleasant-looking trees. (*Rambam, Mishneh Torah, Hilchos Berachos* 10:13). See the commentary of R. Ovadiah of Bartenura to this *mishnah.*
36. *Devarim* 4:9.
37. *Ibid.*

WHENEVER ANYONE FORGETS ANY OF HIS TORAH KNOWLEDGE, THE TORAH CONSIDERS IT AS IF HE WERE GUILTY OF A MORTAL SIN — We are commanded[38] to obliterate the memory of Amalek. This appears to contradict the injunction mentioned in this *mishnah*, for there are several passages in the Torah which mention Amalek, and obliterating the memory of this nation would seemingly require forgetting these passages.

This difficulty can be resolved as follows: It is forbidden to think about Amalek for any purpose other than the destruction of that nation. When, however, the remembrance has as its goal — as do the Torah passages associated with that nation — the utter annihilation of the people and all its possessions, the remembrance of Amalek fulfills a *mitzvah*.[39] Obliterating Amalek's memory thus does not relate to the Torah passages concerning that nation, but to the actual existence of the nation.

Homiletically speaking, there is a connection between the battle against Amalek and Torah study, as reflected by the fact that Amalek first attacked the Jewish people after the Exodus from Egypt, when they were on their way to receive the Torah.

Amalek represents the cold rationality which makes us question everything we do or experience.[40] This interferes with our ability to internalize the Torah within our personalities (the key to memory). Wiping out our inner Amalek makes it easier to ingrain the Torah in every aspect of our being, and this will prevent it from be easily forgotten.

(Likkutei Sichos, Vol. XIV, p. 91; Vol. XXI, p. 190ff)

---

38 . *Ibid.* 25:18.

39 . Note the *Rambam, Sefer HaMitzvos* (pos. *mitzvah* 189), who associates the *mitzvah* to remember Amalek with "arousing a desire... to battle them." See *Midrash Tanchuma, Parshas Seitze,* sec. 9; *Rashi, Devarim* 25:18; *Sefer HaMaamarim* 5679, p. 294.

40 . Cf. *Sefer HaMaamarim* 5679, *ibid.,* which focuses on the numerical equivalence between the name (עמלק) Amalek and the word ספק, meaning doubt. See also *ibid.,* p. 65.

ONE IS NOT GUILTY OF A MORTAL SIN UNTIL HE
SITS AND CAUSES THEM TO BE REMOVED FROM HIS
HEART." — In his *Hilchos Talmud Torah* (2:10), the Alter
Rebbe writes that the majority of a person's study should focus
on the practical application of Torah law, and that the person
should review those laws so that he does not forget them. He
should, however, take a portion of his study time to learn the
Talmud and the *Midrashim,* so that he will have studied the
entire Oral Law.

Although he will surely forget what he studies, he need not
worry, "in the Era of the Redemption, he will be reminded of
all that he forgot against his will." The forgetting of this
material is thus not permanent. Moreover, "before the Throne
Your glory, there is no forgetting,"[41] and even in the present
era, in the spiritual realms, a person's Torah study serves as a
continuous positive influence.

When does the prohibition against forgetting the Torah
apply? When the person "sequesters himself from the
Torah."[42] In one sense, this refers to a person who instead of
studying devotes his attention to idle matters.[43] Moreover,
even when a person studies other subjects in Torah, but
intentionally ignores reviewing a subject he has studied, he can
be considered to have "sequestered himself from it." If,
however, his forgetfulness comes against his will, it is not
considered as a negative quality.

(Likkutei Sichos, Vaes'chanan, 5747)

ט רַבִּי חֲנִינָא בֶּן דּוֹסָא אוֹמֵר : כֹּל שֶׁיִּרְאַת חֶטְאוֹ קוֹדֶמֶת לְחָכְמָתוֹ,
חָכְמָתוֹ מִתְקַיֶּמֶת. וְכֹל שֶׁחָכְמָתוֹ קוֹדֶמֶת לְיִרְאַת חֶטְאוֹ, אֵין חָכְמָתוֹ
מִתְקַיֶּמֶת.

---

41 . *Berachos* 32b.
42 . *Sefer Mitzvos Gadol,* neg. *mitzvah* 13.
43 . *Yereim.*

9. RABBI CHANINA BEN DOSA SAID: "WHENEVER A PERSON'S FEAR OF SIN COMES BEFORE HIS WISDOM, HIS WISDOM WILL ENDURE; BUT WHEN A PERSON'S WISDOM COMES BEFORE HIS FEAR OF SIN, HIS WISDOM WILL NOT ENDURE."

WHENEVER A PERSON'S FEAR OF SIN COMES BEFORE HIS WISDOM — Fear of sin involves self-nullification; a person restricts his own self-expression lest he violate G-d's will. Such an approach is developed through prayer, for prayer helps a person redefine his identity. Instead of remaining conscious only of his ego, through prayer a person develops a connection with the inner "I" of his G-dly nature.

Such an approach expands his conceptual horizons and ensures that his wisdom will endure. He will not view the Torah he studies as merely an abstract, intellectual discipline, but as G-dly truth that should permeate every dimension of his existence. This approach will cause his Torah knowledge to become a lasting part of his being.

(Sichos Shabbos Parshas Ki Savo, 5728)

*The lesson taught by our *mishnah* is particularly relevant in the area of *chinuch*, education. First and foremost, it is important to establish a foundation of fear of G-d. This foundation will enable knowledge to flourish. Moreover, the order of precedence taught by the *mishnah* is not merely chronological. Fear of G-d represents a higher rung and a more desirable quality than mere wisdom.

(Likkutei Sichos, Vol. XXII, p. 402)

י הוּא הָיָה אוֹמֵר: כֹּל שֶׁמַּעֲשָׂיו מְרֻבִּין מֵחָכְמָתוֹ, חָכְמָתוֹ מִתְקַיֶּמֶת. וְכֹל שֶׁחָכְמָתוֹ מְרֻבָּה מִמַּעֲשָׂיו, אֵין חָכְמָתוֹ מִתְקַיֶּמֶת. הוּא הָיָה

אוֹמֵר: כֹּל, שֶׁרוּחַ הַבְּרִיּוֹת נוֹחָה הֵימֶנּוּ, רוּחַ הַמָּקוֹם נוֹחָה הֵימֶנּוּ.
וְכֹל שֶׁאֵין רוּחַ הַבְּרִיּוֹת נוֹחָה הֵימֶנּוּ, אֵין רוּחַ הַמָּקוֹם נוֹחָה הֵימֶנּוּ.
רַבִּי דוֹסָא בֶּן הַרְכִּינַס אוֹמֵר: שֵׁנָה שֶׁל שַׁחֲרִית, וְיַיִן שֶׁל צָהֳרַיִם,
וְשִׂיחַת הַיְלָדִים, וִישִׁיבַת בָּתֵּי כְנֵסִיּוֹת שֶׁל עַמֵּי הָאָרֶץ, מוֹצִיאִין אֶת
הָאָדָם מִן הָעוֹלָם.

10. HE USED TO SAY: "WHENEVER A PERSON'S [GOOD] DEEDS EXCEED HIS WISDOM, HIS WISDOM WILL ENDURE; BUT WHEN A PERSON'S WISDOM EXCEEDS HIS [GOOD] DEEDS, HIS WISDOM WILL NOT ENDURE."

HE USED TO SAY: "WHENEVER A PERSON'S FELLOWMEN ARE PLEASED WITH HIM, G-D IS ALSO PLEASED WITH HIM; BUT WHEN A PERSON'S FELLOWMEN ARE NOT PLEASED WITH HIM, G-D IS ALSO NOT PLEASED WITH HIM."

RABBI DOSA BEN HARKINAS SAID: "THE SLEEP OF THE [LATE] MORNING, WINE AT MIDDAY, CHILDREN'S PRATTLE, AND SITTING IN THE GATHERING PLACES OF THE IGNORANT DRIVE A MAN FROM THE WORLD."

*WHENEVER A PERSON'S [GOOD] DEEDS EXCEED HIS WISDOM, HIS WISDOM WILL ENDURE — The lessons of this *mishnah* should also be applied in the area of *chinuch*. A school should endeavor to both impart wisdom to its students, and train them in the performance of good deeds. Of the two, however, the primary focus should be good deeds. Indeed, it is through such deeds that knowledge will thrive.

(Likkutei Sichos, Vol. XXII, pgs. 399-400, 420)

יא רַבִּי אֶלְעָזָר הַמּוֹדָעִי אוֹמֵר: הַמְחַלֵּל אֶת הַקֳּדָשִׁים, וְהַמְבַזֶּה אֶת
הַמּוֹעֲדוֹת, וְהַמַּלְבִּין פְּנֵי חֲבֵרוֹ בָּרַבִּים, וְהַמֵּפֵר בְּרִיתוֹ שֶׁל אַבְרָהָם

אָבִינוּ, וְהַמְגַלֶּה פָנִים בַּתּוֹרָה שֶׁלֹּא כַהֲלָכָה, אַף עַל פִּי שֶׁיֵּשׁ בְּיָדוֹ
תּוֹרָה וּמַעֲשִׂים טוֹבִים, אֵין לוֹ חֵלֶק לָעוֹלָם הַבָּא.

11. RABBI ELAZAR OF MODIN SAID: "WHEN A PERSON PROFANES SACRED THINGS, DEGRADES THE FESTIVALS, PUBLICLY HUMILIATES HIS COLLEAGUE, ABROGATES THE COVENANT OF OUR FATHER AVRAHAM, OR INTERPRETS THE TORAH IN A MANNER CONTRADICTORY TO ITS TRUE INTENT, EVEN THOUGH HE MAY POSSESS TORAH AND GOOD DEEDS, HE HAS NO SHARE IN THE WORLD TO COME."

WHEN A PERSON WHO PROFANES SACRED THINGS, ... HAS NO SHARE IN THE WORLD TO COME — A Jew has the power to make the mundane holy, to imbue every dimension of worldly experience with G-dliness. In the World to Come, the Era of the Resurrection, the ultimate worth of these efforts will be revealed, for then the barrier separating the spiritual from the physical will be dissolved.

All the acts mentioned by the *mishnah* involve making the sacred profane. A person who conducts himself in this manner acts in direct opposition to the intent of the World to Come. Therefore he will not be granted a share in this revelation.

More specifically, the different sacred entities mentioned by the *mishnah* refer to holiness brought about through man's efforts. "Sacred things" refers to animals or other objects consecrated for the altar. By and large, it is man who consecrates such offerings. "The festivals" are also consecrated through the divine service of the Jewish people. Thus in our holiday prayers,[44] we praise G-d who "sanctifies Israel and the festive sea-

---

44 . *Siddur Tehillat HaShem*, p. 254.

sons." For as our Sages comment,[45] G-d sanctifies Israel, and Israel in turn consecrates the festive seasons.[46]

With regard to one who publicly humiliates his colleague, it can be explained that although all Jews share a fundamental unity, the fact that a person is one's colleague, i.e., that these inner bonds have been given outward expression, is a result of human activity. By publicly humiliating his colleague, a person betrays the bonds of friendship that have been established.

The covenant of our father Avraham was originally established by human activity — Avraham's act of circumcision — and is renewed by man's deeds. Similarly, the interpretation of Torah law and its application in our lives is an area in which man is granted the potential for achievement. When, however, a person interprets the Torah in a manner contradictory to its true intent, he misuses this potential and profanes the sanctity of a Torah lifestyle.

It must, however, be emphasized that the *mishnah*'s statement applies only to a person who has not turned to G-d in *teshuvah*. *Teshuvah* has the potential not only to erase the negative effects of a person's conduct, but to actually transform his sins into merits,[47] and assure him a full portion in the World to Come.

(Sichos Shabbos Parshas Shelach, 5738)

EVEN THOUGH HE MAY POSSESS TORAH AND GOOD DEEDS — The literal meaning of the Hebrew words is "Even if he has Torah and good deeds in his hand." It is impossible for a person who commits such sins to have made the Torah part of his being. He may have studied Torah and performed good deeds, but they are "in his hand" — at a level of

---

45 . *Berachos* 49a.
46 . For this reason, the *mishnah* mentions the festivals and not the *Shabbasos*. For the sanctification of the *Shabbos* is not dependent on the Jewish people, but is a natural function of the weekly spiritual cycle. See *Beitzah* 17a.
47 . *Yoma* 86b; cf. *Tanya*, ch. 7.

his being that does not affect his true self. And therefore they do not endow the person with a portion in the World to Come.

(Sichos Shabbos Parshas Devarim, 5747)

יב רַבִּי יִשְׁמָעֵאל אוֹמֵר: הֱוֵי קַל לְרֹאשׁ, וְנוֹחַ לְתִשְׁחֹרֶת, וֶהֱוֵי מְקַבֵּל אֶת כָּל הָאָדָם בְּשִׂמְחָה.

12. RABBI YISHMAEL SAID: "BE READILY SUBMISSIVE TO A SUPERIOR AND BE AFFABLE TO A YOUNGER PERSON; RECEIVE EVERY PERSON CHEERFULLY."

RABBI YISHMAEL SAID — Rabbi Yishmael was a priest,[48] and according to certain opinions a High Priest.[49] Despite his standing, he was prepared to show respect and warmth to all others.[50]

(Sichos Shabbos Parshas Acharei-Kedoshim, 5728)

RECEIVE EVERY PERSON CHEERFULLY — This directive is connected to the instruction to adopt a submissive and flexible approach. A person might show humility and deference to others, but without enthusiasm, manifesting these qualities against his nature. With this directive, Rabbi Yishmael emphasizes that a person should internalize a high regard for his fellow man, and feel genuine happiness in his relations with him.

(Ibid.)

---

48. *Chulin* 49a.
49. *Rashi, op. cit.*, mentions this view.
50. Herein we see a connection to his ancestor Aharon, who "loved peace and pursued peace," as mentioned in ch. 1, *mishnah* 12.

יג רַבִּי עֲקִיבָא אוֹמֵר: שְׂחוֹק וְקַלּוּת רֹאשׁ, מַרְגִּילִין אֶת הָאָדָם לְעֶרְוָה, מַסֹּרֶת סְיָג לַתּוֹרָה, מַעַשְׂרוֹת סְיָג לָעֹשֶׁר, נְדָרִים סְיָג לַפְּרִישׁוּת, סְיָג לַחָכְמָה שְׁתִיקָה.

13. RABBI AKIVA SAID: "LAUGHTER AND FRI-VOLITY ACCUSTOM A MAN TO LEWDNESS. THE ORAL TRADITION IS A FENCE AROUND THE TORAH; TITHES ARE A FENCE FOR RICHES; VOWS ARE A FENCE FOR ABSTINENCE; A FENCE FOR WISDOM IS SILENCE."

RABBI AKIVA SAID — Rabbi Akiva came from a family of converts,[51] and himself did not begin the study of Torah until the age of 40.[52] Our Sages explain that a convert[53] has a tendency to return to his former ways.[54] Similarly, a person who has adopted a worldly outlook for many years is inclined to be materially oriented. For this reason, Rabbi Akiva emphasizes the importance of adopting "fences" — safeguards that protect a person from overindulgence in worldly matters.

(Ibid., Sichos Shabbos Parshas Shelach, 5740)

VOWS ARE A FENCE FOR ABSTINENCE — On one hand, abstinence is a positive quality, for worldly involvement is a self-reinforcing cycle that often leads to overindulgence. On the other hand, our Sages have also counseled[55] against taking such vows, stating: "It is sufficient, what the Torah has forbidden."

---

51. The *Rambam*'s Introduction to the *Mishneh Torah; Seder HaDoros.*
52. *Avos d'Rabbi Nossan* 6:2.
53. See *Rambam, Mishneh Torah, Hilchos Isurei Bi'ah* 15:8, which states that for several generations, the descendants of converts can be considered as if they themselves are converts with regard to certain matters.
54. *Bava Metzia* 59b; *Likkutei Sichos*, Vol. XI, pgs. 107-108.
55. *Jerusalem Talmud, Nedarim* 9:1.

Moreover, despite the drawbacks of crass materialism, there is an advantage to worldly involvement. Through it, a person elevates his environment and reveals its G-dly source.

Both thrusts are valid Torah approaches. The question is: which is appropriate at any given time? In making this determination, a historical perspective is useful. During the time of the First *Beis HaMikdash*, the Sages did not institute many safeguards. By and large, these were instituted in the era of the Second *Beis HaMikdash*, in a period when G-dly revelation had decreased. And in subsequent generations, beginning with the destruction of the *Beis HaMikdash* and the exile of our people, the number of these safeguards increased.

What is the fundamental principle at work? During a time when G-dliness is revealed in the world at large, it is easier to bring out the G-dliness contained within each material entity. But when the world is in darkness, it is more difficult to carry out this task, and it becomes advisable to limit one's worldly involvement.

Although ours is an era of great spiritual darkness, so that restraint would seem to be called for, there is no need to curb our worldly involvement. We need merely reorient our perspective. For we are approaching the Era of the Redemption, when the G-dliness that permeates every element of existence will be revealed. In the present time, close as we are to that era, we have the potential to anticipate this revelation, and carry out the directive to "know G-d in all your ways"[56] by appreciating His presence in all aspects of the world.

(Likkutei Sichos, Vol. IV, p. 1076ff; Sichos Shabbos Parshas Vayigash, 5752)

יד הוּא הָיָה אוֹמֵר: חָבִיב אָדָם שֶׁנִּבְרָא בְּצֶלֶם, חִבָּה יְתֵרָה נוֹדַעַת
לוֹ, שֶׁנִּבְרָא בְּצֶלֶם, שֶׁנֶּאֱמַר: כִּי בְּצֶלֶם אֱלֹהִי-ם עָשָׂה אֶת הָאָדָם.

---

56 . *Mishlei* 3:6.

חֲבִיבִין יִשְׂרָאֵל שֶׁנִּקְרְאוּ בָנִים לַמָּקוֹם, חִבָּה יְתֵרָה נוֹדַעַת לָהֶם,
שֶׁנִּקְרְאוּ בָנִים לַמָּקוֹם, שֶׁנֶּאֱמַר: בָּנִים אַתֶּם לַי-י אֱלֹהֵי-כֶם. חֲבִיבִין
יִשְׂרָאֵל שֶׁנִּתַּן לָהֶם כְּלִי חֶמְדָּה, חִבָּה יְתֵרָה נוֹדַעַת לָהֶם, שֶׁנִּתַּן לָהֶם
כְּלִי חֶמְדָּה, שֶׁנֶּאֱמַר: כִּי לֶקַח טוֹב נָתַתִּי לָכֶם, תּוֹרָתִי אַל תַּעֲזֹבוּ.

14. HE USED TO SAY: "BELOVED IS MAN, FOR HE WAS CREATED IN THE IMAGE [OF G-D]; AN EVEN GREATER EXPRESSION OF LOVE IS THAT IT WAS MADE KNOWN TO HIM THAT HE WAS CREATED IN THE IMAGE [OF G-D], AS IT IS STATED:[57] 'FOR IN THE IMAGE OF G-D HE MADE MAN.'

"BELOVED ARE THE PEOPLE ISRAEL, FOR THEY ARE CALLED CHILDREN OF G-D; AN EVEN GREATER EXPRESSION OF LOVE IS THAT IT WAS MADE KNOWN TO THEM THAT THEY ARE CALLED CHILDREN OF G-D, AS IT IS SAID:[58] 'YOU ARE THE CHILDREN OF THE L-RD YOUR G-D.'

"BELOVED ARE THE PEOPLE ISRAEL, FOR A PRECIOUS ARTICLE WAS GIVEN TO THEM; AN EVEN GREATER EXPRESSION OF LOVE IS THAT IT WAS MADE KNOWN TO THEM THAT THEY WERE GIVEN A PRECIOUS ARTICLE, AS IT IS SAID:[59] 'I HAVE GIVEN YOU GOOD TEACHING; DO NOT FORSAKE MY TORAH.'"

HE USED TO SAY — There are three clauses in this *mishnah*: one which expresses the positive virtues of mankind as a whole, one which indicates the virtues possessed by the Jewish people without considering their connection to the Torah, and one which highlights the virtues which the bond with Torah contributes to our people.

These three stages are reflected within the history of the world at large. In the beginning, man was created in the image

---

57 . *Bereishis* 9:6.
58 . *Devarim* 14:1.
59 . *Mishlei* 4:2.

of G-d. At the time of the Exodus from Egypt, the Jews were distinguished as G-d's children, as it is written:[60] "My son, My firstborn, Israel." It was not until the Giving of the Torah that the Jews were endowed with the possibility of acquiring the third attribute through their connection with the Torah.

These three phases are also mirrored in the personal history of every individual. As a child, one is more concerned with physical existence and gaining practical knowledge — traits which a Jew shares with all mankind. After *Bar Mitzvah*, he gains the potential to establish a bond with G-d through the observance of *mitzvos*, this being the unique heritage of the Jewish people. And as he matures and his understanding blossoms, he has the potential to delve into our precious Torah heritage.[61]

These three clauses can be applied to Rabbi Akiva's own history. He came from a family of converts.[62] Thus he was able to appreciate the virtues possessed by mankind as a whole. For the first 40 years of his life, he was unlearned,[63] and thus understood the innate virtues which the Jews possess, even when they have not been cultivated by the Torah. And he spent the latter 80 years[64] of his life devoted to the study of the "precious article" which G-d entrusted to the Jewish people.

(Sichos Shabbos Parshas Acharei-Kedoshim, 5728;
Sichos Motzoei Shabbos Parshas Shelach, 5739;
Sichos Shabbos Parshas Shelach, 5741)

---

60 . *Shmos* 4:22.
61 . We also see such a pattern within the daily cycle of a person's life. As a person rises and recites *Modeh Ani*, he should strive to attain the virtues seemly in one "created in the image of G-d." In prayer, he should seek to attain an ever-higher rung, realizing his potential as one of the children of G-d. And afterwards, he should proceed from the house of prayer to the house of study (*Berachos* 64a), striving to reach the higher distinction that comes from employing G-d's "precious article."
62 . The *Rambam*'s Introduction to the *Mishneh Torah; Seder HaDoros.*
63 . *Avos d'Rabbi Nossan* 6:2.
64 . *Sifri, Berachah* 34:7; *Yalkut Shimoni* end of *Parshas Berachah*, sec. 965.

*BELOVED IS MAN, FOR HE WAS CREATED IN THE IMAGE [OF G-D] — In his *Guide to the Perplexed*,[65] the *Rambam* interprets this as referring to our capacity to conceive of intellectual ideas and to be conscious of "He who spoke and brought the world into being." The ability to use our minds creatively and direct our thoughts to G-d is the most precious of our human potentials.

Creating a setting which leads to the realization of these values should be the purpose of every society. In an ultimate sense, it is in the Era of the Redemption that the above goals will be realized, for then *Mashiach* will "perfect the entire world, [motivating all the nations] to serve G-d together,"[66] and in that era, "the occupation of the entire world will be solely to know G-d."[67]

We need not, however, wait for the future. A foretaste is possible in our days, for we are standing at the threshold of Redemption. We have the potential to anticipate the heightened spiritual awareness which will characterize the Era of the Redemption and incorporate it within the fabric of our society. And by doing so, we will help precipitate the coming of that ultimate era.

(Sichos Shabbos Parshas Ki Seitzei, 5751[68])

BELOVED ARE THE PEOPLE ISRAEL, FOR THEY ARE CALLED CHILDREN OF G-D — There are two levels in our divine service: that of servants and that of children. The *Zohar*[69] explains that the advantage of a son over a servant is that because of a father's love for his son, he gives him the opportunity to look through all his treasures and see all the secret resources that have been cherished for ages. This concept introduces the third clause, which relates that "Beloved are the

---

65. Vol. I, ch. 1.
66. *Rambam, Mishneh Torah, Hilchos Melachim* 11:4.
67. *Ibid.* 12:5.
68. See *Sound the Great Shofar* (Kehot, N.Y., 1992), where these ideas are explained at length.
69. III, 111b.

people Israel, for a precious article was given to them." G-d's love for His people is so great that He granted them the Torah — an article so precious that it transcends all mortal limits.

(Sichos Shabbos Parshas Ki Savo, 5743)

The Hebrew words כלי חמדה, translated as "a precious article," can have a more specific meaning. כלי also means "utensil,"[70] and חמדה is associated with pleasure. The Torah is a utensil given to the Jewish people to bring out the pleasure which G-d desired to derive from the world.

(Sichos Shabbos Parshas Shelach, 5737)

טו הַכֹּל צָפוּי, וְהָרְשׁוּת נְתוּנָה, וּבְטוֹב הָעוֹלָם נִדּוֹן, וְהַכֹּל לְפִי רוֹב הַמַּעֲשֶׂה.

15. EVERYTHING IS FORESEEN, YET FREEDOM OF CHOICE IS GRANTED; THE WORLD IS JUDGED WITH GOODNESS, AND EVERYTHING IS ACCORDING TO THE PREPONDERANCE OF [GOOD] DEEDS.

EVERYTHING IS FORESEEN — This statement can be interpreted as a support for the Baal Shem Tov's teaching[71] that everything — not only the events that involve man, but even those which influence inanimate matter, plants, and animals — comes about with Divine knowledge. Everything, even the most seemingly insignificant aspects of creation, such as a

---

70. This interpretation is reflected in the statement at the beginning of *Bereishis Rabbah*, which quotes the Torah as saying: "I was the tool (כלי) used by G-d to fashion His handiwork."

71. Rabbi Yisrael Baal Shem Tov as quoted in *Kesser Shem Tov, Hosafos*, sec. 119ff. See the essay entitled "Masterplan: The Baal Shem Tov's Unique Conception of Divine Providence" (Sichos In English, 5752).

leaf fluttering in the wind, is foreseen by G-d and controlled by His providence.

(Sichos Shabbos Parshas Ki Savo, 5746)

Alternatively, this phrase can be interpreted within the context of the *mishnah* at hand. By saying "everything," the *mishnah* teaches that all of a person's potentials and the challenges he will encounter are "foreseen." G-d knows His creations and does not confront them with unfair demands.[72] Every person is granted a mission which he has the potential to fulfill.

YET FREEDOM OF CHOICE IS GRANTED — Every person has the potential to fulfill his personal destiny, but the choice to fulfill that destiny is his alone. No one can stand in his way, nor is there anyone compelling him.

(Sichos Shabbos Parshas Acharei-Kedoshim, 5728)

This clause also shares a connection to its author, Rabbi Akiva. As mentioned, Rabbi Akiva descended from a family of converts. On one hand, every convert is destined to convert. This is reflected in our Sages'[73] use of the expression גר שנתגייר, (lit., "a convert who converts") rather than גוי שנתגייר ("a gentile who converts"). For even before a person actually converts, he possesses the spark of a holy soul.[74] Nevertheless, there is no *obligation* for a convert to convert; indeed, the Rabbis are obligated to try to dissuade him. The decision to become a Jew is his alone.

(Sichos Motzoei Shabbos Parshas Emor, 5738; Sichos Shabbos Parshas Shelach, 5740)

THE WORLD IS JUDGED WITH GOODNESS — Even when for various reasons a person does not completely fulfill

---

72 . *Avodah Zarah* 3a.
73 . *Yevamos* 22a, 47a.
74 . *Chidah, Midbar Kadmos, Erech Gimmel.* See *Likkutei Sichos*, Vol. X, p. 89, note 14.

the mission with which he was charged, G-d judges him favorably and finds grounds on which his flaws can be excused.

This concept also serves as a directive for man to imitate this trait and always view a colleague with a favorable eye. When a person conducts himself in this fashion, G-d will deal similarly with him.

(Ibid.)

EVERYTHING IS ACCORDING TO THE PRE-PONDERANCE OF [GOOD] DEEDS — The *Rambam* interprets this *mishnah*[75] to mean that the number of times one performs a positive act is significant; it is therefore preferable to give charity in the form of many different gifts than it is to give the same sum as a single donation. By giving repeatedly, a person ingrains the trait of generosity within his character.

In *Tanya*,[76] the Alter Rebbe gives a different rationale for the same principle: that each time one performs a *mitzvah*, one creates a spiritual bond with G-d, drawing down Divine influence to our material world. The more often one gives, the more often one draws down Divine influence.

(Sichos Shabbos Parshas Devarim, 5744)

טז הוּא הָיָה אוֹמֵר: הַכֹּל נָתוּן בָּעֵרָבוֹן, וּמְצוּדָה פְרוּסָה עַל כָּל הַחַיִּים, הֶחָנוּת פְּתוּחָה, וְהַחֶנְוָנִי מַקִּיף, וְהַפִּנְקָס פָּתוּחַ, וְהַיָּד כּוֹתֶבֶת, וְכָל הָרוֹצֶה לִלְווֹת יָבֹא וְיִלְוֶה, וְהַגַּבָּאִין מַחֲזִירִין תָּדִיר בְּכָל יוֹם, וְנִפְרָעִין מִן הָאָדָם, מִדַּעְתּוֹ וְשֶׁלֹּא מִדַּעְתּוֹ, וְיֵשׁ לָהֶם עַל מַה שֶּׁיִּסְמוֹכוּ, וְהַדִּין דִּין אֱמֶת, וְהַכֹּל מְתֻקָּן לִסְעוּדָה.

16. HE USED TO SAY: "EVERYTHING IS GIVEN ON COLLATERAL AND A NET IS SPREAD OVER

---

75 . *Avos, loc. cit.*
76 . *Iggeres HaKodesh*, Epistle 21.

ALL THE LIVING. THE SHOP IS OPEN, THE
SHOPKEEPER EXTENDS CREDIT, THE LEDGER IS
OPEN, THE HAND WRITES, AND WHOEVER WISHES TO
BORROW, LET HIM COME AND BORROW. THE
COLLECTORS MAKE THEIR ROUNDS REGULARLY,
EACH DAY, AND EXACT PAYMENT FROM MAN WITH OR
WITHOUT HIS KNOWLEDGE; AND THEY HAVE ON
WHAT TO RELY. THE JUDGMENT IS A JUDGMENT OF
TRUTH, AND EVERYTHING IS PREPARED FOR THE
FEAST."

**THE COLLECTORS... EXACT PAYMENT FROM MAN
WITH OR WITHOUT HIS KNOWLEDGE** — The Baal Shem
Tov explains[77] it is impossible for any being — even the angels
of the Heavenly Court — to judge a Jew. For a Jew's soul is
"an actual part of G-d from above;[78] even if he sins, this
essential virtue remains intact.

How then is payment exacted? Divine Providence gives
the person the opportunity, in casual discussions with a friend
or the like, to judge a colleague who has performed a deed
similar to his own. Afterwards, the judgment made with his
knowledge about a colleague is "without his knowledge"
applied to himself[79] by the Heavenly Court.

(Likkutei Sichos, Vol. IV, p. 1207)

*EVERYTHING IS PREPARED FOR THE FEAST —
"The feast" refers to the World to Come,[80] the pinnacle of the

---

77 . *Likkutei Maharan*, sec. 113.

78 . *Tanya*, ch. 2.

79 . This also explains the expression (Avos 3:1) "and before whom you are destined
to give a דין וחשבון (lit., a judgment and an accounting)." One might suppose that
it would be proper to say "an accounting and a judgment," for first a reckoning is
made of a person's deeds, and then a judgment is issued. The explanation,
however, is that first a person is given the opportunity to judge a colleague, and
then, on the basis of this judgment, an accounting is made with regard to his own
deeds.

80 . See the Commentary of R. Ovadiah of Bartenura and others.

Era of the Redemption. In the present age, this teaching is particularly relevant for, to echo the analogy, the table has already been set, the food has already been served, *Mashiach* is sitting with us at the table. All we need to do is open our eyes.

Our Sages[81] describe *Mashiach* as waiting anxiously to come. In previous generations, however, his coming was delayed by the fact that the Jewish people had not completed the tasks expected of them. Now, however, those tasks have been accomplished; there is nothing lacking. To return to the above analogy: the feast is prepared; now we have to prepare ourselves. We have to ready ourselves to accept *Mashiach*.

(Sefer HaSichos, 5752, Vol. I, p. 151ff[82])

יז רַבִּי אֶלְעָזָר בֶּן עֲזַרְיָה אוֹמֵר: אִם אֵין תּוֹרָה אֵין דֶּרֶךְ אֶרֶץ, אִם אֵין דֶּרֶךְ אֶרֶץ אֵין תּוֹרָה, אִם אֵין חָכְמָה אֵין יִרְאָה, אִם אֵין יִרְאָה אֵין חָכְמָה, אִם אֵין דַּעַת אֵין בִּינָה, אִם אֵין בִּינָה אֵין דַּעַת, אִם אֵין קֶמַח אֵין תּוֹרָה, אִם אֵין תּוֹרָה אֵין קֶמַח. הוּא הָיָה אוֹמֵר: כֹּל שֶׁחָכְמָתוֹ מְרֻבָּה מִמַּעֲשָׂיו, לְמָה הוּא דוֹמֶה: לְאִילָן שֶׁעֲנָפָיו מְרֻבִּין וְשָׁרָשָׁיו מוּעָטִין, וְהָרוּחַ בָּאָה וְעוֹקַרְתּוֹ וְהוֹפַכְתּוֹ עַל פָּנָיו, שֶׁנֶּאֱמַר: וְהָיָה כְּעַרְעָר בָּעֲרָבָה, וְלֹא יִרְאֶה כִּי יָבֹא טוֹב, וְשָׁכַן חֲרֵרִים בַּמִּדְבָּר, אֶרֶץ מְלֵחָה וְלֹא תֵשֵׁב. אֲבָל, כֹּל שֶׁמַּעֲשָׂיו מְרֻבִּין מֵחָכְמָתוֹ, לְמָה הוּא דוֹמֶה: לְאִילָן, שֶׁעֲנָפָיו מוּעָטִין וְשָׁרָשָׁיו מְרֻבִּין, שֶׁאֲפִילוּ כָּל הָרוּחוֹת שֶׁבָּעוֹלָם בָּאוֹת וְנוֹשְׁבוֹת בּוֹ, אֵין מְזִיזִין אוֹתוֹ מִמְּקוֹמוֹ, שֶׁנֶּאֱמַר: וְהָיָה כְּעֵץ שָׁתוּל עַל מַיִם, וְעַל יוּבַל יְשַׁלַּח שָׁרָשָׁיו, וְלֹא יִרְאֶה כִּי יָבֹא חֹם, וְהָיָה עָלֵהוּ רַעֲנָן, וּבִשְׁנַת בַּצֹּרֶת לֹא יִדְאָג, וְלֹא יָמִישׁ מֵעֲשׂוֹת פֶּרִי.

17. RABBI ELAZAR BEN AZARYAH SAID: "IF THERE IS NO TORAH, THERE IS NO PROPER SOCIAL CONDUCT. IF THERE IS NO PROPER SOCIAL

---

81. *Sanhedrin* 98a.
82. See *Sound the Great Shofar* (Kehot, N.Y., 1992).

CONDUCT, THERE IS NO TORAH. IF THERE IS NO
WISDOM, THERE IS NO FEAR [OF G-D]. IF THERE IS NO
FEAR [OF G-D], THERE IS NO WISDOM.

"IF THERE IS NO KNOWLEDGE, THERE IS NO UN-
DERSTANDING. IF THERE IS NO UNDERSTANDING,
THERE IS NO KNOWLEDGE. IF THERE IS NO FLOUR,
THERE IS NO TORAH. IF THERE IS NO TORAH, THERE
IS NO FLOUR."

HE USED TO SAY: "ANYONE WHOSE WISDOM EXCEEDS
HIS [GOOD] DEEDS, TO WHAT CAN HE BE COMPARED?
TO A TREE WHOSE BRANCHES ARE NUMEROUS BUT
WHOSE ROOTS ARE FEW. THE WIND WILL COME AND
UPROOT IT AND TURN IT UPSIDE DOWN; AS IT IS
STATED:[83] 'AND HE SHALL BE LIKE A LONELY TREE IN
ARID LAND, AND SHALL NOT SEE WHEN GOOD COMES;
HE SHALL DWELL ON PARCHED SOIL IN THE WIL-
DERNESS, ON UNINHABITABLE SALT-LAND.'

"IN CONTRAST, ANYONE WHOSE [GOOD] DEEDS
EXCEED HIS WISDOM, TO WHAT CAN HE BE COM-
PARED? TO A TREE WHOSE BRANCHES ARE FEW BUT
WHOSE ROOTS ARE NUMEROUS, SO THAT EVEN IF ALL
THE WINDS IN THE WORLD WERE TO COME AND BLOW
AGAINST IT, THEY COULD NOT MOVE IT FROM ITS
PLACE; AS IT IS STATED:[84] 'AND HE SHALL BE LIKE A
TREE PLANTED BY WATERS, TOWARD THE STREAM
SPREADING ITS ROOTS, AND IT SHALL NOT FEEL
WHEN THE HEAT COMES, AND ITS FOLIAGE SHALL BE
VERDANT; IN THE YEAR OF DROUGHT IT SHALL NOT
WORRY, NOR SHALL IT CEASE FROM YIELDING
FRUIT.'"

ANYONE WHOSE WISDOM EXCEEDS HIS [GOOD] DEEDS, TO WHAT CAN HE BE COMPARED? TO A TREE

---

83 . *Yirmeyahu* 17:6.
84 . *Ibid.* 17:8.

WHOSE BRANCHES ARE NUMEROUS BUT WHOSE ROOTS ARE FEW — The analogy compares a person's wisdom to branches, and his deeds to roots. But since one's deeds are an outgrowth of one's understanding, seemingly the reverse would be proper.

This difficulty can be resolved as follows: With the expression "[good] deeds," the *mishnah* is referring to the ultimate source of motivation for our positive acts — the power of *kabbalas ol*, the acceptance of G-d's yoke.

Wisdom has an unlimited potential, though the effect it has on our conduct has its bounds. *Kabbalas ol* connects a person to the G-dly source of his soul, and enables him to tap this infinite potential. Making an unreserved commitment to fulfill G-d's will thus serves as the "root" for all expressions of our personality, including wisdom, infusing them with unbounded strength and energy.

(Likkutei Sichos, Vol. IV, p. 1210ff)

יח רַבִּי אֱלִיעֶזֶר (בֶּן) חִסְמָא אוֹמֵר, קִנִּין, וּפִתְחֵי נִדָּה, הֵן הֵן גּוּפֵי הֲלָכוֹת, תְּקוּפוֹת, וְגִמַטְרִיָאוֹת, פַּרְפְּרָאוֹת לַחָכְמָה.

18. RABBI ELIEZER (BEN) CHISMA SAID: "THE LAWS PERTAINING TO THE BIRD-SACRIFICES AND THE CALCULATION OF THE ONSET OF THE *NIDDAH* STATE ARE ESSENTIALS OF TORAH LAW; THE CALCULATION OF THE HEAVENLY CYCLES AND GEOMETRY ARE CONDIMENTS TO WISDOM."

THE LAWS PERTAINING TO THE BIRD-SACRIFICES AND THE CALCULATION OF THE ONSET OF THE *NIDDAH* STATE — As the commentaries explain,[85] calcula-

---

85 . R. Ovadiah of Bartenura.

tions become necessary when a doubt arises with regard to these matters, and one must bring more bird-offerings or immerse oneself in the *mikveh* on more occasions than would be required had such doubt not arisen. Although these may appear of secondary importance

THESE ARE ESSENTIALS OF TORAH LAW, — and must be studied with the same dedication that is given to other matters of Torah law. Ignoring them diminishes one's comprehension of the Torah as a whole.

Rabbi Eliezer was an expert in mathematics and physics; Rabbi Yehoshua[86] stated that he could calculate the number of drops of water in the ocean. It is thus implied that he could appreciate how even the most minute particle contributes a dimension of perfection to the entity of which it is a part. Similarly, he understood how even the apparently insignificant aspects of Torah law are essential.

(Sichos Shabbos Parshas Korach, 5741)

---

86 . *Horios* 10b. See *Tosafos Yom Tov* who explains that this is reflected in his reference to astronomy (the knowledge of the heavens) and geometry (the knowledge of earthly wisdom).

CHAPTER FOUR

CHAPTER FOUR

א בֶּן זוֹמָא אוֹמֵר: אֵיזֶהוּ חָכָם הַלוֹמֵד מִכָּל אָדָם, שֶׁנֶּאֱמַר: מִכָּל
מְלַמְּדַי הִשְׂכַּלְתִּי, כִּי עֵדְוֹתֶיךָ שִׂיחָה לִי. אֵיזֶהוּ גִבּוֹר, הַכּוֹבֵשׁ אֶת
יִצְרוֹ, שֶׁנֶּאֱמַר: טוֹב אֶרֶךְ אַפַּיִם מִגִּבּוֹר, וּמוֹשֵׁל בְּרוּחוֹ, מִלֹּכֵד עִיר.
אֵיזֶהוּ עָשִׁיר הַשָּׂמֵחַ בְּחֶלְקוֹ, שֶׁנֶּאֱמַר: יְגִיעַ כַּפֶּיךָ כִּי תֹאכֵל, אַשְׁרֶיךָ
וְטוֹב לָךְ, אַשְׁרֶיךָ בָּעוֹלָם הַזֶּה, וְטוֹב לָךְ לָעוֹלָם הַבָּא. אֵיזֶהוּ מְכֻבָּד,
הַמְכַבֵּד אֶת הַבְּרִיּוֹת, שֶׁנֶּאֱמַר: כִּי מְכַבְּדַי אֲכַבֵּד וּבֹזַי יֵקַלּוּ.

1. BEN ZOMA SAYS: "WHO IS WISE? HE WHO LEARNS FROM EVERY PERSON, AS IT IS STATED:[1] 'FROM ALL THOSE WHO HAVE TAUGHT ME, I HAVE GAINED WISDOM, FOR YOUR TESTIMONIES ARE MY CONVERSATION.'

"WHO IS MIGHTY? HE WHO SUBDUES HIS INCLI-NATION, AS IT IS STATED:[2] 'A PATIENT PERSON IS BETTER THAN A STRONG MAN, AND HE WHO MASTERS HIS SPIRIT IS BETTER THAN ONE WHO CONQUERS A CITY.'

"WHO IS RICH? HE WHO IS HAPPY WITH HIS PORTION, AS IT IS STATED:[3] 'WHEN YOU EAT OF THE LABOR OF YOUR HANDS, YOU WILL BE HAPPY, AND IT WILL BE GOOD FOR YOU.' 'YOU WILL BE HAPPY' IN THIS WORLD; 'IT WILL BE GOOD FOR YOU' IN THE WORLD TO COME.

---

1. *Tehillim* 119:99.
2. *Mishlei* 16:32.
3. *Tehillim* 128:2.

"WHO IS HONORED? HE WHO HONORS OTHERS, AS IT IS STATED:[4] 'I WILL HONOR THOSE WHO HONOR ME, AND THOSE WHO DESPISE ME WILL BE DEGRADED.' "

WHO IS WISE? HE WHO LEARNS FROM EVERY PERSON — A wise man sees other peoples' weaknesses. Thus it would be natural for him to regard those who are less developed than he with a condescending attitude. One who is truly wise, however, focuses his attention on the positive characteristics which every person possesses. He will surely be able to discover such positive traits, for every man was created in the image of G-d,[5] and thus possesses innate virtue. By opening himself to learn from the virtues of others, a wise man expands his horizons and enhances his own wisdom.

WHO IS MIGHTY? — Might is different from physical strength. It refers to the ability to call upon inner resources of energy.

HE WHO SUBDUES HIS INCLINATION — The *mishnah* is referring not merely to one's evil inclination, the *yetzer hora*, but rather all of one's natural inclinations. When a person masters his natural tendencies, he expresses true power, for exercising such mastery requires deep resources of inner strength.

WHO IS RICH? HE WHO IS HAPPY WITH HIS PORTION — The tendency of the wealthy is to seek to increase their assets, as our Sages have commented:[6] "A person who possesses 100 desires 200; one who possesses 200 desires 400." One who is truly wealthy is one who does not become

---

4.   *I Shmuel* 2:30.
5.   *Bereishis* 1:27.
6.   See *Koheles Rabbah* 1:34; *Ramban* and *Bechaye* end of *Parshas Chaye Sarah.*

caught up by such desires, but rather maintains inner peace and calm. Nor will this approach force him to sacrifice wealth. On the contrary a person at peace with himself is far more able to take advantage of opportunities which present themselves, and thus achieve success in the world at large.

(Adapted from Sichos Shabbos Parshas Korach and Parshas Balak, 5740)

*WHEN YOU EAT OF THE LABOR OF YOUR HANDS — The prooftext complements the teachings of our Sages, highlighting the idea that one's work must be merely "the labor of your hands." A person's heart and mind, by contrast, should be directed towards seeking spiritual fulfillment.

And it promises that the outcome of such an approach will be: "You will be happy" in this world. By contrast, over-involvement in one's business may bring material success, but not happiness. Happiness comes only from the inner fulfillment a person feels when motivated by spiritual goals.

(Likkutei Sichos, Vol. I, p. 62)

WHO IS HONORED? HE WHO HONORS OTHERS — It might be said that the natural tendency of a person worthy of honor is to remain aloof from those at a lower level. Moreover, the Hebrew word הבריות, translated as "others," literally means "creations," and refers to[7] individuals who seem to have no redeeming virtue other than the fact that they are G-d's creations.

How and why would an honorable man give honor to such people?

The prooftext provides the answer: "I will honor those who honor Me." G-d represents the epitome of honor, and yet He gives honor to His creations, for they all exist to increase His

---

7. See ch. 1, *mishnah* 12, as explained in *Tanya*, ch. 32.

glory, as it is stated:[8] "Everything which the Holy One, blessed be He, created in this world, He created solely for His glory."

Just as G-d appreciates the virtues possessed by every created being — and for that reason grants it honor — so too, a human should honor others, aware that, at the very least, they possess the potential for virtues and achievements which are worthy of honor.

AND THOSE WHO DESPISE ME WILL BE DEGRADED
— It is difficult to understand why this portion of the prooftext was included in the *mishnah*. What does it add?

It can be explained that when a person fails to honor a colleague, he is in effect showing disrespect to G-d. To cite a narrative:[9] R. Eliezar ben R. Shimon once insulted a person whose appearance belied the possession of any virtues. The person replied: "Go to the Craftsman who created me." By failing to appreciate the person's positive qualities, R. Eliezar was detracting from G-d's creative potential.

Developing this concept further, it can be explained that the verse, "and those who despise Me will be degraded," does not refer to a punishment; it is rather a tendency which G-d has built into the very fabric of nature. When a person cannot appreciate the positive potentials possessed by others, his colleagues will fail to appreciate the virtues which he possesses.

(Adapted from Sichos Shabbos Parshas Korach and Parshas Balak, 5740)

ב בֶּן עַזַּאי אוֹמֵר: הֱוֵי רָץ לְמִצְוָה קַלָּה, וּבוֹרֵחַ מִן הָעֲבֵרָה, שֶׁמִּצְוָה, גּוֹרֶרֶת מִצְוָה, וַעֲבֵרָה גּוֹרֶרֶת עֲבֵרָה, שֶׁשְּׂכַר מִצְוָה מִצְוָה, וּשְׂכַר עֲבֵרָה עֲבֵרָה.

8 .　*Pirkei Avos*, the conclusion of ch. 6.
9 .　*Taanis* 20a ff.

2. BEN AZZAI SAYS: "RUN TO [PERFORM EVEN] AN EASY *MITZVAH*, AND FLEE FROM TRANSGRESSION; FOR ONE *MITZVAH* BRINGS ABOUT ANOTHER *MITZVAH*, AND ONE TRANSGRESSION BRINGS ABOUT ANOTHER; FOR THE REWARD OF A *MITZVAH* IS THE *MITZVAH*, AND THE RECOMPENSE OF A TRANSGRESSION IS A TRANSGRESSION."

RUN TO [PERFORM EVEN] AN EASY *MITZVAH* — The intent is not merely that we actually run to perform a *mitzvah*,[10] but that we should observe the *mitzvos* with joy, vitality and vigor. Even a *mitzvah* which appears easy and insignificant should be observed with enthusiasm and devotion.

Why? Because...

ONE *MITZVAH* BRINGS ABOUT ANOTHER *MITZVAH* — On a simple level, the *mishnah* is teaching us a lesson in causality; fulfilling one *mitzvah* will make it possible for us to fulfill others. This phrase, however, also has a deeper meaning:[11] Every *mitzvah* leads to a *tzavsa* (connection) with G-d. Moreover...

THE REWARD OF A *MITZVAH* IS THE *MITZVAH* — Even a person concerned with reward, i.e., the benefit he will receive, should realize the infinite bond with G-d that is established through the performance of a *mitzvah*. This will grant him immeasurable satisfaction. As a person begins to appreciate the infinite nature of this connection, he will feel a growing commitment to the observance of the *mitzvos*.

(Likkutei Sichos, Vol. XVII, p. 371ff)

---

10 . The obligation to run to perform certain *mitzvos* is an explicit duty (see *Berachos* 6b, *Shulchan Aruch HaRav* 90:13), and thus need not be mentioned in *Pirkei Avos*, which is intended to teach a commitment beyond the measure of the law. Moreover, there are many *mitzvos* for which it is impossible to literally run.

11 . *Likkutei Amarim* of the Maggid of Mezeritch, sec. 259.

Alternatively, this phrase can be interpreted to mean that the reward for fulfilling one *mitzvah* is the opportunity to perform another. In a life dedicated to one goal — closer connection with G-d — there can be nothing more satisfying than the performance of an act which strengthens that connection. Single-minded, wholehearted service to G-d is thus best rewarded by the opportunity to continue serving G-d in this manner.

(Sichos Shabbos Parshas Re'eh, 5749)

ONE TRANSGRESSION BRINGS ABOUT ANOTHER — This teaching demonstrates the importance of forebearing from even the smallest of transgressions. For any trespass, however slight, begins a chain of negative causality that can ultimately lead a person to the most serious sins.

(Likkutei Sichos, Vol. XX, p. 355)

ג הוּא הָיָה אוֹמֵר: אַל תְּהִי בָז לְכָל אָדָם וְאַל תְּהִי מַפְלִיג לְכָל דָּבָר, שֶׁאֵין לְךָ אָדָם שֶׁאֵין לוֹ שָׁעָה, וְאֵין לְךָ דָּבָר שֶׁאֵין לוֹ מָקוֹם.

3. HE WOULD SAY: "DO NOT REGARD ANYONE WITH CONTEMPT, AND DO NOT REJECT ANYTHING, FOR THERE IS NO MAN WHO DOES NOT HAVE HIS HOUR, AND NOTHING WHICH DOES NOT HAVE ITS PLACE."

THERE IS NO MAN WHO DOES NOT HAVE HIS HOUR — That hour of positive activity will have a lasting effect on a person, although the effects may not be seen immediately.

(Sefer HaSichos 5751, Vol. II, p. 625)

***THERE IS... NOTHING WHICH DOES NOT HAVE
ITS PLACE** — Even a mortal architect strives to ensure that
every part of the building he designs is functional. This tendency has its source in the creativity of G-d Himself. Every
particle which He creates exists for a purpose; there is a specific divine intent which cannot be completed without it.[12]

(Likkutei Sichos, Vol. XXI, p. 42)

ד רַבִּי לְוִיטַס אִישׁ יַבְנֶה אוֹמֵר: מְאֹד מְאֹד הֱוֵי שְׁפַל רוּחַ, שֶׁתִּקְוַת
אֱנוֹשׁ רִמָּה. רַבִּי יוֹחָנָן בֶּן בְּרוֹקָה אוֹמֵר: כָּל הַמְחַלֵּל שֵׁם שָׁמַיִם
בַּסֵּתֶר, נִפְרָעִין מִמֶּנּוּ בְּגָלוּי, אֶחָד שׁוֹגֵג וְאֶחָד מֵזִיד בְּחִלּוּל הַשֵּׁם.

4. RABBI LEVITAS OF YAVNEH SAID: "BE OF AN
EXCEEDINGLY HUMBLE SPIRIT, FOR THE EXPEC-
TATION OF MORTAL MAN IS BUT WORMS."[13]

RABBI YOCHANAN BEN BEROKAH SAID: "WHOEVER
DESECRATES THE HEAVENLY NAME IN SECRET,
PUNISHMENT WILL BE METED OUT TO HIM IN PUBLIC;
UNWITTINGLY OR INTENTIONALLY, IT IS ALL THE
SAME IN REGARD TO THE DESECRATION OF [G-D'S]
NAME."

*BE OF AN EXCEEDINGLY HUMBLE SPIRIT — With
regard to pride, the *Rambam* writes:[14] "Any person who has the
slightest trace of a haughty spirit is worthy of being placed
under a ban of ostracism." The commentaries explain that the
Rambam is rejecting the view in the *Talmud*,[15] which permits a
sage to possess an eighth of an eighth measure of pride.

---

12 . *Shabbos* 77b. See also the *Guide to the Perplexed*, Vol. III, ch. 25.
13 . *V. supra, Pirkei Avos* 3:1.
14 . *Mishneh Torah, Hilchos De'os* 2:3
15 . *Sotah* 5a.

The Alter Rebbe explains[16] that the small measure of pride our Sages mentioned is necessary. Were a person to lack it, "he would not desire to approach divine service, for he would think: 'Who am I, and what are my efforts worth?'"

There is not, however, necessarily a contradiction between the two views. The Alter Rebbe is speaking with regard to a person in the initial phases of divine service. In such an instance, unless the person realizes that divine service will enhance his self-esteem, he will not be motivated to apply himself. When, however, a person has progressed in his divine service, he must cultivate the application of the *Rambam's* teaching and shun haughtiness entirely.

(Sefer HaSichos 5749, p. 101ff)

*UNWITTINGLY OR INTENTIONALLY, IT IS ALL THE SAME IN REGARD TO THE DESECRATION OF [G-D'S] NAME — The sanctification or desecration of G-d's Name is not dependent on a person's intent, but on the impression created in the world at large. A person may have the highest intentions when performing a given act. Nevertheless, if the performance gives other people an unfavorable view of the Torah or a Torah personality, G-d's Name has been desecrated.

When, by contrast, a person's behavior — both intentional and unintentional — causes the Torah to be revered, so that people look at him and say: "See what a personality the Torah has molded!"[17] he is sanctifying G-d's name.

---

16. *Torah Or, Megillas Esther* 91b.
17. Cf. *Yoma* 86a.

ה רַבִּי יִשְׁמָעֵאל בַּר רַבִּי יוֹסֵי אוֹמֵר: הַלּוֹמֵד תּוֹרָה עַל מְנָת לְלַמֵּד,
מַסְפִּיקִין בְּיָדוֹ לִלְמוֹד וּלְלַמֵּד, וְהַלּוֹמֵד עַל מְנָת לַעֲשׂוֹת, מַסְפִּיקִין
בְּיָדוֹ לִלְמוֹד וּלְלַמֵּד לִשְׁמוֹר וְלַעֲשׂוֹת. רַבִּי צָדוֹק אוֹמֵר: אַל תִּפְרוֹשׁ
מִן הַצִּבּוּר, וְאַל תַּעַשׂ עַצְמְךָ כְּעוֹרְכֵי הַדַּיָּנִין, וְאַל תַּעֲשֶׂהָ עֲטָרָה
לְהִתְגַּדֵּל בָּהּ, וְלֹא קַרְדּוֹם לַחְתָּךְ בָּהּ, וְכָךְ הָיָה הִלֵּל אוֹמֵר:
וּדְאִשְׁתַּמֵּשׁ בְּתַגָּא חֲלָף, הָא לָמַדְתָּ, כָּל הַנֶּהֱנֶה מִדִּבְרֵי תוֹרָה, נוֹטֵל
חַיָּיו מִן הָעוֹלָם.

5. RABBI YISHMAEL BEN RABBI YOSSE SAID: "HE WHO STUDIES TORAH IN ORDER TO TEACH IS GIVEN THE OPPORTUNITY TO STUDY AND TEACH; AND HE WHO STUDIES IN ORDER TO PRACTICE IS GIVEN THE OPPORTUNITY TO STUDY AND TEACH, TO OBSERVE AND TO PRACTICE."

RABBI TZADOK SAID: "DO NOT SEPARATE YOURSELF FROM THE COMMUNITY, AND DO NOT ACT AS A COUNSELOR [WHEN SITTING AS A JUDGE]. DO NOT MAKE IT [THE TORAH] A CROWN FOR SELF-AGGRANDIZEMENT, NOR AN AXE WITH WHICH TO CUT."

SO TOO HILLEL USED TO SAY: "HE WHO EXPLOITS THE CROWN [OF TORAH FOR HIS OWN ENDS] SHALL PERISH."[18] INDEED, YOU HAVE LEARNED FROM THIS THAT WHOEVER DERIVES PERSONAL GAIN FROM THE WORDS OF TORAH REMOVES HIS LIFE FROM THE WORLD.

DO NOT MAKE IT [THE TORAH]... AN AXE WITH WHICH TO CUT — The intent is that the Torah should not serve as the means by which one earns one's livelihood.[19] Over the centuries, however, we see that the Jewish community has always paid salaries to its rabbis and teachers.

---

18 . *V. supra*, 1:13.
19 . See the commentary of R. Ovadiah of Bartenura and others.

In *Hilchos Talmud Torah*,[20] the Alter Rebbe resolves this issue as follows: A person should never begin studying Torah so that he will be able to earn a salary as a teacher or rabbi. If, however, he begins studying with the proper intention, and then the expenses of his household require him to seek a livelihood, he is permitted to earn a salary based on his Torah knowledge.

We should not look to earn wealth[21] from the study of Torah. Nevertheless, Torah study should not prevent a person from supporting himself and his family.

(Likkutei Sichos, Vol. XX, p. 49-50)

WHOEVER DERIVES PERSONAL GAIN FROM THE WORDS OF TORAH REMOVES HIS LIFE FROM THE WORLD — Nevertheless, the Alter Rebbe writes[22] that even a person who seeks to study Torah for his own aggrandizement should do so, because "A person should always involve himself with the Torah, [even] for a selfish motive. For out of [involvement for] a selfish motive will come involvement for the sake of the Torah itself."[23]

On a simple level, this means that the study of Torah molds each student's thinking processes to the point that he will eventually devote himself to Torah with a selfless intent. There is, however, the possibility for an extended interpretation. שמתוך — rendered as "For out of" — can also mean "In the depths of." Regardless of a person's conscious motives, the inner incentive for him to study the Torah and fulfill its *mitzvos* is always commitment for the sake of the Torah itself.

(Ibid.)

---

20 . 4:15.
21 . Given to us as a wage, in contrast to wealth that comes from G-d.
22 . *Loc. cit.*:14.
23 . *Pesachim* 50b, *Jerusalem Talmud, Chagigah* 1:7.

ו רַבִּי יוֹסֵי אוֹמֵר: כָּל הַמְכַבֵּד אֶת הַתּוֹרָה, גּוּפוֹ מְכֻבָּד עַל הַבְּרִיּוֹת,
וְכָל הַמְחַלֵּל אֶת הַתּוֹרָה גּוּפוֹ מְחֻלָּל עַל הַבְּרִיּוֹת.

6. RABBI YOSSE SAID: "WHOEVER HONORS THE
TORAH IS HIMSELF GIVEN HONOR BY MEN, AND
WHOEVER DISHONORS THE TORAH IS HIMSELF
DISHONORED BY MEN."

WHOEVER HONORS THE TORAH — The *Midrash*[24]
tells us of a dialogue between Rabbi Yosse and a Roman
matron. She asked questions based on the Torah and Rabbi
Yosse attempted to offer her rational explanations.

That narrative can be seen as an extension of this teaching:
Why did Rabbi Yosse enter into such a dialogue? Only for the
honor of Torah; he desired that even non-Jews perceive its wisdom.

On that basis, we can appreciate the reward promised by
the *mishnah*:

IS HIMSELF GIVEN HONOR BY MEN — The Hebrew
term for "himself" — גופו — also means his physical body, and
the term translated as "men" — הבריות — refers, as explained
previously,[25] to people whose only redeeming quality is that
they are G-d's creations.

When a person endeavors to see that all men honor the
Torah, he in turn will receive honor from all people — even
those who are merely G-d's creations. Moreover, since such
individuals have no conception of things spiritual, the honor
they give him will affect his physical person — the dimension
to which they relate.

(Sichos Motzoei Shabbos Parshas Korach, 5738)

---

24 . *Bereishis Rabbah* 68:4.
25 . 1:2, 4:1.

ז רַבִּי יִשְׁמָעֵאל בְּנוֹ אוֹמֵר: הַחֹשֵׂךְ עַצְמוֹ מִן הַדִּין, פּוֹרֵק מִמֶּנּוּ אֵיבָה וְגָזֵל וּשְׁבוּעַת שָׁוְא, וְהַגַּס לִבּוֹ בְּהוֹרָאָה: שׁוֹטֶה רָשָׁע וְגַס רוּחַ.

7. RABBI YISHMAEL HIS SON SAID: "[A JUDGE] WHO REFRAINS FROM HANDING DOWN LEGAL JUDGMENTS [BUT INSTEAD SEEKS COMPROMISE BETWEEN THE LITIGANTS] REMOVES FROM HIMSELF ENMITY, THEFT, AND [THE RESPONSIBILITY FOR] AN UNNECESSARY OATH; BUT ONE WHO AGGRANDIZES HIMSELF BY [EAGERLY] ISSUING LEGAL DECISIONS IS A FOOL, WICKED AND ARROGANT."

*SEEKS COMPROMISE BETWEEN THE LITIGANTS — In a business dispute, the ability to accept compromise is important, for it demonstrates that an individual is able to see beyond his own position and make concessions for the sake of another person.

There are, however, certain matters, such as Jewish education and Torah law, where compromise must be avoided. For the Torah is eternal, G-dly truth — containing absolute values that must not be mitigated by human notions of right and wrong.

(Likkutei Sichos, Vol. XX, p. 356-357)

ח הוּא הָיָה אוֹמֵר: אַל תְּהִי דָן יְחִידִי, שֶׁאֵין דָּן יְחִידִי, אֶלָּא אֶחָד, וְאַל תֹּאמַר קַבְּלוּ דַעְתִּי, שֶׁהֵן רַשָּׁאִין וְלֹא אָתָּה.

8. HE USED TO SAY: "DO NOT JUDGE ALONE, FOR NONE MAY JUDGE ALONE EXCEPT ONE; AND DO NOT SAY [TO YOUR FELLOW JUDGES], 'ACCEPT MY VIEW,' FOR THEY [THE MAJORITY] HAVE THAT PREROGATIVE, NOT YOU."

DO NOT JUDGE ALONE — This principle also applies when judging oneself. A person's self-interest blurs his perspective, so even with regard to one's own affairs, one should always seek the counsel of another.

(Likkutei Sichos, Vol. V, p. 21)

ט רַבִּי יוֹנָתָן אוֹמֵר: כָּל הַמְקַיֵּם אֶת הַתּוֹרָה מֵעֹנִי, סוֹפוֹ לְקַיְּמָהּ מֵעֹשֶׁר, וְכָל הַמְבַטֵּל אֶת הַתּוֹרָה מֵעֹשֶׁר, סוֹפוֹ לְבַטְּלָהּ מֵעֹנִי.

9. RABBI YONASAN SAID: "WHOEVER FULFILLS THE TORAH IN POVERTY WILL ULTIMATELY FULFILL IT IN WEALTH; BUT WHOEVER NEGLECTS THE TORAH IN WEALTH WILL ULTIMATELY NEGLECT IT IN POVERTY."

WHOEVER FULFILLS THE TORAH IN POVERTY — Poverty is not necessarily measured in financial terms. On the contrary, our Sages commented[26] that it is with regard to one's knowledge that one is defined as being rich or poor. And poverty in knowledge is relative. Just as a member of the middle-class is dwarfed by a magnate's wealth, so too, all of us feel impoverished when we realize the infinite scope of the Torah's wisdom.

This sense of poverty should awaken a thirst which will motivate earnest and sincere effort in Torah study.

(Sichos Shabbos Parshas Naso, 5746)

WHOEVER NEGLECTS THE TORAH IN WEALTH — One should not interpret the *mishnah* as implying that wealth is undesirable or a hindrance to Torah study. On the contrary, our

---

26 . *Kesubos* 68a.

Sages explain[27] that material wealth assists Torah study, enabling one to broaden one's perspective. And when a wealthy
person devotes himself to Torah study, he will be granted even
greater prosperity.

(Sichos Chag HaShavuos, 5746)

י רַבִּי מֵאִיר אוֹמֵר: הֱוֵי מְמַעֵט בְּעֵסֶק וַעֲסוֹק בַּתּוֹרָה, וֶהֱוֵי שְׁפַל רוּחַ
בִּפְנֵי כָל אָדָם, וְאִם בָּטַלְתָּ מִן הַתּוֹרָה, יֶשׁ לָךְ בְּטֵלִים הַרְבֵּה כְּנֶגְדָּךְ,
וְאִם עָמַלְתָּ בַּתּוֹרָה הַרְבֵּה, יֶשׁ שָׂכָר הַרְבֵּה לִתֶּן לָךְ.

10. RABBI MEIR SAID: "MINIMIZE YOUR BUSINESS ACTIVITIES AND OCCUPY YOURSELF WITH THE TORAH. BE OF HUMBLE SPIRIT BEFORE EVERY PERSON.

"IF YOU SHOULD NEGLECT THE [STUDY OF] TORAH,
YOU WILL HAVE MANY CAUSES FOR NEGLECTING [IT]
CONFRONTING YOU, BUT IF YOU TOIL MUCH IN THE
TORAH, THERE IS AMPLE REWARD TO BE GIVEN YOU."

**MINIMIZE YOUR BUSINESS ACTIVITIES AND
OCCUPY YOURSELF WITH THE TORAH** — This teaching
is directed at a person for whom earning a living requires
activities other than the study of Torah. Although he is allowed
to follow such a course, the *mishnah* encourages him to minimize such activity and devote his energies primarily to the
study of Torah. If he must choose to either devote his spare
time to the study of Torah or to the performance of charitable
deeds, he should choose Torah study.

---

27 . See *Sotah* 28a. Note also the comments of the *Maharil (Likkutim)*, who relates that
when *Rabbeinu Tam* wished to broaden his understanding of a difficult passage, he
would place golden coins on his study table.

A person who is productively involved in both the study of Torah and commercial activity is likely to feel pride. For after all, there are few who are successful in both fields. Therefore the *mishnah* continues...

BE OF HUMBLE SPIRIT BEFORE EVERY PERSON — Despite your own virtues, look for the virtue in others, and regard yourself humbly. Such a person is promised...

IF YOU TOIL MUCH IN THE TORAH, THERE IS AMPLE REWARD TO BE GIVEN YOU — The word "toil" implies a struggle. In consideration of such efforts, the reward one receives is "ample" — above the limits of our world.

(Sichos Shabbos Parshas Eikev, 5728)

BE OF HUMBLE SPIRIT BEFORE EVERY PERSON — There are two reasons for approaching others with humility: a) The entire Jewish people is compared, by analogy, to a human body.[28] No organ or limb can exist alone. Moreover, every limb complements the functioning of the others. Thus, regardless of the extent of an individual's virtue, every other Jew can contribute something to his growth. Therefore humility is always in order.

b) Everyone possesses weaknesses and failings. When considering others, we must always look at them favorably and attribute their failures to extenuating circumstances. But such rationalizations should not be offered with regard to oneself. We must confront ourselves and the challenges we face honestly. When taking this factor into account, there is reason to be humble before every person — Jew or gentile, regardless of his upbringing or background.

These concepts enable us to appreciate a difference of opinion regarding the appropriate version of the text of this

---

28 . *Yerushalmi, Nedarim* 9:4; *Likkutei Torah* beginning of *Parshas Nitzavim.*

mishnah: For the term "every person," some texts use the Hebrew word האדם, while others use the word אדם, without using the ה as a modifier. The commentaries explain that האדם refers to Jews and gentiles alike,[29] while אדם refers to Jews alone. The first explanation is relevant only with regard to Jews, for complementary unity applies only within our own people. The second explanation, by contrast, applies with regard to both Jews and gentiles. For when a person fails to live up to the potential he was granted, he should feel humble before all the rest of G-d's creations.

In his text of the *mishnah*, the Alter Rebbe chooses the version that employs the word אדם, for the *mishnah* emphasizes how a person's efforts in Torah study should not lead him to pride, and this is primarily relevant with regard to the Jewish people. When referring to the *mishnah* in other contexts,[30] however, he uses the term האדם, for his intent is to emphasize the humility that stems from self-confrontation.

(Likkutei Sichos, Vol. IV, p. 1211ff)

יא רַבִּי אֱלִיעֶזֶר בֶּן יַעֲקֹב אוֹמֵר: הָעוֹשֶׂה מִצְוָה אַחַת, קוֹנֶה לוֹ פְּרַקְלִיט אֶחָד, וְהָעוֹבֵר עֲבֵרָה אַחַת, קוֹנֶה לוֹ קַטֵּגוֹר אֶחָד, תְּשׁוּבָה וּמַעֲשִׂים טוֹבִים כִּתְרִיס בִּפְנֵי הַפֻּרְעָנוּת. רַבִּי יוֹחָנָן הַסַּנְדְּלָר אוֹמֵר: כָּל כְּנֵסִיָּה שֶׁהִיא לְשֵׁם שָׁמַיִם סוֹפָהּ לְהִתְקַיֵּם, וְשֶׁאֵינָהּ לְשֵׁם שָׁמַיִם אֵין סוֹפָהּ לְהִתְקַיֵּם.

11. RABBI ELIEZER BEN YAAKOV SAID: "HE WHO FULFILLS ONE *MITZVAH* ACQUIRES FOR HIMSELF ONE ADVOCATE, AND HE WHO COMMITS ONE TRANSGRESSION ACQUIRES AGAINST HIMSELF ONE

---

29. See *Tosafos, Yevamos* 61a.
30. *Tanya*, ch. 30.

ACCUSER. REPENTANCE AND GOOD DEEDS ARE LIKE A
SHIELD AGAINST RETRIBUTION."

RABBI YOCHANAN HASANDLAR SAID: "EVERY
ASSEMBLY [WHOSE PURPOSE IS] FOR THE SAKE OF
HEAVEN WILL BE PERPETUATED, BUT THAT WHICH IS
NOT FOR THE SAKE OF HEAVEN WILL NOT BE
PERPETUATED."

**HE WHO FULFILLS ONE *MITZVAH* ACQUIRES FOR
HIMSELF ONE ADVOCATE** — The simple meaning of this
mishnah is that the performance of a *mitzvah* creates an angel
that will act as an advocate for the person in his final judgment.[31] Nevertheless, the fact that the *mishnah* uses the expression "acquires" rather than "creates" implies something
deeper. In addition to the angel **created** by each *mitzvah* he
performs, a person **acquires** One advocate; the One becomes
an advocate for him. For every *mitzvah* a person performs, regardless of his intent,[32] connects him to G-d. Conversely...

**HE WHO COMMITS ONE TRANSGRESSION AC-
QUIRES AGAINST HIMSELF ONE ACCUSER** — Here also,
the intent is that "the One" becomes an accuser, because
through sin, a person disrupts the connection between himself
and G-d.

(Sichos Motzoei Shabbos Parshas Eikev, 5738; Sichos Shabbos Parshas Bechukosai, 5741)

**REPENTANCE AND GOOD DEEDS ARE LIKE A
SHIELD AGAINST RETRIBUTION** — Here we are not
speaking about a person's individual judgment, but about a
defense against the spirit of retribution that causes hardship
and misfortune in the world at large. When a person performs a
mitzvah and turns to G-d in *teshuvah*, he gains a shield. This can

---

31 . R. Ovadiah of Bartenura. See also *Likkutei Torah, Bamidbar* 11a.
32 . In contrast, the strength of the angel the person created through the performance
of a *mitzvah* depends on the person's intent.

be compared to a soldier who goes into battle wearing a helmet. Because of the dangers of combat, he takes protective measures. Although our world is fraught with danger, by fulfilling the Torah and its *mitzvos* — and particularly those *mitzvos* associated with protection (e.g., *tefillin* and *mezuzah*) — a person can ward off harm.

(Sichos Motzoei Shabbos Parshas Eikev, 5738)

Every assembly [whose purpose is] for the sake of Heaven will be perpetuated — An "assembly" — a grouping together of different people — runs contrary to the nature of our world, which is characterized by division and self-interest. For such an assembly to "be perpetuated," i.e., that the oneness achieved be extended over time, requires a Divine blessing. This blessing is encouraged when the intent of the participants is for the sake of Heaven.

(Ibid.)

When many people come together for the sake of strengthening each other in the observance of the Torah and its *mitzvos*, the gathering inspires each individual and endows him with the strength to overcome challenges. Moreover, the bonds established between the participants will also be perpetuated. For the bond established through the shared observance of the Torah and its *mitzvos* is eternal, transcending the boundaries of time and space.

(Sichos Shabbos Parshas Emor, 5734; Yechidus Klalis, Rosh Chodesh MarCheshvan, 5752)

יב רַבִּי אֶלְעָזָר בֶּן שַׁמּוּעַ אוֹמֵר: יְהִי כְבוֹד תַּלְמִידְךָ חָבִיב עָלֶיךָ
כְּשֶׁלָּךְ, וּכְבוֹד חֲבֵרְךָ כְּמוֹרָא רַבָּךְ, וּמוֹרָא רַבָּךְ, כְּמוֹרָא שָׁמָיִם.

12. RABBI ELAZAR BEN SHAMMUA SAID: "LET THE HONOR OF YOUR STUDENT BE AS DEAR

TO YOU AS YOUR OWN, THE HONOR OF YOUR
COLLEAGUE AS THE REVERENCE FOR YOUR TEACHER,
AND THE REVERENCE FOR YOUR TEACHER AS THE
FEAR OF HEAVEN."

**LET THE HONOR OF YOUR STUDENT BE AS DEAR
TO YOU AS YOUR OWN** — A student is obligated to revere
his master and sit before him in awe.[33] Therefore, it is out of
place for a teacher to conspicuously honor his student. He
should, however, take care to protect his student's dignity.

(Sichos Shabbos Parshas Bamidbar, 5733)

יג רַבִּי יְהוּדָה אוֹמֵר: הֱוֵי זָהִיר בְּתַלְמוּד, שֶׁשִּׁגְגַת תַּלְמוּד עוֹלָה
זָדוֹן. רַבִּי שִׁמְעוֹן אוֹמֵר: שְׁלֹשָׁה כְתָרִים הֵן כֶּתֶר תּוֹרָה, וְכֶתֶר כְּהֻנָּה,
וְכֶתֶר מַלְכוּת, וְכֶתֶר שֵׁם טוֹב עוֹלֶה עַל גַּבֵּיהֶן.

13. RABBI YEHUDAH SAID: "BE CAUTIOUS IN
STUDY, FOR AN UNWITTING ERROR IN
[OBSERVANCE DUE TO INSUFFICIENT] STUDY IS
ACCOUNTED AS WANTON TRANSGRESSION."

RABBI SHIMON SAID: "THERE ARE THREE CROWNS —
THE CROWN OF TORAH, THE CROWN OF PRIESTHOOD,
AND THE CROWN OF KINGSHIP — BUT THE CROWN OF
A GOOD NAME SURPASSES THEM ALL."

BE CAUTIOUS IN STUDY — זהיר, rendered as "be cautious," shares the same root as the word זוהר, "radiance." A Jew
should always endeavor to add radiance to his Torah study. Al-

---

33 . See *Shabbos* 30b, *Rambam, Mishneh Torah, Hilchos Talmud Torah*, ch. 5.

though the Torah is G-dly, every Jew has the potential to increase its light.[34]

This also explains the need for caution. The fact that there is a potential for increase implies that there is a possibility of error.

(Sichos Shabbos Parshas Bechukosai, 5744)

RABBI SHIMON SAID: "THERE ARE THREE CROWNS — THE CROWN OF TORAH, THE CROWN OF PRIESTHOOD, AND THE CROWN OF KINGSHIP — BUT THE CROWN OF A GOOD NAME SURPASSES THEM ALL" — The wording of the *mishnah* raises an obvious question, for it begins by stating that there are three crowns, and then proceeds to mention four.

This difficulty can be resolved by interpreting the *mishnah* in terms of our divine service, and appreciating each of these crowns as representative of a different spiritual thrust.

The crown of kingship refers to acceptance of the yoke of G-d's kingship — the first step in establishing a bond with G-d.[35] First and foremost, a Jew must give himself over to G-d with the absolute and total commitment of a subject towards his ruler.

The acceptance of G-d's kingship is itself insufficient, for this relationship implies the existence of a gap between subject and Ruler. This shortcoming is overcome by the remaining "crowns," which enable a person to develop an inner bond with G-d.

The crown of priesthood refers to the High Priest, who entered the Holy of Holies, the place which held the Tablets

---

34. In particular, the word the *mishnah* uses for Torah study, *talmud*, is also significant. *Talmud* refers to the didactic analysis of Torah law. In this area, as opposed to the study of the Written Law or straightforward *halachic* directives, man has a greater opportunity to express his potential. This is also the area were greater caution is necessary lest error occur.
35. *Tanya*, ch. 41.

of the Ten Commandments. The Tablets represent a perfect state of unity with the Torah, for unlike letters written on parchment or paper, the Ten Commandments were carved into the stone itself.[36] This refers to a person whose desire and pleasure are identified with the Torah.

The crown of Torah refers to a deeper connection. When a person studies Torah, his thoughts become permeated by the Torah's wisdom, and he is able to internalize his connection with G-dliness. G-dliness becomes not merely the focus of his desire and pleasure, but an expression of who he is.

Nevertheless, even when a person has attained these three crowns, he is still a self-contained entity; he has infused his being with the Torah, but has not transcended himself. This is the thrust of the crown of a good name, which refers to a person's involvement with others and with his environment. For when a person is alone, he does not require a name. When is a name necessary? When one communicates.[37]

A good name is achieved when a person lives his every day life according to the Torah. For then, the deeds he performs spread G-dly light throughout the world.

Nevertheless, the G-dliness encouraged by the performance of *mitzvos* is often not openly revealed, neither within the world at large, nor even within our souls. Frequently, although a person performs many good deeds, the influence they have on his character is neither immediate, nor direct.

On this basis, we can comprehend our *mishnah*. In principle, there are only three crowns, for the achievement of a good name — the spreading of G-dliness throughout the world — is not necessarily a crown; it does not always bring personal fulfillment.

When does a good name become a crown? When, as the *mishnah* continues, it is עולה על גביהן. This phrase, translated as

---

36 . See the essay entitled "Repairing the Breaches," *Timeless Patterns in Time*, Vol. II, p. 128ff (Kehot, N.Y., 1994) and the sources mentioned there.

37 . See *Torah Or* 79c; *Likkutei Torah, Behar* 41c; *Balak* 67c.

"are superior," literally means "ascends upon them." When the service of spreading G-dliness in one's environment follows "upon them" i.e., when it comes as an extension of the three inward thrusts of kingship, priesthood and Torah, it also becomes a "crown."

When a person has developed himself through these three mediums of divine service, his efforts to spread light in the world also generate inner light, which guides him to a deeper and more encompassing relationship with G-d.

(Likkutei Sichos, Vol. IV, p. 1214ff)

The concept that the crown of a good name follows after the crown of Torah has a corollary: one's study of Torah should not be directed merely towards personal development, but should motivate efforts to share this wisdom with others.

Significantly, the author of this teaching is Rabbi Shimon bar Yochai, of whom it is said, *Toraso umanaso*,[38] "his profession was Torah." He devoted himself solely to Torah study, remaining completely uninvolved in worldly concerns. Nevertheless, Rabbi Shimon did not stand aloof from other people, and realized the importance of spreading Torah to individuals who were themselves worldly inclined.[39]

(Likkutei Sichos, Vol. XVII, p. 305ff)

---

38. *Shabbos* 11a.
39. The number of this *mishnah*, 13, also contributes an allusion which adds depth to this concept. *Shabbos* 33b relates that Rabbi Shimon and his son Rabbi Elazar spent 12 years hiding in a cave from their Roman pursuers. When they emerged, they encountered people involved in their day-to-day affairs.

   They were unable to understand, "How can people abandon eternal life (i.e., Torah study) and occupy themselves with temporal concerns?" When G-d saw that they were utterly unable to appreciate the value of other people's worldly involvement, he ordered them to return to the cave for an additional year. After this thirteenth year, Rabbi Shimon was able to comprehend the Divine intent in worldly involvement, and was motivated to share his Torah knowledge, and use it to refine his environment.

   (This concept also points to the spiritual significance of the number 13, which as reflected by the Thirteen Attributes of Mercy, relates to a transcendent dimension of G-dliness. This transcendence enables one to infuse spirituality within our material world. See *Or HaTorah, Bereishis* 7a and other sources.)

יד רַבִּי נְהוֹרַאי אוֹמֵר: הֱוֵי גוֹלֶה לִמְקוֹם תּוֹרָה, וְאַל תֹּאמַר שֶׁהִיא תָבוֹא אַחֲרֶיךָ, שֶׁחֲבֵרֶיךָ יְקַיְּמוּהָ בְיָדֶךָ וְאֶל בִּינָתְךָ אַל תִּשָּׁעֵן.

14. RABBI NEHORA'EY SAID: "EXILE YOURSELF TO A PLACE OF TORAH, AND DO NOT ASSUME THAT IT WILL COME AFTER YOU, FOR IT IS YOUR COLLEAGUES WHO [THROUGH DISCUSSION AND DELIBERATION] WILL CAUSE IT TO BE CLEARLY ESTABLISHED IN YOUR GRASP; AND DO NOT RELY ON YOUR OWN UNDERSTANDING."[40]

DO NOT RELY ON YOUR OWN UNDERSTANDING — This phrase is an explicit quotation from the *Tanach*. Why does Rabbi Nehora'ey include it in his directive without mentioning his source? Also, why is this instruction quoted in *Pirkei Avos*, which teaches pious conduct beyond the measure of the law?

These questions can be answered as follows: In its source, the verse "do not rely on your own understanding" is interpreted[41] as a charge to seek out a teacher rather than remaining content with one's own capacity for comprehension. In our *mishnah*, by contrast, it comes as the final clause. After a person has exiled himself to a place of Torah, and through discussion with his colleagues has brought Torah wisdom within his grasp, he is capable of responding to situations independently. Nevertheless, he should humbly realize the value of consulting with others instead of relying solely on his own knowledge.[42]

Herein we also see a connection to the author of the *mishnah*, Rabbi Nehora'ey. *Nehor* is Aramaic for "light." Rabbi Nehora'ey was given that name because he "illumined the eyes of the wise in the study of Torah law."[43] But despite his

40 . *Mishlei* 3:5.
41 . See *Rashi's* commentary.
42 . See the commentary of Rabbeinu Yonah.
43 . *Eruvin* 13b.

high level of understanding, he taught the virtue of taking counsel with others.

(Sichos Shabbos Parshas Behar, 5733)

טו רַבִּי יַנַּאי אוֹמֵר: אֵין בְּיָדֵינוּ לֹא מִשַּׁלְוַת הָרְשָׁעִים, וְאַף לֹא מִיִּסּוּרֵי הַצַּדִּיקִים. רַבִּי מַתְיָא בֶּן חָרָשׁ אוֹמֵר: הֱוֵי מַקְדִּים בְּשָׁלוֹם כָּל אָדָם, וֶהֱוֵי זָנָב לָאֲרָיוֹת, וְאַל תְּהִי רֹאשׁ לַשּׁוּעָלִים.

15. RABBI YANNAI SAID: "WE ARE UNABLE TO UNDERSTAND EITHER THE WELL-BEING OF THE WICKED OR THE TRIBULATIONS OF THE RIGHTEOUS."

RABBI MATYA BEN CHARASH SAID: "BE THE FIRST TO EXTEND GREETINGS TO ANYONE YOU MEET. RATHER BE A TAIL TO LIONS THAN A HEAD TO FOXES."

WE ARE UNABLE TO UNDERSTAND... THE WELL-BEING OF THE WICKED[44] — The commentaries[45] mention an alternative meaning: "We do not possess either the well-being of the wicked...." To explain: During the time of the *Beis HaMikdash*, the wicked were allowed to prosper. G-d would give them recompense for their few good deeds in this world, and then deny them a portion in the World to Come. In our time — after the destruction of the *Beis HaMikdash* — the wicked are not granted such prosperity.

What is the rationale for such a change? In the time of the *Beis HaMikdash*, G-dliness was openly revealed. Therefore those who ignored this revelation and transgressed were considered as blatantly rebelling against G-d's will and were not

---

44. Our translation follows the first interpretation of the *mishnah* offered by R. Ovadiah of Bartenura.
45. Both interpretations are mentioned by R. Ovadiah of Bartenura.

deemed worthy of a portion in the World to Come. After the destruction of the *Beis HaMikdash*, by contrast, when G-dliness is concealed, the sins which the wicked perform are considered less severe, and they are not denied a portion in the World to Come. They are, however, also not granted the same degree of prosperity in this life.

(Sichos Shabbos Parshas Chayei Sarah, 5730)

*WE ARE UNABLE TO UNDERSTAND... THE TRIBULATIONS OF THE RIGHTEOUS — One of the Maggid of Mezeritch's students asked him how it was possible to accept tribulation with joy. The Maggid sent him to his student, R. Zushya of Anapoli.

R. Zushya was poor; he suffered from physical difficulties, and endured many different types of privation. Nevertheless, he radiated happiness. When the student told him the purpose of his journey, he replied: "I don't know why the Maggid sent you to me. I have never suffered any adversity in my life."

Not knowing — in the positive sense — is the key. When a person makes a commitment to G-dliness that is not bound by the limitations of understanding, he is able to appreciate that everything which G-d grants him is good.

(Likkutei Sichos, Vol. IV, p. 1081ff)

טז רַבִּי יַעֲקֹב אוֹמֵר: הָעוֹלָם הַזֶּה דּוֹמֶה לִפְרוֹזְדוֹר, בִּפְנֵי הָעוֹלָם הַבָּא, הַתְקֵן עַצְמְךָ בִּפְרוֹזְדוֹר כְּדֵי שֶׁתִּכָּנֵס לִטְרַקְלִין.

16. RABBI YAAKOV SAID: "THIS WORLD IS LIKE AN ANTE-ROOM BEFORE THE WORLD TO COME; PREPARE YOURSELF IN THE ANTE-ROOM SO THAT YOU MAY ENTER THE BANQUET HALL."

*THIS WORLD IS LIKE AN ANTE-ROOM BEFORE THE WORLD TO COME — The World to Come — the Era of the Redemption — reflects the ultimate purpose of creation, when it will be revealed that this world is G-d's dwelling.[46]

To explain the analogy: A person reveals the fundamental nature of his character more easily in his own home. We express ourselves outside our homes as well, but there are always social conventions, personal reservations, and the like. When we're at home, these constrictions do not apply, and our true nature is revealed. In the analogue, our world is G-d's home, the place where His essence and the truth of His Being is manifest.

G-d nevertheless desired that mortals should fashion His dwelling, for man has a natural tendency to appreciate the fruit of his own labors.[47] If, instead, this dwelling were to be granted as an unearned gift from above, the bliss we would enjoy would be tarnished.[48] To borrow the metaphor of our Sages,[49] we would be eating "the bread of shame."

And so, in the present era, man's efforts are directed towards transforming the world into a dwelling for G-d. For this reason, the present era is referred to as an ante-room, a preparatory phase through which we must pass.

(Likkutei Sichos, Vol. V, p. 243ff; Vol. XV, p. 95ff)

*PREPARE YOURSELF IN THE ANTE-ROOM SO THAT YOU MAY ENTER THE BANQUET HALL — These preparations have already been completed. To borrow an expression from the Previous Rebbe:[50] We have already

---

46. Cf. *Midrash Tanchuma, Parshas Bechukosai*, sec. 3; *Tanya*, chs. 33 and 36.
47. *Rashi, Bava Metzia*, 38a, s.v. *kav shelo*.
48. There is also a deeper rationale. G-d's underlying motive in implanting this tendency in man is a desire that man be not only a passive recipient (*mekabeil*), but also a contributing partner (*mashpia*) in the work of creation.
49. Cf. *Jerusalem Talmud, Orlah* 1:3; *Likkutei Torah, Parshas Tzav* 7d.
50. *Sichas Simchas Torah*, 5689.

"polished the buttons" — everything necessary to bring about
the Redemption has already been accomplished.

(Sefer HaSichos 5752, Vol. I, p. 151ff)

יז הוּא הָיָה אוֹמֵר: יָפָה שָׁעָה אַחַת בִּתְשׁוּבָה וּמַעֲשִׂים טוֹבִים
בָּעוֹלָם הַזֶּה, מִכָּל חַיֵּי הָעוֹלָם הַבָּא, וְיָפָה שָׁעָה אַחַת שֶׁל קוֹרַת רוּחַ
בָּעוֹלָם הַבָּא, מִכָּל חַיֵּי הָעוֹלָם הַזֶּה.

17. HE USED TO SAY: "ONE HOUR OF
REPENTANCE AND GOOD DEEDS IN THIS
WORLD IS BETTER THAN ALL THE LIFE OF THE
WORLD TO COME. AND ONE HOUR OF BLISS IN THE
WORLD TO COME IS BETTER THAN ALL THE LIFE OF
THIS WORLD."

REPENTANCE AND GOOD DEEDS — According to the
ordinary conception, the function of *teshuvah* is to compensate
for past faults. Were this its only function, the order of the
mishnah should have been reversed, with "good deeds" preceding "*teshuvah.*"

This would imply that a person's life work is the performance of good deeds, with *teshuvah* operating only when there is
a need to compensate for error. By placing *teshuvah* first, the
mishnah indicates that the service of G-d through *teshuvah* takes
precedence. For *teshuvah* means "return," the connection of the
soul to its G-dly core. This aspect of *teshuvah* is of universal
relevance, applying even to those who have not sinned.

It is *teshuvah* of this nature that makes our deeds "good"
and grants them luminance;[51] i.e., it endows them with a higher

---

51 . See *Likkutei Torah, Matos* 82a.

level of good than they possessed in their own right.[52] For the intense yearning for a connection with G-d which characterizes the drive to *teshuvah* invigorates and elevates every aspect of our observance of the Torah.

(Sefer HaSichos 5749, Vol. II, p. 653)

ONE HOUR OF REPENTANCE AND GOOD DEEDS IN THIS WORLD IS BETTER THAN ALL THE LIFE OF THE WORLD TO COME — G-d's essence cannot be grasped or comprehended. Nevertheless, through repentance and the performance of good deeds in one's daily life, a person can establish a connection with this essence. This is the peak of all experience, the ultimate purpose for the creation of the world.

(Likkutei Sichos, Vol. V, p. 244ff)

ONE HOUR OF BLISS IN THE WORLD TO COME IS BETTER THAN ALL THE LIFE OF THIS WORLD — The connection to G-d's essence generated by the performance of *mitzvos* in this world is not openly revealed. In the World to Come, by contrast, we will consciously appreciate the bond we share with G-d.

When seen in this context, the World to Come highlights the pleasure experienced by man, while the present era is characterized by the pleasure generated for G-d, as our Sages commented:[53] "It is pleasing before Me, that I decreed and My will was done." This is problematic; for the World to Come, the final stage of existence, should be completely satisfying, not only to man, but also to G-d.

Nevertheless, this is only a limited perspective. The Era of the Redemption and the Era of the Resurrection of the Dead are, to quote *Tanya*,[54] "the ultimate perfection of the creation of this world... and the intent for which it was brought into

---

52. See the essay entitled "*Teshuvah* — Return, not Repentance," *Timeless Patterns in Time*, Vol. I, p. 33ff (Kehot, N.Y., 1993).
53. *Rashi, Vayikra* 1:9.
54. Ch. 36.

being." It is in that era that it will be openly revealed that our world is G-d's dwelling, the place where His essence is manifest.

To explain: In contrast to all the other entities in the physical and spiritual realms, the concepts of revelation or hiddenness do not apply with regard to G-d's essence. Even when His presence is not revealed, He is there. Indeed, all revelation is by nature limited, and therefore fails to fully express His essence. Therefore, it is in a realm where He is absolutely concealed, our material world, that His essence is manifest.

Nevertheless, just as G-d's essence can remain concealed, it also can be revealed. Although the ordinary channels of revelation are not mediums for its expression, it is not compelled to remain hidden. In coming into expression, it remakes and redefines these channels of revelation.

It is a revelation of this nature that will characterize the World to Come. And thus the World to Come reflects a positive advantage for G-d Himself, as it were, for it is in this era that His essence will be truly revealed in our material world.

(Ibid.)

יח רַבִּי שִׁמְעוֹן בֶּן אֶלְעָזָר אוֹמֵר: אַל תְּרַצֶּה אֶת חֲבֵרֶךָ בְּשַׁעַת כַּעֲסוֹ, וְאַל תְּנַחֲמֵהוּ בְּשָׁעָה שֶׁמֵּתוֹ מֻטָּל לְפָנָיו, וְאַל תִּשְׁאַל לוֹ בִּשְׁעַת נִדְרוֹ, וְאַל תִּשְׁתַּדֵּל לִרְאוֹתוֹ בִּשְׁעַת קַלְקָלָתוֹ.

18. RABBI SHIMON BEN ELAZAR SAID: "DO NOT PLACATE YOUR FELLOW IN THE MOMENT OF HIS ANGER; DO NOT COMFORT HIM WHILE HIS DEAD LIES BEFORE HIM. DO NOT QUESTION HIM [ABOUT THE DETAILS] OF HIS VOW AT THE MOMENT HE MAKES IT; AND DO NOT SEEK TO SEE HIM AT THE TIME OF HIS DEGRADATION."

*DO NOT COMFORT HIM WHILE HIS DEAD LIES BEFORE HIM — The concept of descent for the sake of ascent is ingrained in the fabric of our existence. The soul has its source in the spiritual realm, and descends to this material plane because this will enable it to achieve a deeper bond with G-d in the spiritual realms after death.

By the same token, the period of mourning is clearly a phase of descent, but through it — and this is its purpose — one is able to ascend to a higher rung than was experienced before. Nevertheless, much striving and effort is required for a person to actually feel, while in the midst of a phase of descent, that this downward thrust is intended solely for the purpose of ascent.

This should be the intent of those who comfort mourners — to help them come to such a realization.[55] While a person's dead lies before him, however, this is impossible, for then his feelings of grief are too powerful to be overcome.

(Sichos Yud-Tes Iyar, 5712)

יט שְׁמוּאֵל הַקָּטָן אוֹמֵר: בִּנְפֹל אוֹיִבְךָ אַל תִּשְׂמָח, וּבִכָּשְׁלוֹ אַל יָגֵל לִבֶּךָ, פֶּן יִרְאֶה יְ-י וְרַע בְּעֵינָיו, וְהֵשִׁיב מֵעָלָיו אַפּוֹ.

19. SHMUEL *HAKATAN* SAID: "WHEN YOUR ENEMY FALLS, DO NOT REJOICE, AND WHEN HE STUMBLES LET YOUR HEART NOT BE GLAD, LEST THE L-RD SEE, AND REGARD IT WITH DISPLEASURE, AND DIVERT HIS WRATH FROM HIM [TO YOU]."

---

55. This concept is also implied by the traditional expression of comfort, "May the Omnipresent comfort you among the other mourners of Zion and Jerusalem." For the destruction of the *Beis HaMikdash* is also a descent for the purpose of ascent — a phase in our progress to the ultimate peaks we will reach in the Era of the Redemption.

SHMUEL *HaKATAN* SAID — It is difficult to understand why this teaching is attributed to Shmuel *HaKatan*; it is an exact quote of a verse in *Mishlei*.[56] Among the explanations offered[57] is that the verse in *Mishlei* refers to conflicts with regard to worldly affairs, while Shmuel *HaKatan* is speaking about conflicts within the realm of Torah, such as when there is a difference between two sages regarding a *halachic* ruling.[58] When the view of one sage prevails over that of another, he should not see it as a personal victory. Rather than focus on the fact that it was his conception that triumphed, he should feel happy that the *halachah* was clarified. That alone should be the source of his joy.

This teaching reflects the character of its author, Shmuel *HaKatan* ("Shmuel, the small"), for he was given that title because he always regarded himself humbly.[59] Although he was one of the leading Sages of his time, he applied himself to his studies modestly, without taking pride in his achievements.

(Likkutei Sichos, Vol. XIX, p. 44ff)

Alternatively, it can be explained that the verse in *Mishlei* is referring to a person with whom one shares personal enmity,[60] while the teaching of Shmuel *HaKatan* refers to a person with whom one has no personal disagreement, and who is called an enemy only because he is wicked, and therefore, "it is a *mitzvah* to hate him."[61]

The verse is teaching us that even when an individual's enemy is wicked, he should not rejoice in his downfall, because the satisfaction that he feels is private in nature, and is not

---

56 . 24:17-18.
57 . *Machzor Vitri, Midrash Shmuel.*
58 . In this context, compare the prayer of R. Nechumia ben HaKanah (*Berachos* 28b).
59 . *Jerusalem Talmud, Sotah* 9:13.
60 . This concept is reflected by the preceding verses, which warn a wicked man "not to lie in wait against the dwelling of the righteous, nor to plunder his resting place."
61 . *Pesachim* 113b.

necessarily a reflection of the joy that accompanies "the perishing of the wicked."[62]

Shmuel *HaKatan* teaches a further lesson. Even when one has no personal reason for rejoicing at the downfall of a wicked person, one should not feel happiness. As the Baal Shem Tov taught,[63] when a person sees a fault in a colleague, he should realize that he possesses a similar fault. Thus, were he to take pleasure in the fall of a wicked person, he would invite similar retribution upon himself.[64]

There is an intrinsic connection between this teaching and Shmuel *HaKatan's* own life. Shmuel *HaKatan* was the Sage chosen to author the blessing *VeLamalshinin*[65] ("Let there be no hope for the informers..."[66]) which curses non-believers. Why was this task assigned to him? Because his zealousness bore no trace of hate, but was a reflection of his unbounded love for G-d.

(Sichos Shabbos Parshas Chukas, 5741)

כ אֱלִישָׁע בֶּן אֲבוּיָה אוֹמֵר: הַלּוֹמֵד יֶלֶד לְמָה הוּא דוֹמֶה: לִדְיוֹ כְתוּבָה עַל נְיָר חָדָשׁ, וְהַלּוֹמֵד זָקֵן לְמָה הוּא דוֹמֶה: לִדְיוֹ כְתוּבָה עַל נְיָר מָחוּק. רַבִּי יוֹסֵי בַּר יְהוּדָה אִישׁ כְּפַר הַבַּבְלִי אוֹמֵר: הַלּוֹמֵד מִן הַקְּטַנִּים, לְמָה הוּא דוֹמֶה: לְאוֹכֵל עֲנָבִים קֵהוֹת, וְשׁוֹתֶה יַיִן מִגִּתּוֹ, וְהַלּוֹמֵד מִן הַזְּקֵנִים, לְמָה הוּא דוֹמֶה: לְאוֹכֵל עֲנָבִים בְּשׁוּלוֹת, וְשׁוֹתֶה יַיִן יָשָׁן. רַבִּי מֵאִיר אוֹמֵר: אַל תִּסְתַּכֵּל בְּקַנְקַן, אֶלָּא, בְּמַה שֶּׁיֶּשׁ בּוֹ, יֵשׁ קַנְקַן חָדָשׁ מָלֵא יָשָׁן, וְיָשָׁן, שֶׁאֲפִילוּ חָדָשׁ אֵין בּוֹ.

---

62 . Cf. *Mishlei* 11:10.
63 . *Meor Einayim*, the beginning of *Parshas Chukas*. Note the explanation in *Likkutei Sichos*, Vol. X, p. 24.
64 . See the notes to ch. 3, *mishnah* 16.
65 . *Berachos* 28b.
66 . *Siddur Tehillat HaShem*, p. 55.

20.

ELISHA BEN AVUYA SAID: "HE WHO STUDIES TORAH AS A CHILD, TO WHAT CAN HE BE COMPARED? TO INK WRITTEN ON FRESH PAPER. AND HE WHO STUDIES TORAH AS AN OLD MAN, TO WHAT CAN HE BE COMPARED? TO INK WRITTEN ON PAPER THAT HAS BEEN ERASED."

RABBI YOSSE BAR YEHUDAH OF KFAR HABAVLI SAID: "HE WHO LEARNS TORAH FROM THE YOUNG, TO WHAT CAN HE BE COMPARED? TO ONE WHO EATS UNRIPE GRAPES OR DRINKS WINE FROM HIS VAT; WHILE HE WHO LEARNS TORAH FROM THE OLD, TO WHAT CAN HE BE COMPARED? TO ONE WHO EATS RIPE GRAPES OR DRINKS AGED WINE."

RABBI MEIR SAID: "DO NOT LOOK AT THE VESSEL, BUT RATHER AT WHAT IT CONTAINS; THERE MAY BE A NEW VESSEL FILLED WITH AGED WINE, OR AN OLD VESSEL IN WHICH THERE IS NOT EVEN NEW [WINE]."

ELISHA BEN AVUYA SAID: HE WHO STUDIES TORAH AS A CHILD, TO WHAT CAN HE BE COMPARED? TO INK WRITTEN ON FRESH PAPER — R. Ovadiah of Bartenura explains that the advantage of writing on fresh paper is that the writing lasts. The concepts a person learns in his childhood will be retained. This teaching was personified by its author, Elisha ben Avuya. In his childhood, his father had him focus his attention on Torah study.[67] When Elisha matured, he was attracted to heretical teachings,[68] and ultimately forsook the Torah life-style. Nevertheless, he retained his Torah knowledge, and was able to teach Rabbi Meir many concepts. Since the ink was written on fresh paper, even when the paper was sullied, the writing remained.

---

67 . *Jerusalem Talmud, Chagigah* 2:1.
68 . See *Chagigah* 15b.

The connection between Rabbi Meir and Elisha ben Avuya also enhances our comprehension of the teaching of Rabbi Meir which is included in this *mishnah*....

DO NOT LOOK AT THE VESSEL, BUT RATHER AT WHAT IT CONTAINS — In addition to the obvious lesson, this clause also explains why Rabbi Meir could study Torah from Elisha. Rabbi Meir did not look at the "vessel" — Elisha and his conduct — "but rather at what it contains" — the Torah knowledge he possessed. "Rabbi Meir found a pomegranate. He ate its contents and discarded its shell."[69]

(It must, however, be emphasized that this approach is only appropriate for a Sage of the stature of Rabbi Meir. By and large, our Sages have given us the directive:[70] "If a teacher resembles an angel of the L-rd of Hosts, seek Torah from him. If not, do not seek Torah from him.")

(Sichos Shabbos Parshas Emor, 5742)

HE WHO STUDIES TORAH AS AN OLD MAN, TO WHAT CAN HE BE COMPARED? TO INK WRITTEN ON PAPER THAT HAS BEEN ERASED — The first clause of this *mishnah* is readily understandable. Emphasizing the advantage of studying when young will encourage a person to make the most of his childhood years, and gain as much Torah knowledge as possible. Why, though, does the *mishnah* continue, stressing the shortcomings of studying when older? What positive lesson can be derived from this?

The point of the *mishnah* is that age has a meaning beyond that expressed on one's passport. There are childlike traits of humility, openness and creative spontaneity that should be nurtured throughout one's lifetime. When a person displays these traits, he will succeed in the study of Torah.

---

69. *Ibid.*
70. *Ibid.*

When, by contrast, a person puts an emphasis on wisdom in its own right, his approach becomes rigid and self-contained, for he will learn only what he already appreciates as right, and this prevents him from apprehending the infinite dimensions of G-d's Torah.

(Likkutei Sichos, Vol. XIX, p. 40ff)

כא רַבִּי אֶלְעָזָר הַקַּפָּר אוֹמֵר: הַקִּנְאָה וְהַתַּאֲוָה וְהַכָּבוֹד, מוֹצִיאִין אֶת הָאָדָם מִן הָעוֹלָם.

21. RABBI ELAZAR HAKAPPAR SAID: "ENVY, DESIRE, AND HONOR-SEEKING DRIVE A MAN FROM THE WORLD."

*DESIRE... DRIVE[S] A MAN FROM THE WORLD — The intent of the *mishnah* is that the mindless drive to satisfy physical desires generally prevents a person from living a well-balanced life.

On the other hand, although a person may think he wants material objects as ends in themselves, his desire may actually be rooted in the depths of his soul.

Consider. Everything in the world contains sparks of G-dliness. Mankind has been given the task of refining the material and revealing its innate G-dliness. Every individual is destined to elevate certain sparks, and this divine service is necessary for his personal growth.

We may be unaware of the spiritual motivation underlying our physical desires and consider them to be physiological or psychological. In truth, however, a deeper force motivates our will. Why does a Jew want children, possessions, or material success? Because his soul has an unarticulated desire to fulfill the G-dly purpose associated with these seemingly material blessings.

Therefore, when a person feels a desire for a material entity, he need not deem it bad and reject it entirely. He must, however, determine whether this desire stems from selfish motives, or is an expression of his soul's longing.

(Likkutei Sichos, Vol. XIX, p. 291ff)

כב הוּא הָיָה אוֹמֵר: הַיִּלוֹדִים לָמוּת, וְהַמֵּתִים לַחֲיוֹת (נ״א לְהֵחָיוֹת), וְהַחַיִּים לָדוֹן, לֵידַע, וּלְהוֹדִיעַ, וּלְהִנָּדַע, שֶׁהוּא אֵ-ל, הוּא הַיּוֹצֵר, הוּא הַבּוֹרֵא, הוּא הַמֵּבִין, הוּא הַדַּיָּן, הוּא הָעֵד, הוּא בַּעַל דִּין, הוּא עָתִיד לָדוֹן. בָּרוּךְ הוּא, שֶׁאֵין לְפָנָיו, לֹא עַוְלָה, וְלֹא שִׁכְחָה, וְלֹא מַשּׂוֹא פָנִים, וְלֹא מִקַּח שֹׁחַד, וְדַע שֶׁהַכֹּל, לְפִי הַחֶשְׁבּוֹן. וְאַל יַבְטִיחֲךָ יִצְרֶךָ, שֶׁהַשְּׁאוֹל בֵּית מָנוֹס לָךְ, שֶׁעַל כָּרְחֲךָ אַתָּה נוֹצָר, וְעַל כָּרְחֲךָ אַתָּה נוֹלָד, וְעַל כָּרְחֲךָ אַתָּה חַי, וְעַל כָּרְחֲךָ אַתָּה מֵת, וְעַל כָּרְחֲךָ אַתָּה עָתִיד לִתֵּן דִּין וְחֶשְׁבּוֹן לִפְנֵי מֶלֶךְ, מַלְכֵי הַמְּלָכִים, הַקָּדוֹשׁ, בָּרוּךְ הוּא:

22. HE USED TO SAY: "THOSE WHO ARE BORN ARE DESTINED TO DIE; THOSE WHO ARE DEAD ARE DESTINED TO LIVE AGAIN; AND THOSE WHO LIVE [AGAIN] ARE DESTINED TO BE JUDGED. [THEREFORE, LET MAN] KNOW, MAKE KNOWN, AND BECOME AWARE THAT HE IS G-D, HE IS THE FASHIONER, HE IS THE CREATOR, HE IS THE DISCERNER, HE IS THE JUDGE, HE IS THE WITNESS, HE IS THE PLAINTIFF, HE WILL HEREAFTER SIT IN JUDGMENT. BLESSED IS HE, BEFORE WHOM THERE IS NO INIQUITY, NOR FORGETTING, NOR PARTIALITY, NOR BRIBE-TAKING; AND KNOW THAT ALL IS ACCORDING TO THE RECKONING.

"AND LET NOT YOUR EVIL INCLINATION ASSURE YOU
THAT THE GRAVE WILL BE A PLACE OF REFUGE FOR
YOU, FOR AGAINST YOUR WILL YOU WERE CREATED,
AGAINST YOUR WILL YOU WERE BORN; AGAINST YOUR
WILL YOU LIVE; AGAINST YOUR WILL YOU DIE, AND
AGAINST YOUR WILL YOU ARE DESTINED TO GIVE AN
ACCOUNT BEFORE THE SUPREME KING OF KINGS, THE
HOLY ONE, BLESSED BE HE."

BRIBE-TAKING — In his *Commentary to the Mishnah*, the
Rambam explains that this clause teaches that G-d will not accept the bribe of a *mitzvah*. Even when a person has performed
1,000 good deeds and only one evil act, the good deeds will not
eclipse the evil act. He will receive ample and fair reward for
all the good he has done, and just retribution for his misdeed.

The reckoning which G-d makes of our virtues and shortcomings is not a form of barter. Every *mitzvah* a person performs creates an eternal bond between him and G-d, and every
sin causes separation between the two.

This highlights the importance of repentance, for *teshuvah*
re-establishes the connection with G-d that is broken through
sin, and indeed has the potential to transform one's willful sins
into merits.[71]

For this reason, our Sages[72] refer to *teshuvah* as a bribe, and
state that this is the one bribe G-d does accept.

(Likkutei Sichos, Vol. XXIV, p. 76ff)

**AGAINST YOUR WILL YOU LIVE; AGAINST YOUR
WILL YOU DIE** — By saying that a person lives against his
will, the *mishnah* implies that a person's true desire is to abandon material existence. Saying that a person dies against his

---

71 . *Yoma* 86b.
72 . *Midrash Tehillim* commenting on *Tehillim* 17:2; *Yalkut Shimoni, Tehillim* sec. 670.

will, by contrast, implies that a person desires to continue living within the body.

In truth, both statements are true. On one hand, the soul is a spiritual entity, "an actual part of G-d."[73] Thus it has a natural desire to rise above the limits of material existence and return to its spiritual source.

Why does it remain within the body? Because it perceives G-d's desire for the world to be transformed into a dwelling for Him. And it dedicates itself to the fulfillment of this desire against its own individual will.

Nevertheless, because the soul is an actual part of G-d, G-d's desire for a dwelling in this world is not an external factor, but rather permeates its essential will. Therefore, death — the departure from this material framework — is also against its will.

These two thrusts, though seemingly contradictory, actually reinforce each other. It is only when a person feels the limitations of material existence and desires the spiritual, that he is capable of satisfying G-d's desire for a dwelling within this world. If he lacks the drive for spirituality, it is likely that his involvement in the world will be spurred by ordinary material desires, and not G-d's desire for a dwelling.

These concepts should be reflected in every individual's life. On one hand, he should not shy away from worldly involvement, for through such activity he can fulfill G-d's desire. Simultaneously, a person should feel that this involvement is contrary to his inner nature — against his will — for his true desire is to be one with G-d.

(Likkutei Sichos, Vol. IV, p. 1217ff)

---

73 . *Tanya*, ch. 2.

CHAPTER FIVE

CHAPTER FIVE

א בַּעֲשָׂרָה מַאֲמָרוֹת נִבְרָא הָעוֹלָם, וּמַה תַּלְמוּד לוֹמַר, וַהֲלֹא
בְּמַאֲמָר אֶחָד יָכוֹל לְהִבָּרְאוֹת, אֶלָּא, לְהִפָּרַע מִן הָרְשָׁעִים שֶׁמְּאַבְּדִין
אֶת הָעוֹלָם שֶׁנִּבְרָא בַּעֲשָׂרָה מַאֲמָרוֹת, וְלִתֵּן שָׂכָר טוֹב לַצַּדִּיקִים
שֶׁמְּקַיְּמִין אֶת הָעוֹלָם שֶׁנִּבְרָא בַּעֲשָׂרָה מַאֲמָרוֹת.

1. THE WORLD WAS CREATED BY MEANS OF TEN [DIVINE] UTTERANCES. WHAT DOES THIS COME TO TEACH US, FOR INDEED, IT COULD HAVE BEEN CREATED BY ONE UTTERANCE? BUT IT WAS SO TO BRING RETRIBUTION UPON THE WICKED WHO DESTROY THE WORLD WHICH WAS CREATED BY TEN UTTERANCES, AND TO BESTOW AMPLE REWARD UPON THE RIGHTEOUS WHO SUSTAIN THE WORLD WHICH WAS CREATED BY TEN UTTERANCES.

CHAPTER FIVE: THE WORLD WAS CREATED BY MEANS OF TEN [DIVINE] UTTERANCES — According to the principles of Torah numerology, five represents a level of G-dliness above all limitation,[1] while ten reflects the structure of our finite, material world. The intent of this chapter of *Pirkei Avos* is to reveal the G-dliness which transcends all limitation within the context of our material existence.

(Sefer HaSichos 5751, Vol. II, p. 772)

Significantly, although the *mishnah* mentions several sets of ten, it does not mention the Ten Commandments. The explanation for this omission is that all the sets of ten mentioned in

---

1. See *Likkutei Torah, Shir HaShirim* 24d; *Sefer HaMaamarim* 5570, p. 92.

this chapter — even "the ten miracles which transpired... in the *Beis HaMikdash*" — reflect how G-dliness descends and takes on the limitations of our worldly existence.

To clothe Himself with the Torah, by contrast, is not a descent for G-d. On the contrary, "the Torah and the Holy One, blessed be He, are one."[2] Therefore, when a person studies Torah for its own sake, he can rise above his worldly limitations.

(Likkutei Sichos, Vol. IV, p. 1226).

There is, however, a parallel between the Ten Commandments and the ten utterances of creation,[3] for the Torah is the purpose for which the world was created,[4] and it is through the Torah that the world's existence is maintained. This represents the goal of man's divine service: to endow every element of the world's existence with its essential G-dliness as revealed through the Torah.

(Sefer HaSichos 5751, Vol. II, p. 537ff)

INDEED, IT COULD HAVE BEEN CREATED BY ONE UTTERANCE — If, however, the world had been created with one utterance, its nature would be fundamentally different than it is today.[5] One utterance would have brought into being a material world, but there would have been no qualitative distinction between the various created beings. All existence would have reflected His oneness.

By creating the world with ten utterances, G-d endowed each order of being with a nature of its own. For the ten utterances of creation reflect the ten *sefiros*, which combine and subdivide into an infinite array of Divine powers. Each of these powers is associated with a particular element of existence.

---

2 .   *Tanya*, ch. 4 and beginning of ch. 23, in the name of the *Zohar;* see *Zohar* II, 60a; *Likkutei Torah, Nitzavim* 46a.
3 .   *Zohar* III, p. 11b.
4 .   See *Rashi, Bereishis* 1:1.
5 .   *Sefer HaMaamarim* 5659, p. 144.

Thus, through these ten mediums, a world which appears to have an identity other than G-dliness came into being. By associating every element of existence with the dimension of the Torah that parallels it, man can demonstrate how the world is one with G-d, not only from the perspective of transcendent oneness, but also within the context of its own particular existence.

(Sefer HaSichos 5750, Vol. II, p. 473ff; 5751, Vol. II, p. 538ff)

IT WAS SO TO BRING RETRIBUTION UPON THE WICKED WHO DESTROY THE WORLD WHICH WAS CREATED BY TEN UTTERANCES — One might ask: why did G-d, the ultimate of good and kindness, create the world for this seemingly negative purpose?

It is possible to answer as follows. On the verse:[6] "G-d has made everything for His sake, also the wicked for his *evil day*," the Alter Rebbe explains[7] that G-d created the wicked so that they will transform their "evil" into "day"; i.e., so that they will turn to Him and allow the G-dly life-force hidden within them to shine forth.

To apply this concept in the present context: The word להפרע, translated as "bring retribution" literally means "collect His due." G-d does not bring retribution in order to punish, heaven forbid, but as a prod. He desires "to collect His due," to prompt every individual to carry out the divine service for which he was created. When a person transgresses G-d's will, he can "pay his due" by turning to Him in *teshuvah*, for *teshuvah* transforms one's sins into merits.[8]

Yes, by creating the world with ten utterances rather than one, G-d allowed for the existence of a greater potential for

---

6. *Mishlei* 16:4.
7. *Tanya*, ch. 27.
8. *Yoma* 86b; see *Tanya*, ch. 7. See also the essay entitled *"Teshuvah* — Return, not Repentance," *Timeless Patterns in Time*, Vol. I, p. 33ff (Kehot, N.Y., 5753), where this concept is explained at length.

evil. But this evil will not be permanent. Through *teshuvah*, it will be transformed into light and holiness.

To highlight this concept, our *mishnah* mentions the wicked before the righteous. For as our Sages declared:[9] "In the place where *baalei teshuvah* stand, even those who are completely righteous cannot stand."

(Sichos Shabbos Parshas Nitzavim, 5741, Likkutei Sichos, Vol. 30, p. 1ff.)

ב עֲשָׂרָה דוֹרוֹת מֵאָדָם וְעַד נֹחַ, לְהוֹדִיעַ כַּמָּה אֶרֶךְ אַפַּיִם לְפָנָיו, שֶׁכָּל הַדּוֹרוֹת הָיוּ מַכְעִיסִין וּבָאִין, עַד שֶׁהֵבִיא עֲלֵיהֶם אֶת מֵי הַמַּבּוּל. עֲשָׂרָה דוֹרוֹת מִנֹּחַ וְעַד אַבְרָהָם, לְהוֹדִיעַ כַּמָּה אֶרֶךְ אַפַּיִם לְפָנָיו, שֶׁכָּל הַדּוֹרוֹת הָיוּ מַכְעִיסִין וּבָאִין, עַד שֶׁבָּא אַבְרָהָם אָבִינוּ וְקִבֵּל שְׂכַר כֻּלָּם.

2. THERE WERE TEN GENERATIONS FROM ADAM TO NOACH TO INDICATE HOW GREAT IS HIS PATIENCE; FOR ALL THOSE GENERATIONS REPEATEDLY ANGERED HIM, UNTIL HE BROUGHT UPON THEM THE WATERS OF THE FLOOD.

THERE WERE TEN GENERATIONS FROM NOACH TO AVRAHAM TO INDICATE HOW GREAT IS HIS PATIENCE, FOR ALL THOSE GENERATIONS REPEATEDLY ANGERED HIM, UNTIL AVRAHAM OUR FATHER CAME AND RECEIVED THE REWARD OF THEM ALL.

THERE WERE TEN GENERATIONS... TO INDICATE HOW GREAT IS HIS PATIENCE — Ten represents the full cycle of worldly existence. G-d waits patiently for man to return to Him. When, however, man's evil grows to encompasses all ten dimensions of his existence, G-d initiates a change (the

---

9 .   *Berachos* 34b; *Rambam, Hilchos Teshuvah* 7:4.

Flood, or the emergence of Avraham) which is intended to transform the nature of the entire world.

(Likkutei Sichos, Vol. XV, p. 71)

UNTIL AVRAHAM OUR FATHER CAME AND RECEIVED THE REWARD OF THEM ALL — The *mishnah* does not make such a statement concerning Noach, for two differences separate Noach and the generations which preceded him from Avraham and the generations before him.

The generations before Noach had no redeeming virtues whatsoever. They "repeatedly angered G-d," and lived in constant friction, conflict, and discord. In contrast, although the generations that preceded Avraham also "repeatedly angered G-d," they at least shared a kindred spirit and treated each other with love.[10] Hence, their conduct generated reward; they themselves, however, were unfit to receive it.

There was also a basic difference between Noach and Avraham. Noach did not seek to influence the behavior of the people around him,[11] while Avraham tried to make all mankind conscious of G-d.[12] Through this conduct, Avraham "received the reward" generated by all the comradely deeds done by the generations which preceded him.

(Likkutei Sichos, Vol. III, p. 753)

ג עֲשָׂרָה נִסְיוֹנוֹת נִתְנַסָּה אַבְרָהָם אָבִינוּ וְעָמַד בְּכֻלָּם, לְהוֹדִיעַ כַּמָּה חִבָּתוֹ שֶׁל אַבְרָהָם אָבִינוּ.

3. OUR PATRIARCH AVRAHAM WAS TESTED WITH TEN TESTS, AND HE WITHSTOOD THEM ALL TO

---

10 . *Sanhedrin* 109a.
11 . *Zohar* I, 67b.
12 . *Sotah* 10a.

SHOW HOW GREAT WAS OUR PATRIARCH AVRAHAM'S
LOVE [FOR G-D].

TEN TESTS — As mentioned, the number ten reflects the
full scope of our personal potential. Avraham showed his devotion to G-d with every dimension of his being.

**TEN TESTS... TO SHOW HOW GREAT WAS OUR
PATRIARCH AVRAHAM'S LOVE [FOR G-D]** — The purpose of the tests which Avraham underwent — and of the challenges which his descendants, each and every member of the
Jewish people, confronts — is to bring into expression a more
powerful love for G-d, as it is written:[13] "G-d... is testing you to
see if you love G-d... with all your heart and with all your soul."

OUR PATRIARCH AVRAHAM — Avraham is described
as אבינו, our Patriarch (literally "our father"). Just as a father
bequeaths his estate to his descendants, Avraham bequeathed
his spiritual legacy to the entire Jewish people. His spiritual
legacy empowers each of us, endowing us with the strength to
withstand the challenges we face in our divine service.

(Sichos Shabbos Parshas Chukas, 5737)

ד עֲשָׂרָה נִסִּים נַעֲשׂוּ לַאֲבוֹתֵינוּ בְּמִצְרַיִם, וַעֲשָׂרָה עַל הַיָּם, עֶשֶׂר
מַכּוֹת הֵבִיא הַקָּדוֹשׁ בָּרוּךְ הוּא עַל הַמִּצְרִיִּם, בְּמִצְרַיִם, וְעֶשֶׂר עַל
הַיָּם. עֲשָׂרָה נִסְיוֹנוֹת נִסּוּ אֲבוֹתֵינוּ אֶת הַקָּדוֹשׁ בָּרוּךְ הוּא בַּמִּדְבָּר,
שֶׁנֶּאֱמַר: וַיְנַסּוּ אוֹתִי זֶה עֶשֶׂר פְּעָמִים וְלֹא שָׁמְעוּ בְּקוֹלִי.

---

13. *Devarim* 13:4.

4. TEN MIRACLES WERE PERFORMED FOR OUR FOREFATHERS IN EGYPT, AND TEN AT THE SEA. THE HOLY ONE, BLESSED BE HE, BROUGHT TEN PLAGUES UPON THE EGYPTIANS IN EGYPT AND TEN AT THE SEA. OUR FOREFATHERS SUBJECTED THE HOLY ONE, BLESSED BE HE, TO TEN TRIALS IN THE DESERT, AS IT IS STATED: "BY NOW THEY HAVE TESTED ME TEN TIMES, AND DID NOT HEED MY VOICE."[14]

TEN MIRACLES WERE PERFORMED FOR OUR FOREFATHERS — *Pirkei Avos* is intended to teach us pious conduct — how to serve G-d beyond the measure of the law. What lesson in pious conduct can we learn from these points of history?

This question can be answered as follows: The fact that G-d wrought miracles for the Jews in Egypt made the people aware of their true identity. Although they were still in exile, the miracles made them conscious that they were G-d's servants, rather than slaves of the Egyptians.

This is also true today. Although we are still in exile, we are G-d's servants, and subject to no other authority. Our commitment to Him need not be limited in any way. On the contrary, just as miracles represent a departure from nature, our commitment can rise above ordinary mortal constraints.

(Sichos Shabbos Parshas Nitzavim, 5738)

TEN MIRACLES... TEN TRIALS — Miracles make a powerful impression on a person, for they reveal to him a reality above his own. Nevertheless, the impression is not internalized. This allows for the possibility — as reflected by the ten trials to which the Jews subjected G-d in the desert — of forgetfulness and descent. Nevertheless, this fall is merely a

---

14 . *Bamidbar* 14:22.

phase in the "journey through the desert" — the march of our people (and of mankind) to *Eretz Yisrael* and Redemption.

(Sichos Shabbos Parshas Re'eh, 5736)

TEN TRIALS — The *mishnah* uses the expression "trials," rather than "sins" or "transgressions." The Jews' conduct in the desert tried G-d's power. But He proved Himself, and removed all their doubts, elevating the newborn nation to a higher level of faith. This is also indicated by the word "trial," for the Hebrew original, נסיון, also connotes "elevation."[15]

(Sichos Shabbos Parshas Chukas, 5743)

ה עֲשָׂרָה נִסִּים נַעֲשׂוּ לַאֲבוֹתֵינוּ בְּבֵית הַמִּקְדָּשׁ: לֹא הִפִּילָה אִשָּׁה
מֵרֵיחַ בְּשַׂר הַקֹּדֶשׁ, וְלֹא הִסְרִיחַ בְּשַׂר הַקֹּדֶשׁ מֵעוֹלָם, וְלֹא נִרְאָה
זְבוּב בְּבֵית הַמִּטְבָּחַיִם, וְלֹא אֵירַע קֶרִי לְכֹהֵן גָּדוֹל בְּיוֹם הַכִּפֻּרִים,
וְלֹא כִבּוּ הַגְּשָׁמִים אֵשׁ שֶׁל עֲצֵי הַמַּעֲרָכָה, וְלֹא נִצְּחָה הָרוּחַ אֶת
עַמּוּד הֶעָשָׁן, וְלֹא נִמְצָא פְּסוּל בָּעֹמֶר, וּבִשְׁתֵּי הַלֶּחֶם וּבְלֶחֶם הַפָּנִים,
עוֹמְדִים צְפוּפִים וּמִשְׁתַּחֲוִים רְוָחִים, וְלֹא הִזִּיק נָחָשׁ וְעַקְרָב
בִּירוּשָׁלַיִם, וְלֹא אָמַר אָדָם לַחֲבֵרוֹ צַר לִי הַמָּקוֹם שֶׁאָלִין בִּירוּשָׁלָיִם.

5. TEN MIRACLES WERE WROUGHT FOR OUR ANCESTORS IN THE *BEIS HAMIKDASH*:

A)　NO WOMAN EVER MISCARRIED BECAUSE OF THE AROMA OF THE MEAT OF THE HOLY SACRIFICES;

B)　THE MEAT OF THE HOLY SACRIFICES NEVER BECAME PUTRID;

C)　NO FLY WAS EVER SEEN IN THE SLAUGHTER-HOUSE;

---

15 . *Sefer HaMaamarim* 5689, p. 203ff.

D) NO BODILY IMPURITY EVER BEFELL THE HIGH
PRIEST ON YOM KIPPUR;

E) RAIN NEVER EXTINGUISHED THE FIRE ON THE
WOOD-PILE OF THE ALTAR;

F) THE WIND NEVER PREVAILED OVER THE COLUMN
OF SMOKE [RISING FROM THE ALTAR, TO DIS-
SIPATE IT];

G) NO DISQUALIFYING DEFECT WAS EVER FOUND IN
THE *OMER*,[16] OR IN THE TWO [SHAVUOS]
LOAVES,[17] OR IN THE SHOWBREAD;[18]

H) WHEN THE PEOPLE STOOD, THEY WERE CROWDED
TOGETHER, YET WHEN THEY PROSTRATED
THEMSELVES, THEY HAD AMPLE SPACE;

I) NO SNAKE OR SCORPION EVER CAUSED HARM IN
JERUSALEM;

J) NOR DID ANY MAN EVER SAY TO HIS FELLOWMAN:
"THE PLACE IS TOO CROWDED FOR ME TO LODGE
OVERNIGHT IN JERUSALEM."

**TEN MIRACLES WERE WROUGHT FOR OUR
ANCESTORS IN THE *BEIS HAMIKDASH*** — *Pirkei Avos* is
intended to teach us *mili dechassidusa*, pious conduct beyond
the measure of the law. Of what relevance is this point of historical information in that context?

The intent in relating these miracles is to make us conscious of the great love and care G-d shows for our people. This
knowledge in turn will inspire us to make a more complete
commitment to our divine service. Moreover, by emphasizing
the uniqueness of the *Beis HaMikdash*, the *mishnah* awakens our
longing for those miracles to be revealed again, and spurs us to

16. *Vayikra* 23:9-14.
17. *Ibid.* 23:16-17.
18. V. *Shmos* 25:30; *Vayikra* 24:5-8.

carry out those activities which will lead to the rebuilding of
the *Beis HaMikdash.*

(Sichos Shabbos Behar-Bechukosai, 5731)

**NO WOMAN EVER MISCARRIED BECAUSE OF THE
AROMA OF THE MEAT OF THE HOLY SACRIFICES —** It
might seem that the first miracle mentioned by the *mishnah*
should involve spiritual matters — those concerns which lie at
the heart of our people's sacrificial worship. The *mishnah*, however, wants to emphasize how dear every Jew is in G-d's eyes,
and therefore cites an example which affects people on a personal level.

(Ibid.)

**WHEN THE PEOPLE STOOD, THEY WERE CROWDED
TOGETHER,   YET   WHEN   THEY   PROSTRATED
THEMSELVES, THEY HAD AMPLE SPACE —** This mira-
cle reflects the necessities of our people's prayer service. They
would confess their sins when they prostrated themselves.
Therefore ample space was necessary so that one person would
not hear another's confession.[19] When standing in prayer, there
was no religious difficulty concomitant with being crowded.
Hence, no miracle transpired.

(Sichos Motzoei Shabbos Parshas Re'eh, 5738)

Alternatively, the miracle can be interpreted as a *result* of
the people's divine service. When they surrendered themselves totally to G-d — the spiritual counterpart of prostration
— they were blessed with ample space.

(Likkutei Sichos, Vol. XXV, p. 300-301)

**NO SNAKE OR SCORPION EVER CAUSED HARM IN
JERUSALEM —** Although this and the following miracle took
place outside the *Beis HaMikdash*, they are counted among the

---

19 . *Vayikra Rabbah* 10:9.

"ten miracles... wrought for our ancestors in the *Beis HaMik-dash*,"[20] because:

a) these miracles came about as a result of the influence of the sacrifices;

b) these miracles prevented the marring of the festive atmosphere during the pilgrimage holidays.

(Sichos Shabbos Parshas Chukas-Balak, 5736)

This miracle can also be appreciated in a homiletical sense. Jerusalem is associated with *ahavas Yisrael* and *achdus Yisrael*, love for every member of our people and the unity they share.[21] Snakes and scorpions, by contrast, can be understood as analogies for strife and coldness. The positive influence of Jerusalem prevented these interpersonal flaws from coming to the surface.

(Sichos Motzoei Shabbos Parshas Re'eh, 5738)

NOR DID ANY MAN EVER SAY TO HIS FEL-LOWMAN: "THE PLACE IS TOO CROWDED FOR ME TO LODGE OVERNIGHT IN JERUSALEM" — This miracle can also be understood as an expression of the unity generated by Jerusalem. The *mishnah* does not say that the city was not crowded. On the contrary, it is highly likely that it was, for the multitude of festive pilgrims could not easily have found lodging. Nevertheless, the unity which the city inspired moti-vated both hosts and guests to be accommodating, and every-one accepted the crowded conditions willingly, without allow-ing the congestion to detract from their love for the holy city.

(Ibid.)

---

20 . Note *Yoma* 21a, which focuses on this issue. Significantly, it is not mentioned by the classic commentaries on *Pirkei Avos* (*Rashi, Rambam,* or R. Ovadiah of Bartenura), implying that it is understood that these miracles came about only as a result of the influence of the *Beis HaMikdash*.
21 . See the *Jerusalem Talmud, Chagigah* 3:6 commenting on *Tehillim* 122:3.

ו עֲשָׂרָה דְבָרִים נִבְרְאוּ בְּעֶרֶב שַׁבָּת בֵּין הַשְּׁמָשׁוֹת, וְאֵלוּ הֵן: פִּי הָאָרֶץ, פִּי הַבְּאֵר, פִּי הָאָתוֹן, הַקֶּשֶׁת, וְהַמָּן, וְהַמַּטֶּה, וְהַשָּׁמִיר, הַכְּתָב, וְהַמִּכְתָּב, וְהַלֻּחֹת. וְיֵשׁ אוֹמְרִים אַף קִבְרוֹ שֶׁל מֹשֶׁה רַבֵּנוּ, וְאֵילוֹ שֶׁל אַבְרָהָם אָבִינוּ, וְיֵשׁ אוֹמְרִים אַף הַמַּזִּיקִין, וְאַף צְבַת בִּצְבַת עֲשׂוּיָה.

6. TEN ENTITIES WERE CREATED ON SHABBOS EVE AT TWILIGHT. THEY ARE:

A) THE OPENING OF THE EARTH [TO SWALLOW KORACH];[22]

B) THE MOUTH OF THE WELL [IN THE WILDERNESS];[23]

C) THE MOUTH OF THE DONKEY [OF BILAAM];[24]

D) THE RAINBOW;[25]

E) THE MANNAH;[26]

F) THE STAFF [OF MOSHE];[27]

G) THE *SHAMIR* WORM [WHICH SPLIT STONES FOR THE *BEIS HAMIKDASH*];[28]

H) THE WRITING [OF THE SECOND TABLETS];[29]

I) THE INSCRIPTION [OF THE FIRST TABLETS];[30]

J) AND THE TABLETS.[31]

SOME SAY ALSO THE BURIAL PLACE OF MOSHE[32] AND THE RAM OF AVRAHAM OUR PATRIARCH.[33] AND SOME

22. *Bamidbar* 16:32.
23. *Ibid.* 21:16-18; *Shmos* 17:6.
24. *Bamidbar* 22:28.
25. *Bereishis* 9:13.
26. *Shmos* 16:11-15, 31-36.
27. *Shmos* 4:17.
28. V. *Gittin* 68a; *Sotah* 48b.
29. *Shmos* 34:1.
30. *Ibid.* 32:16.
31. *Loc. cit.*
32. V. *Devarim* 34:6.

SAY ALSO THE SPIRITS OF DESTRUCTION[34] AS WELL AS
THE [ORIGINAL] TONGS, FOR TONGS MUST BE MADE
WITH TONGS.

**TEN ENTITIES WERE CREATED ON SHABBOS EVE
AT TWILIGHT** — Twilight — *bein hashamashos* — on Friday
represents the instant of transition from the natural order of the
weekdays to the *Shabbos*. Therefore entities created at that
time represent a fusion of the natural and the infinite.[35]

This *mishnah* also has particular relevance for the present
age. For, according to the conception that each of the days of
creation parallels a millennia of existence,[36] we are approaching
twilight on Friday.[37] Just as in the narrative of creation, miraculous entities which completed the work of creation as a whole
were created at that time, we too are living in a time of miracles
in which perfection can be granted to all existence.

(Likkutei Sichos, Vol. IV, p. 1224ff)

The *mishnah* can also be appreciated as teaching us the importance of using every moment. Twilight — the last moments
before the commencement of the *Shabbos* — was used to
enhance creation in its totality. Similarly, we have the potential
to use every moment granted us to influence and improve our
environment as a whole.

(Sichos Shabbos Parshas Behar-Bechukosai, 5747)

---

33 . V. *Bereishis* 22:13.
34 . V. *Bereishis Rabbah* 7:5; *Midrash Tanchuma Bereishis*, sec. 17; *Yalkut Shimoni,
Bereishis*, sec. 12.
35 . These miracles represent a more complete expression of infinity than those
which occurred in the *Beis HaMikdash*. For the latter involved the negation of
undesirable influences, while the entities created at twilight were totally positive
in nature.
36 . See the commentary of the *Ramban, Bereishis* 2:3.
37 . See *Sefer HaSichos* 5750, Vol. I, p. 254ff.

**THE INSCRIPTION [OF THE FIRST TABLETS]...
AND THE TABLETS** — The Tablets are symbolic of the
deepest possible connection between Torah and man, for the
letters of the Ten Commandments were hewn into the stones
themselves.

When the letters of a Torah scroll are inscribed with ink on
parchment, the words thus formed never become an integral
part of the parchment. In the Tablets, they and the Torah were
one and inseparable.[38]

This complete unity reflects a state in which one is totally
united with the Torah. A person in this state does not see the
Torah as an entity separate from himself, which he must study
and whose laws he must follow, but rather as part and parcel of
his own being. He and the Torah form a single whole.[39]

Just as the Tablets and their inscription were created at
twilight on Friday, so too, this single-minded commitment to
Torah is relevant in the present age — only moments before
the twilight preceding "the day which is all *Shabbos* and rest for
eternity."[40]

The Era of the Redemption will be characterized by such a
unified mindset, and this attitude both anticipates and precipi-
tates its coming.

(Sichos Shabbos Parshas Nitzavim Vayeilech, 5742)

THE SPIRITS OF DESTRUCTION — The purpose of
these spirits' creation is that they will eventually be transformed into positive influences.[41] Nevertheless, it is beyond
the ability of man alone to affect this transformation. Therefore
these spirits were created at twilight on the eve of the *Shabbos*,
connecting their existence and the transcendent nature of that

---

38. See *Likkutei Torah, Parshas Bechukosai*, p. 45a.
39. For a broader exposition of this concept, see *Likkutei Sichos*, Vol. II, *Parshas
Chukas*, and the sources listed there.
40. The conclusion of *Tractate Tamid*.
41. See *Toras Kohanim, Bechukosai* 26:6.

time. This transcendent power makes possible their transformation.

(Likkutei Sichos, Vol. XVII, p. 383-384)

THE [ORIGINAL] TONGS, FOR TONGS MUST BE MADE WITH TONGS — Tongs represent man's ability to change and mold his environment. The *mishnah* emphasizes that this potential (the original tongs) is a gift given to man by G-d.

The tongs were created on Friday at twilight, i.e., they were the very last creations brought into being. This indicates that man's efforts represent the ultimate goal of creation, for it is man's efforts which will bring all existence to perfection.

(Sefer HaSichos 5748, Vol. II, p. 605)

ז שִׁבְעָה דְבָרִים בְּגֹלֶם וְשִׁבְעָה בְחָכָם, חָכָם: אֵינוֹ מְדַבֵּר לִפְנֵי מִי שֶׁגָּדוֹל מִמֶּנּוּ בְּחָכְמָה וּבְמִנְיָן, וְאֵינוֹ נִכְנָס לְתוֹךְ דִּבְרֵי חֲבֵרוֹ, וְאֵינוֹ נִבְהָל לְהָשִׁיב, שׁוֹאֵל כְּעִנְיָן וּמֵשִׁיב כַּהֲלָכָה, וְאוֹמֵר עַל רִאשׁוֹן רִאשׁוֹן וְעַל אַחֲרוֹן אַחֲרוֹן, וְעַל מַה שֶּׁלֹּא שָׁמַע אוֹמֵר לֹא שָׁמַעְתִּי, וּמוֹדֶה עַל הָאֱמֶת, וְחִלּוּפֵיהֶן בְּגֹלֶם.

7. SEVEN THINGS CHARACTERIZE A STUPID PERSON, AND SEVEN A WISE ONE. A WISE MAN DOES NOT SPEAK BEFORE ONE WHO IS GREATER THAN HE IN WISDOM OR IN YEARS; HE DOES NOT INTERRUPT THE WORDS OF HIS FELLOW; HE DOES NOT RUSH TO ANSWER; HE ASKS WHAT IS RELEVANT TO THE SUBJECT MATTER AND REPLIES TO THE POINT. HE SPEAKS OF FIRST THINGS FIRST AND OF LAST THINGS LAST; CONCERNING THAT WHICH HE HAS NOT HEARD, HE SAYS, "I HAVE NOT HEARD," AND HE ACKNOWLEDGES THE TRUTH.

AND THE REVERSE OF THESE CHARACTERIZE A
STUPID PERSON.

**CONCERNING THAT WHICH HE HAS NOT HEARD,
HE SAYS, "I HAVE NOT HEARD"** — In his commentary on
this *Mishnah*, *Rashi* (and similarly, R. Ovadiah of Bartenura)
interprets this as referring to a wise man's reluctance to render
a *halachic* decision based on only his own reasoning. Unless he
has heard a ruling from an authoritative source, he refrains from
stating his opinion.

Without discounting Rashi's view, it is also possible to
interpret the *mishnah*'s statements simply: a wise man is not
ashamed to admit his lack of knowledge. He has the humility
to acknowledge the limits of his wisdom.

(Likkutei Sichos, Vol. XVII, p. 110)

ח שִׁבְעָה מִינֵי פֻרְעָנִיּוֹת בָּאִין לְעוֹלָם, עַל שִׁבְעָה גּוּפֵי עֲבֵרָה:
מִקְצָתָן מְעַשְּׂרִין וּמִקְצָתָן אֵינָן מְעַשְּׂרִין, רָעָב שֶׁל מְהוּמָה בָּא,
מִקְצָתָן רְעֵבִים וּמִקְצָתָן שְׂבֵעִים. גָּמְרוּ שֶׁלֹּא לְעַשֵּׂר, רָעָב שֶׁל בַּצֹּרֶת
בָּא. וְשֶׁלֹּא לִטּוֹל אֶת הַחַלָּה, רָעָב שֶׁל כְּלָיָה בָּא. דֶּבֶר בָּא לְעוֹלָם:
עַל מִיתוֹת הָאֲמוּרוֹת בַּתּוֹרָה שֶׁלֹּא נִמְסְרוּ לְבֵית דִּין, וְעַל פֵּרוֹת
שְׁבִיעִית. חֶרֶב בָּאָה לְעוֹלָם, עַל עִנּוּי הַדִּין, וְעַל עִוּוּת הַדִּין, וְעַל
הַמּוֹרִים בַּתּוֹרָה שֶׁלֹּא כַהֲלָכָה.

8. SEVEN KINDS OF PUNISHMENT COME TO THE
WORLD FOR SEVEN KINDS OF TRANSGRESSIONS.

IF SOME TITHE AND SOME DO NOT, A FAMINE OF
[WAR] PANIC ENSUES: SOME SUFFER HUNGER AND
SOME HAVE PLENTY.

IF ALL DECIDE NOT TO TITHE, A FAMINE OF
DROUGHT ENSUES; AND [IF THEY ALSO DECIDE] NOT

TO SEPARATE THE *CHALLAH*,[42] A FAMINE OF DE-
STRUCTION ENSUES.

PESTILENCE COMES TO THE WORLD [AS RETRI-
BUTION FOR THE TRANSGRESSIONS WHICH] THE
TORAH MENTIONS THAT ARE PUNISHABLE BY DEATH,
BUT WHICH THE COURT OF JUSTICE WAS NOT
EMPOWERED TO CARRY OUT; AND FOR [MAKING
FORBIDDEN USE OF] THE FRUITS OF THE SABBATICAL
YEAR.[43]

WAR COMES TO THE WORLD FOR THE DELAY OF
JUSTICE, FOR THE PERVERSION OF JUSTICE AND FOR
RENDERING A TORAH DECISION NOT IN ACCORDANCE
WITH HALACHAH.

***WAR COMES TO THE WORLD... FOR RENDERING A
TORAH DECISION NOT IN ACCORDANCE WITH
HALACHAH** — This *mishnah* indicates that there is a direct
connection between peace and the integrity of Torah law.
Flaunting Torah law is not only a question of religious observance, it's a matter of security. The converse is also true;
adherence to the Torah promotes peace and safety for our
people, both in *Eretz Yisrael* and throughout the world.

ט חַיָּה רָעָה בָּאָה לְעוֹלָם, עַל שְׁבוּעַת שָׁוְא וְעַל חִלּוּל הַשֵּׁם. גָּלוּת
בָּא לְעוֹלָם, עַל עֲבוֹדָה זָרָה, וְעַל גִּלּוּי עֲרָיוֹת, וְעַל שְׁפִיכוּת דָּמִים,
וְעַל שְׁמִטַּת הָאָרֶץ. בְּאַרְבָּעָה פְּרָקִים הַדֶּבֶר מִתְרַבֶּה, בָּרְבִיעִית,
וּבַשְּׁבִיעִית, וּבְמוֹצָאֵי שְׁבִיעִית, וּבְמוֹצָאֵי הֶחָג שֶׁבְּכָל שָׁנָה וְשָׁנָה.
בָּרְבִיעִית, מִפְּנֵי מַעְשַׂר עָנִי שֶׁבַּשְּׁלִישִׁית. בַּשְּׁבִיעִית, מִפְּנֵי מַעְשַׂר

---

42 . V. *Bamidbar* 15:20; *Yechezkel* 44:30.
43 . V. *Shmos* 23:11; *Vayikra* 25:1-7.

עָנִי שֶׁבַּשְּׁשִׁית. בְּמוֹצָאֵי שְׁבִיעִית, מִפְּנֵי פֵּרוֹת שְׁבִיעִית. בְּמוֹצָאֵי הֶחָג שֶׁבְּכָל שָׁנָה וְשָׁנָה, מִפְּנֵי גֶזֶל מַתְּנוֹת עֲנִיִּים.

9. WILD BEASTS COME UPON THE WORLD FOR SWEARING FALSELY AND PROFANING THE DIVINE NAME. EXILE COMES TO THE WORLD FOR IDOLATRY, FOR PROHIBITED SEXUAL RELATIONS, FOR MURDER, AND FOR NOT LEAVING THE EARTH AT REST DURING THE *SABBATICAL* YEAR.

AT FOUR PERIODS [WITHIN THE SEVEN-YEAR AGRICULTURAL CYCLE] PESTILENCE INCREASES: IN THE FOURTH YEAR, IN THE SEVENTH YEAR, IN THE YEAR FOLLOWING THE *SABBATICAL* YEAR, AND ANNUALLY AT THE CONCLUSION OF THE FESTIVAL OF SUKKOS.

IN THE FOURTH YEAR FOR NOT HAVING GIVEN THE TITHE FOR THE POOR IN THE THIRD. IN THE SEVENTH YEAR FOR NOT HAVING GIVEN THE TITHE FOR THE POOR IN THE SIXTH. IN THE YEAR FOLLOWING THE *SABBATICAL* YEAR FOR [NOT OBSERVING THE LAWS PERTAINING TO] THE PRODUCE OF THE *SABBATICAL* YEAR. ANNUALLY, AT THE CONCLUSION OF THE FESTIVAL OF SUKKOS FOR ROBBING THE POOR OF THEIR [HARVEST] GIFTS.[44]

EXILE COMES TO THE WORLD FOR IDOLATRY... — This teaches us that exile runs contrary to the very nature of the world. Were these four sins not to be committed — even if other transgressions were, heaven forbid — there would be no exile. Although the natural order of the world requires that G-dliness be concealed to a certain extent, the deeper hiddenness brought about by exile is unnatural.

---

44 . *Vayikra* 19:9-10; 23:22. *Devarim* 24:19-22.

Since exile runs contrary to nature, one may ask: Why did G-d give man the potential to bring about exile?[45] The answer reflects G-d's kindness. G-d desired that man reach a level of connection with Him that surpasses the limits of creation — an "unnatural" bond as it were. This will be realized in the Era of the Redemption. Moreover, in His kindness, G-d desired that man attain this level through his own efforts. For this to be possible, He employed a catalyst, exile. For exile also runs contrary to the natural order, but can be brought about by man's conduct.

(Sichos Shabbos Parshas Balak, 5744)

IDOLATRY, FOR PROHIBITED SEXUAL RELATIONS, FOR MURDER, AND FOR NOT LEAVING THE EARTH AT REST DURING THE *SABBATICAL* YEAR — Since, as is frequently mentioned, *Pirkei Avos* teaches *mili dechassidusa*, pious behavior beyond the measure of the law, of what importance is the mention of these four sins? Even people who are not overly pious do not commit them.

The answer lies in the homiletic interpretation of these four transgressions. When mentioning idol worship, the *mishnah* does not refer merely to one who bows to a statue. The intent is to indicate anyone who even conceives of the existence of a power other than G-d. This, unfortunately, is a fault found in many. Is it not natural for a person to think, "It was my strength and the power of my hand which brought me this prosperity"?[46] And do not people make idols out of wisdom or achievement?

With regard to sexual impropriety, even a person who would never consider performing such acts may from time to time relax his standards of modesty. And with regard to mur-

---

45 . This question is based on the premise that exile comes because G-d gave man free choice, and man chose to commit these four severe sins. Nevertheless, since exile runs contrary to the nature of the world, one might ask why the ability to unleash such a catastrophe was given to man.

46 . *Devarim* 8:17.

der, our Sages[47] equate embarrassing a person in public with homicide.

Similarly, with regard to the observance of the *Sabbatical* year, in addition to the implied geographic conception of *Eretz Yisrael*, there is also a spiritual conception, the reaffirmation of G-d's creation,[48] and the observance of the *Sabbatical* year in this context is relevant to all Jews, wherever and whenever they live.[49]

(Ibid.)

י אַרְבַּע מִדּוֹת בָּאָדָם: הָאוֹמֵר שֶׁלִּי שֶׁלָּךְ, וְשֶׁלָּךְ שֶׁלִּי, עַם הָאָרֶץ. שֶׁלִּי שֶׁלִּי, וְשֶׁלָּךְ שֶׁלָּךְ, זוֹ מִדָּה בֵּינוֹנִית, וְיֵשׁ אוֹמְרִים זוֹ מִדַּת סְדוֹם. שֶׁלִּי שֶׁלָּךְ, וְשֶׁלָּךְ שֶׁלָּךְ, חָסִיד. שֶׁלָּךְ שֶׁלִּי, וְשֶׁלִּי שֶׁלִּי, רָשָׁע.

10.

THERE ARE FOUR [CHARACTER] TYPES AMONG MEN: HE WHO SAYS, "WHAT IS MINE IS YOURS, AND WHAT IS YOURS IS MINE" IS AN IGNORAMUS. [HE WHO SAYS,] "WHAT IS MINE IS MINE, AND WHAT IS YOURS IS YOURS" THIS IS A MEDIAN CHARACTERISTIC; SOME SAY THIS IS THE CHARACTERISTIC OF [THE PEOPLE OF] SODOM. [HE WHO SAYS,] "WHAT IS MINE IS YOURS, AND WHAT IS YOURS IS YOURS" IS PIOUS. AND [HE WHO SAYS,] "WHAT IS YOURS IS MINE, AND WHAT IS MINE IS MINE" IS WICKED.

---

47 . *Bava Metzia* 58b.
48 . See *Sefer HaChinuch, mitzvah* 84.
49 . The severity of the violation of the *Sabbatical* laws is reflected by the fact that they are grouped together with these three sins — sins so severe that, in contrast to all other sins mentioned in the Torah, if forced to choose between death and committing them, one should choose death (*Sanhedrin* 74a).

[HE WHO SAYS,] "WHAT IS MINE IS YOURS, AND
WHAT IS YOURS IS YOURS," IS PIOUS — The *mishnah* is
talking about a person who may not have the financial means to
give generously. Nevertheless, while giving the little he can,
he bolsters the spirits of the poor person[50] by explaining that
even the little which he himself owns belongs equally to the
poor man.

This attitude is sufficient to have him termed pious.

(Sichos Motzoei Shabbos Parshas Re'eh, 5739)

[HE WHO SAYS,] "WHAT IS YOURS IS MINE, AND
WHAT IS MINE IS MINE," IS WICKED — As mentioned
several times, *Pirkei Avos* concerns *mili dechassidusa* — pious
conduct beyond the measure of the law. Why should a wicked
man who says "What is yours is mine" be mentioned at all in
such a text?

It can be explained that such a person merely *says* "What is
yours is mine..."; in practice, he gives and even gives generously. Nevertheless, from the perspective of *mili dechassidusa*,
since he frequently makes such statements, belittling the poor
who receive his generosity, he is considered wicked.

(Ibid.)

יא אַרְבַּע מִדּוֹת בְּדֵעוֹת: נוֹחַ לִכְעוֹס וְנוֹחַ לֵרָצוֹת, יָצָא הֶפְסֵדוֹ
בִּשְׂכָרוֹ. קָשֶׁה לִכְעוֹס וְקָשֶׁה לֵרָצוֹת, יָצָא שְׂכָרוֹ בְּהֶפְסֵדוֹ. קָשֶׁה
לִכְעוֹס וְנוֹחַ לֵרָצוֹת, חָסִיד. נוֹחַ לִכְעוֹס וְקָשֶׁה לֵרָצוֹת, רָשָׁע.

11. THERE ARE FOUR TYPES OF
TEMPERAMENTS: EASILY ANGERED AND
EASILY PACIFIED — HIS LOSS IS OUTWEIGHED BY HIS

---

50. See *Bava Basra* 9b, which states that a person who does not have the means to
give charity should endeavor to lift the spirits of a poor person who asks for a gift.

MERIT; HARD TO ANGER AND HARD TO PACIFY — HIS
MERIT IS OUTWEIGHED BY HIS LOSS; HARD TO ANGER
AND EASY TO PACIFY — PIOUS; EASILY ANGERED AND
HARD TO PACIFY — WICKED.

**EASILY ANGERED AND HARD TO PACIFY —
WICKED** — Again, one might ask why *Pirkei Avos* should concern itself with a person of this nature?

Here, too, a similar resolution can be offered. "Easily angered and hard to pacify"[51] refers to the person's temperament, not to his conduct. In practice, the person is able to restrain himself, and should he lose his temper, he becomes mollified quickly. Nevertheless, since he possesses such a tendency, *Pirkei Avos* terms him "wicked" so he should realize the challenge he faces.

Similarly, people who are only "easily angered" or "hard to pacify" must realize the importance of going beyond that nature and eradicating such traits.

(Sichos Shabbos Parshas Nitzavim-Vayeilech, 5739)

יב אַרְבַּע מִדּוֹת בְּתַלְמִידִים: מַהֵר לִשְׁמוֹעַ וּמַהֵר לְאַבֵּד, יָצָא שְׂכָרוֹ
בְּהֶפְסֵדוֹ. קָשֶׁה לִשְׁמוֹעַ וְקָשֶׁה לְאַבֵּד, יָצָא הֶפְסֵדוֹ בִּשְׂכָרוֹ. מַהֵר
לִשְׁמוֹעַ וְקָשֶׁה לְאַבֵּד, זֶה חֵלֶק טוֹב. קָשֶׁה לִשְׁמוֹעַ וּמַהֵר לְאַבֵּד, זֶה
חֵלֶק רָע.

---

51. It must be emphasized that these two traits run directly contrary to the standards established by Torah law. For the *Rambam* states (*Mishneh Torah, Hilchos De'os* 2:3, cited by the *Shulchan Aruch HaRav* 156:3): "Anger is a very undesirable quality... it is proper to maintain the furthest possible distance from it."

With regard to becoming pacified easily, the *Rambam* states (*Hilchos Teshuvah* 2:10): "When a person who wrongs one asks for forgiveness, one should forgive him with a perfect heart and a willing spirit." The *Shulchan Aruch HaRav* 606:8 states that one should grant such forgiveness immediately.

12. THERE ARE FOUR TYPES OF STUDENTS: QUICK TO GRASP AND QUICK TO FORGET — HIS GAIN IS OVERRIDDEN BY HIS LOSS; SLOW TO GRASP AND SLOW TO FORGET — HIS LOSS IS OVERRIDDEN BY HIS GAIN; QUICK TO GRASP AND SLOW TO FORGET — THIS IS A GOOD PORTION; SLOW TO GRASP AND QUICK TO FORGET — THIS IS A BAD PORTION.

THERE ARE FOUR TYPES OF STUDENTS — One might ask: What is the point of this teaching? Seemingly, it is an obvious observation which any teacher could make. Moreover, what connection does it share with *Pirkei Avos*, which teaches pious conduct?

The key to the *mishnah* is that role of a teacher which it attempts to nurture. Generally, we think of a teacher as a person who imparts knowledge. The *mishnah* informs us that the approach of *mili dechassidusa* obligates teachers to accept a more encompassing task.

They should see themselves as being responsible for their students' conceptual development. This necessitates a careful appreciation of their capacities, and conscientious efforts to offset their weaknesses and accentuate their strengths.

When a teacher sees that a student is quick to grasp, he must maintain a connection and observe the student's powers of retention. If the student is by nature quick to forget, the teacher must emphasize the importance of repeatedly reviewing the subject matter.

If he sees that a student is by nature slow to grasp the material being taught, the teacher should not give up and direct his attention to other students. It is possible that the student is also slow to forget, and then "his loss is overridden by his gain."

Even if the student is also quick to forget, the teacher should not despair. Although such a student has been given a bad portion, this reflects merely his natural tendencies. Everyone has the potential to apply himself, and through such effort overcome natural disabilities and succeed in his studies.

Conversely, when a teacher has a student who is quick to grasp and slow to forget, and therefore succeeds in his studies, the teacher should not become overly proud. Instead, he should realize that the student has been given "a good portion," and be content that he was able to nurture these potentials.

(*Sichos Shabbos Parshas Bamidbar, 5744*)

יג אַרְבַּע מִדּוֹת בְּנוֹתְנֵי צְדָקָה: הָרוֹצֶה שֶׁיִּתֵּן וְלֹא יִתְּנוּ אֲחֵרִים, עֵינוֹ רָעָה בְּשֶׁל אֲחֵרִים. יִתְּנוּ אֲחֵרִים וְהוּא לֹא יִתֵּן, עֵינוֹ רָעָה בְּשֶׁלּוֹ. יִתֵּן וְיִתְּנוּ אֲחֵרִים, חָסִיד. לֹא יִתֵּן וְלֹא יִתְּנוּ אֲחֵרִים, רָשָׁע.

13. THERE ARE FOUR TYPES AMONG THOSE WHO GIVE CHARITY: ONE WHO WISHES TO GIVE BUT THAT OTHERS SHOULD NOT — HE BEGRUDGES OTHERS; THAT OTHERS SHOULD GIVE AND HE SHOULD NOT — HE BEGRUDGES HIMSELF; THAT HE SHOULD GIVE AND OTHERS SHOULD TOO — HE IS PIOUS; THAT HE SHOULD NOT GIVE NOR SHOULD OTHERS — HE IS WICKED.

THERE ARE FOUR TYPES AMONG THOSE WHO GIVE CHARITY — One might ask: Why is a person who wishes that "he should not give nor should others" included among those who give charity? The truth is, however, that every Jew is by nature a giver of charity. Even when he does not actually give, his inner desire is to do so, for every Jew wishes to perform all the *mitzvos*, and separate himself from sin. It is merely his evil inclination which sometimes compels him to act otherwise. [52]

And the very awareness of this inner will is itself an impetus bringing it into expression. For the essential nature of every entity seeks expression. This tendency is enhanced when the individual and those around him are conscious of this inner drive.

(Sichos Shabbos Parshas Eikev, 5747)

Alternatively, it can be explained that, in practice, all four types of people give charity, for this is a natural expression of a Jew's nature. Differences will exist only with regard to the thinking processes accompanying the act. There may be those who wish that neither they nor others should give, but in practice all give.

(Sichos Shabbos Parshas Nitzavim-Vayeilech, 5739)

יד אַרְבַּע מִדּוֹת בְּהוֹלְכֵי בֵית הַמִּדְרָשׁ: הוֹלֵךְ וְאֵינוֹ עוֹשֶׂה, שְׂכַר הֲלִיכָה בְּיָדוֹ. עוֹשֶׂה וְאֵינוֹ הוֹלֵךְ, שְׂכַר מַעֲשֶׂה בְּיָדוֹ. הוֹלֵךְ וְעוֹשֶׂה, חָסִיד. לֹא הוֹלֵךְ וְלֹא עוֹשֶׂה, רָשָׁע.

14. THERE ARE FOUR TYPES AMONG THOSE WHO ATTEND THE HOUSE OF STUDY: ONE WHO ATTENDS BUT DOES NOT ENGAGE [IN STUDY] EARNS THE REWARD FOR GOING. ONE WHO ENGAGES [IN STUDY] BUT DOES NOT ATTEND EARNS THE REWARD FOR THE ACT [OF STUDYING]. ONE WHO ATTENDS AND ENGAGES [IN STUDY] IS PIOUS. ONE WHO NEITHER ATTENDS NOR ENGAGES [IN STUDY] IS WICKED.

---

52 . *Rambam, Mishneh Torah, Hilchos Gerushin* 2:20.

THERE ARE FOUR TYPES AMONG THOSE WHO ATTEND THE HOUSE OF STUDY — The natural place for all Jews is the House of Study. Even a person who in fact "neither attends nor engages [in study]," is therefore "among those who attend the House of Study."

(Sichos Shabbos Parshas Eikev, 5747)

Alternatively, we can interpret the reference to one who "neither attends nor engages [in study]" as pertaining to a person prevented from carrying out these activities by circumstances beyond his control. Even so, from the standpoint of *mili dechassidusa*, he is considered wicked.[53] As the Previous Rebbe would say:[54] "A completely righteous man who neglects his Torah study because of the weakness of his body must turn [to G-d] in complete *teshuvah* from the depths of his heart."

(Sichos Shabbos Parshas Nitzavim-Vayeilech, 5739)

טו אַרְבַּע מִדּוֹת בְּיוֹשְׁבִים לִפְנֵי חֲכָמִים: סְפוֹג, וּמַשְׁפֵּךְ, מְשַׁמֶּרֶת, וְנָפָה. סְפוֹג, שֶׁהוּא סוֹפֵג אֶת הַכֹּל. וּמַשְׁפֵּךְ, שֶׁמַּכְנִיס בְּזוֹ וּמוֹצִיא בְזוֹ. מְשַׁמֶּרֶת, שֶׁמּוֹצִיאָה אֶת הַיַּיִן וְקוֹלֶטֶת אֶת הַשְּׁמָרִים. וְנָפָה, שֶׁמּוֹצִיאָה אֶת הַקֶּמַח וְקוֹלֶטֶת אֶת הַסֹּלֶת:

15. THERE ARE FOUR TYPES AMONG THOSE WHO SIT BEFORE THE SAGES. [THEY ARE LIKENED TO] A SPONGE, A FUNNEL, A STRAINER, AND A SIEVE: A SPONGE, WHICH ABSORBS EVERYTHING; A FUNNEL, WHICH TAKES IN FROM ONE END AND SPILLS OUT FROM THE OTHER; A STRAINER, WHICH ALLOWS THE WINE TO FLOW OUT AND RETAINS THE DREGS;

---

53. Here also, the pattern of causality is significant. The fact that a person is prevented by circumstances beyond his control is a sign that he is lacking in this dimension. See *Rambam, Mishneh Torah, Hilchos Teshuvah* 9:2.

54. *Likkutei Dibburim*, Vol. II, p. 65 (English translation).

AND A SIEVE, WHICH ALLOWS THE FLOUR TO PASS
THROUGH AND RETAINS THE FINE FLOUR.

**THERE ARE FOUR TYPES AMONG THOSE WHO SIT
BEFORE THE SAGES** — The previous *mishnah* mentions
"those who attend the House of Study," i.e., students who are
at the early stages of learning. By mentioning "those who sit
before the Sages," our *mishnah* is referring to more developed
students — those who have already grasped the fundamentals
and desire more intensive scholarship. Such individuals must
appreciate that in addition to their own study, they must begin
communicating the wisdom they grasp to others. This is the
focus of the present *mishnah* and its analysis of the four types of
students.

A SPONGE WHICH ABSORBS — It's natural that when a
person hears an interesting concept, he will desire to share it
with others. There are times, however, e.g., in the study of
mystical matters, when our Sages warn against passing on concepts indiscriminately.[55] Similarly, there are occasions[56] when
they have said: "This is the *halachah*, but it should not be
taught publicly." In such instances, a person must struggle
against his natural tendency and, like a sponge, retain the
knowledge within himself.

**A FUNNEL, WHICH TAKES IN FROM ONE END AND
SPILLS OUT FROM THE OTHER** — Such a teacher shares
everything with others, without considering himself at all. On
the contrary, he dedicates himself to the welfare of his colleagues, granting them all the wisdom he possesses.

---

55 . See *Chagigah* 11a.
56 . E.g., *Shabbos* 12b.

A STRAINER, WHICH ALLOWS THE WINE TO FLOW OUT AND RETAINS THE DREGS — Every concept possesses certain dimensions whose positive nature are readily obvious. Like wine, they have a pleasant flavor which can be easily appreciated. And there are other, secondary, dimensions which are like dregs, the usefulness of which cannot be grasped straightaway.

At times, a teacher must allow the "wine" to flow out and retain the "dregs," presenting his students with those ideas which they can readily appreciate.

A SIEVE, WHICH ALLOWS THE FLOUR TO PASS THROUGH AND RETAINS THE FINE FLOUR — Although fine flour is more refined than ordinary flour, it is not suited for as many tasks. Similarly, when it comes to communicating refined ideas, since they may not be comprehended by the listeners, there are times when one should release only the "flour" — the general outline — and retain the "fine flour" — the deeper comprehension of the matter. Otherwise, one's students may become confused.

(Sichos Shabbos Parshas Behar-Bechukosai, 5743)

Alternatively, this *mishnah* can be taken as advice to a teacher with regard to developing his students' potentials. At times — particularly at the beginning of a course of study — a student may be like a sponge which absorbs everything. The teacher must be aware of his student's inability to discriminate.

In other situations — particularly when a student is tired — he becomes like a funnel, which takes in from one end and spills out from the other. When this happens, a teacher should realize that it is more valuable to cease his instruction temporarily.

As a student grows more accomplished, he develops the ability to make distinctions. Nevertheless, it is quite possible that he will grasp only the more concrete dimensions of the subject matter, without attempting to appreciate the more abstract elements — like a strainer, which allows the wine to flow out and retains the dregs. In such an instance, a teacher must train his student until he is like a sieve, which allows the flour to pass through and retains the fine flour.

(Sichos Shabbos Parshas Behar-Bechukosai, 5731)

טז כָּל אַהֲבָה שֶׁהִיא תְלוּיָה בְדָבָר, בָּטֵל דָּבָר בְּטֵלָה אַהֲבָה, וְשֶׁאֵינָהּ תְּלוּיָה בְדָבָר, אֵינָהּ בְּטֵלָה לְעוֹלָם. אֵיזוֹ הִיא אַהֲבָה שֶׁהִיא תְלוּיָה בְדָבָר, זוֹ אַהֲבַת אַמְנוֹן וְתָמָר, וְשֶׁאֵינָהּ תְּלוּיָה בְדָבָר, זוֹ אַהֲבַת דָּוִד וִיהוֹנָתָן.

16. WHENEVER LOVE IS DEPENDENT UPON A SPECIFIC CONSIDERATION, WHEN THAT CONSIDERATION VANISHES, THE LOVE CEASES. IF, BY CONTRAST, IT IS NOT DEPENDENT UPON A SPECIFIC CONSIDERATION, IT WILL NEVER CEASE.

WHICH IS A LOVE THAT IS DEPENDENT UPON A SPECIFIC THING? THE LOVE OF AMNON AND TAMAR.[57] AND ONE WHICH IS NOT DEPENDENT UPON A SPECIFIC THING? THE LOVE OF DAVID AND YONASAN.[58]

WHENEVER LOVE IS DEPENDENT UPON A SPECIFIC CONSIDERATION, WHEN THAT CONSIDERATION VANISHES, THE LOVE CEASES — The lesson this *mishnah* teaches — that love which is dependent on an external factor is no more lasting than the factor on which it is based — though profound and encompassing, is also obvious.

---

57 . *II Shmuel* 13:1ff.
58 . *I Shmuel* 18:1; 20:17; *II Shmuel* 1:26.

Within the wording of the *mishnah* and the examples it provides is a deeper concept.

The *mishnah* uses the expression "is dependent upon a specific consideration" rather than "stems from a specific consideration" to teach that even though love may be based at first on a specific consideration, if it is nurtured and cultivated, it will function as an "essential" love — one that is not dependent on an outside factor.

To illustrate this concept, the *mishnah* cites the love of...

DAVID AND YONASAN — At the outset, there were reasons why these two were attracted to each other. Nevertheless, their relationship developed to the point that it was no longer dependent on its original reasons and flourished into an example of essential love.

Conversely, the other example given by the *mishnah* — the love between Amnon and Tamar — shows how an essential love such as the connection shared by a brother and sister can be corrupted when an external factor is given excessive consideration.

These concepts have parallels in our service of G-d. There are feelings of love that stem from a person's intellectual appreciation of G-dliness, or because of his gratitude for blessings received. On a deeper level, there is an essential love which each person possesses because his soul is "an actual part of G-d."[59] Even when the beginnings of a person's conscious bond with G-d are dependent on external factors, the relationship can become true and lasting, since at all times he shares an essential connection.

(Sichos Shabbos Parshas Bechukosai, 5733)

---

59. See *Tanya*, chs. 2, 18.

יז כָּל מַחֲלֹקֶת שֶׁהִיא לְשֵׁם שָׁמַיִם, סוֹפָהּ לְהִתְקַיֵּם, וְשֶׁאֵינָהּ לְשֵׁם
שָׁמַיִם, אֵין סוֹפָהּ לְהִתְקַיֵּם. אֵיזוֹ הִיא מַחֲלֹקֶת שֶׁהִיא לְשֵׁם שָׁמַיִם, זוֹ
מַחֲלֹקֶת הִלֵּל וְשַׁמַּאי. וְשֶׁאֵינָהּ לְשֵׁם שָׁמַיִם, זוֹ מַחֲלֹקֶת קֹרַח וְכָל
עֲדָתוֹ.

17. ANY CONTROVERSY WHICH IS FOR THE SAKE OF HEAVEN WILL BE PERPETUATED; AND THAT WHICH IS NOT FOR THE SAKE OF HEAVEN WILL NOT BE PERPETUATED.

WHICH IS A CONTROVERSY FOR THE SAKE OF HEAVEN? THE CONTROVERSY BETWEEN HILLEL AND SHAMMAI.[60] AND WHICH IS NOT FOR THE SAKE OF HEAVEN? THE CONTROVERSY OF KORACH AND ALL HIS FACTION.[61]

WHICH IS A CONTROVERSY FOR THE SAKE OF HEAVEN? THE CONTROVERSY BETWEEN HILLEL AND SHAMMAI — The *Zohar*[62] explains that the controversy between Hillel and Shammai stemmed from the fact that Shammai's soul was characterized by the quality of *gevurah*, might, while Hillel's was characterized by the quality of *chesed*, kindness. These attributes are highlighted by several examples in the Talmud which show Shammai as short-tempered and Hillel as gentle and patient.[63] For that reason, Hillel's opinions would generally be more lenient, and Shammai's more stringent.

Nevertheless, the differences of opinion between Hillel and Shammai were not merely expressions of their personal natures; they were "for the sake of Heaven." As proof, we find several instances[64] in which Shammai issued lenient rulings, and Hillel, more stringent ones. Because their study of Torah

---

60 . *Eruvin* 13b.
61 . *Bamidbar*, ch. 16.
62 . III, 245a; see *Tanya, Iggeres HaKodesh*, Epistle 13.
63 . E.g. *Shabbos* 31a.
64 . E.g., *Ediyos*, chs. 4 and 5.

was characterized by a selfless desire to discover G-d's truth, they rose above their individual natures and at times displayed the opposite thrust.

As long as a person's divine service follows his natural tendencies, he can never be sure that his intent is to serve G-d; it is possible that his efforts, however worthy, do not reflect a commitment above his individual nature. When, by contrast, he is required to display tendencies that run contrary to his nature, it is clear that he is being motivated by a commitment to G-d that transcends his personal motives.[65]

(Sichos Shabbos Parshas Bamidbar, 5734)

THE CONTROVERSY OF KORACH AND ALL HIS FACTION — The *mishnah* does not say "the controversy of Korach and Moshe," for Moshe was not involved in controversy. Although Korach aroused strife, Moshe's response was intended solely to preserve the unity of the Jewish people.

(Ibid.)

יח כָּל הַמְזַכֶּה אֶת הָרַבִּים אֵין חֵטְא בָּא עַל יָדוֹ, וְכָל הַמַּחֲטִיא אֶת הָרַבִּים, אֵין מַסְפִּיקִין בְּיָדוֹ לַעֲשׂוֹת תְּשׁוּבָה. מֹשֶׁה זָכָה וְזִכָּה אֶת הָרַבִּים, זְכוּת הָרַבִּים תָּלוּי בּוֹ, שֶׁנֶּאֱמַר: צִדְקַת י-י עָשָׂה, וּמִשְׁפָּטָיו עִם יִשְׂרָאֵל. יָרָבְעָם בֶּן נְבָט חָטָא וְהֶחֱטִיא אֶת הָרַבִּים, חֵטְא הָרַבִּים תָּלוּי בּוֹ, שֶׁנֶּאֱמַר: עַל חַטֹּאות יָרָבְעָם אֲשֶׁר חָטָא, וַאֲשֶׁר הֶחֱטִיא אֶת יִשְׂרָאֵל.

---

65 . This concept is reflected in one of the explanations given for the greatness inherent in Avraham's binding of Yitzchak. Previously, Avraham's divine service involved acts of kindness which reflected his own personal nature. With regard to the binding of Yitzchak, however, it is written (*Bereishis* 22:12): "Now I know that you fear G-d"; i.e., he had to first display qualities that ran contrary to his natural tendencies. See *Sefer HaMaamarim-Kuntreisim*, Vol. II, p. 642; *Likkutei Sichos*, Vol. II, p. 378.

18. WHENEVER A PERSON CAUSES THE MANY TO HAVE MERIT, NO SIN SHALL COME THROUGH HIM; BUT ONE WHO CAUSES THE MANY TO SIN SHALL NOT BE GRANTED THE OPPORTUNITY TO REPENT.

MOSHE WAS HIMSELF MERITORIOUS AND CAUSED THE MANY TO ATTAIN MERIT, [THEREFORE] THE MERITS OF THE MANY ARE ATTRIBUTED TO HIM, AS IT IS STATED: "HE (MOSHE) PERFORMED THE RIGHTEOUSNESS OF THE L-RD AND HIS ORDINANCES TOGETHER WITH ISRAEL."⁶⁶

YEROVAM BEN NEVAT HIMSELF SINNED AND CAUSED THE MANY TO SIN, [THEREFORE] THE SINS OF THE MANY ARE ATTRIBUTED TO HIM, AS IT IS STATED: "FOR THE SINS OF YEROVAM WHICH HE SINNED AND CAUSED ISRAEL TO SIN."⁶⁷

NO SIN SHALL COME THROUGH HIM — This is not to say that such a person's free will is taken away, and he will be prevented from sinning. The intent is that since he endeavored to bring merit to many people, the positive influence these efforts generates will prevent him from becoming involved in circumstances which would cause him to sin accidentally or inadvertently.

(Sichos Shabbos Parshas Bamidbar, 5741)

SHALL NOT BE GRANTED THE OPPORTUNITY TO REPENT — This does not mean that the gates of *teshuvah* will be closed before him. Instead, the intent is to point out that people at large are constantly being encouraged to *teshuvah* by G-d. This positive influence will be withheld from such an individual.⁶⁸

(Ibid.)

---

66 . *Devarim* 33:21.
67 . *I Melachim* 15:30.
68 . See *Tanya*, ch. 25; *Iggeres HaTeshuvah*, ch. 11.

THE MERITS OF THE MANY ARE ATTRIBUTED TO HIM — The merit accrued in this manner is an ongoing process, for positive activity generates a self-reinforcing pattern that continues forever. Thus this clause can be interpreted to mean that the merits of the many, even at the era of the composition of the *Mishnah*, are attributed to Moshe.

(Ibid.)

יט כָּל מִי שֶׁיֵּשׁ בּוֹ שְׁלֹשָׁה דְבָרִים הַלָּלוּ, הוּא מִתַּלְמִידָיו שֶׁל אַבְרָהָם אָבִינוּ, וּשְׁלֹשָׁה דְבָרִים אֲחֵרִים, הוּא מִתַּלְמִידָיו שֶׁל בִּלְעָם הָרָשָׁע. תַּלְמִידָיו שֶׁל אַבְרָהָם אָבִינוּ עַיִן טוֹבָה, וְרוּחַ נְמוּכָה, וְנֶפֶשׁ שְׁפָלָה. תַּלְמִידָיו שֶׁל בִּלְעָם הָרָשָׁע עַיִן רָעָה, וְרוּחַ גְּבוֹהָה, וְנֶפֶשׁ רְחָבָה. מַה בֵּין תַּלְמִידָיו שֶׁל אַבְרָהָם אָבִינוּ לְתַלְמִידָיו שֶׁל בִּלְעָם הָרָשָׁע, תַּלְמִידָיו שֶׁל אַבְרָהָם אָבִינוּ, אוֹכְלִין בָּעוֹלָם הַזֶּה, וְנוֹחֲלִין הָעוֹלָם הַבָּא, שֶׁנֶּאֱמַר: לְהַנְחִיל אֹהֲבַי יֵשׁ, וְאוֹצְרוֹתֵיהֶם אֲמַלֵּא. אֲבָל תַּלְמִידָיו שֶׁל בִּלְעָם הָרָשָׁע יוֹרְשִׁין גֵּיהִנֹּם וְיוֹרְדִין לִבְאֵר שַׁחַת, שֶׁנֶּאֱמַר: וְאַתָּה אֱלֹהִי-ם תּוֹרִדֵם לִבְאֵר שַׁחַת, אַנְשֵׁי דָמִים וּמִרְמָה לֹא יֶחֱצוּ יְמֵיהֶם, וַאֲנִי אֶבְטַח בָּךְ.

19. WHOEVER POSSESSES THE FOLLOWING THREE CHARACTERISTICS IS OF THE DISCIPLES OF AVRAHAM OUR PATRIARCH; AND THE THREE OPPOSITE CHARACTERISTICS, IS OF THE DISCIPLES OF THE WICKED BILAAM.

THE DISCIPLES OF OUR PATRIARCH AVRAHAM POSSESS A GOOD EYE, A HUMBLE SPIRIT, AND A MEEK SOUL. THE DISCIPLES OF THE WICKED BILAAM POSSESS AN EVIL EYE, AN ARROGANT SPIRIT, AND A GREEDY SOUL.

WHAT IS THE DIFFERENCE BETWEEN THE DISCIPLES OF AVRAHAM OUR PATRIARCH AND THE DISCIPLES OF THE WICKED BILAAM? THE DISCIPLES OF AVRAHAM OUR PATRIARCH ENJOY [THE FRUITS OF THEIR GOOD

QUALITIES] IN THIS WORLD AND INHERIT THE
WORLD TO COME, AS IT IS STATED: "TO CAUSE
THOSE WHO LOVE ME TO INHERIT AN EVERLASTING
POSSESSION [THE WORLD TO COME], AND I WILL
FILL THEIR STOREHOUSES [IN THIS WORLD]."[69]

BUT THE DISCIPLES OF THE WICKED BILAAM INHERIT
GEHINOM AND DESCEND INTO THE NETHERMOST
PIT, AS IT IS STATED: "AND YOU, O G-D, WILL BRING
THEM DOWN TO THE NETHERMOST PIT; BLOOD-
THIRSTY AND TREACHEROUS MEN SHALL NOT LIVE
OUT HALF THEIR DAYS, AND I WILL TRUST IN YOU."[70]

**THE DISCIPLES OF AVRAHAM OUR PATRIARCH
ENJOY [THE FRUITS OF THEIR GOOD QUALITIES]** —
Although the ultimate intent is that all positive personal qualities be expressed in one's conduct, the *mishnah* teaches us that,
independent of a person's positive acts, he will receive reward
for his positive character traits alone. Conversely, retribution is
meted out for the possession of undesirable character traits,
even when they are not expressed in actual conduct.

(Sichos Shabbos Parshas Chukas-Balak, 5746)

כ יְהוּדָה בֶּן תֵּימָא אוֹמֵר: הֱוֵי עַז כַּנָּמֵר, וְקַל כַּנֶּשֶׁר, רָץ כַּצְּבִי, וְגִבּוֹר
כָּאֲרִי, לַעֲשׂוֹת רְצוֹן אָבִיךָ שֶׁבַּשָּׁמָיִם. הוּא הָיָה אוֹמֵר: עַז פָּנִים
לְגֵיהִנֹּם, וּבוֹשֶׁת פָּנִים לְגַן עֵדֶן. יְהִי רָצוֹן מִלְּפָנֶיךָ י־י אֱלֹהֵי־נוּ
וֵאלֹהֵ־י אֲבוֹתֵינוּ, שֶׁיִּבָּנֶה בֵּית הַמִּקְדָּשׁ בִּמְהֵרָה בְיָמֵינוּ, וְתֵן חֶלְקֵנוּ
בְּתוֹרָתֶךָ.

20. YEHUDAH BEN TEMA SAID: "BE BOLD AS A
LEOPARD, LIGHT AS AN EAGLE, SWIFT AS A

---

69. *Mishlei* 83:21. Cf. *Uktzin* 3:12.
70. *Tehillim* 55:24.

DEER, AND STRONG AS A LION, TO CARRY OUT THE WILL OF YOUR FATHER IN HEAVEN."

HE USED TO SAY: "THE BRAZEN IS HEADED FOR GEHINOM, BUT THE SHAMEFACED FOR HEAVEN.

"MAY IT BE YOUR WILL, L-RD OUR G-D AND G-D OF OUR FATHERS, THAT THE *BEIS HAMIKDASH* BE REBUILT SPEEDILY IN OUR DAYS, AND GRANT US OUR PORTION IN YOUR TORAH."

A LEOPARD... AN EAGLE — On the verse,[71] "Instruct us from the beasts of the earth; grant us wisdom from the birds of the heaven," our Sages state[72] that even were, (heaven forbid,) the Torah not to have been given, we could learn the positive traits it teaches by meditating on the qualities with which G-d endowed the animals.

As the Baal Shem Tov teaches:[73] "Everything which a person sees or hears should serve as a lesson for him in his divine service." When a person sees a beast or a bird — even a non-kosher species like a leopard or an eagle — he should realize that the purpose is to teach him positive qualities which he should employ in his divine service.

(Likkutei Sichos, Vol. XXI, p. 284ff)

BE BOLD AS A LEOPARD... THE BRAZEN IS HEADED FOR GEHINOM — These two clauses appear to be contradictory. On one hand, the *mishnah* is telling us to display boldness. On the other hand, it states that brazen behavior brings retribution.

This difficulty can be resolved by considering another seeming contradiction in the words of our Sages. In one source,[74] our Sages state that humility is one of the traits which

---

71 . *Iyov* 35:11.
72 . *Eruvin* 102b.
73 . Quoted in *HaYom Yom*, p. 52, *Kesser Shem Tov, Hosafos*, sec. 127.
74 . *Yevamos* 79a.

distinguish the Jewish people. And yet, in another source,[75] they state that Jews are "the most bold of the nations."

Humility and boldness need not be contradictory. When it comes to a person's individual concerns, he should be humble and willing to compromise. With regard to his divine service, however, he should stand proud and boldly assert his rights, remaining unphased in the face of any and all who try to hinder him.

Indeed, this concept is so important that the *Tur* and the Alter Rebbe in his *Shulchan Aruch* chose to begin their compendiums of Jewish law with this directive.[76]

The scope of this directive extends beyond the individual sphere. When the Jewish people are pressured by gentiles with regard to the observance of the Torah and its *mitzvos,* or with regard to a matter concerning the welfare of the Jewish people, they need not be intimidated. Instead, they should proudly and boldly assert their position. When that position is based on the Torah, and presented as such, the gentiles will listen.

The above concepts are particularly appropriate in the present era, short moments before the coming of the Redemption, when G-d will lead us proud and upright to our land.[77] By anticipating the pride and self-esteem of the Redemption at the present time, we can precipitate its coming.

(Ibid., Likkutei Sichos, Vol. XV, p. 256)

MAY IT BE YOUR WILL... THAT THE *BEIS HAMIKDASH* BE REBUILT SPEEDILY IN OUR DAYS, AND GRANT US OUR PORTION IN YOUR TORAH —

---

75 . *Beitzah* 25b.
76 . And if, heaven forbid, a person does not express boldness in his divine service, boldness will become manifest in an undesirable manner. To cite a parallel, our Sages (*Shabbos* 156a) state that a person born under the sign of Mars will become a murderer or a robber or a butcher or a *mohel.* In other words, the person has a tendency towards bloodshed, but the question is: how will he express it? Similarly, with regard to the matter at hand: Jews have boldness in their nature. The question is: In which avenues will they display this quality?
77 . Cf. *Vayikra* 26:13.

The association of the two clauses in this prayer can be explained as follows: In the present era, much of our efforts are devoted to worldly activities. In the Era of the Redemption, when the *Beis HaMikdash* will be rebuilt, we will, by contrast, be able to devote all our energies to the study of Torah.

(Sichas Shabbos Parshas Re'eh, 5741)

כא בֶּן בַּג בַּג אוֹמֵר: הֲפָךְ בָּהּ וַהֲפָךְ בָּהּ, דְּכֹלָּא בָהּ, וּבָהּ תֶּחֱזֵי, וְסִיב וּבְלֵה בָהּ, וּמִנַּהּ לָא תָזוּעַ, שֶׁאֵין לָךְ מִדָּה טוֹבָה הֵימֶנָּה. בֶּן הֵא הֵא אוֹמֵר: לְפוּם צַעֲרָא אַגְרָא:

21. BEN BAG BAG SAID: "LEARN IT AND LEARN IT [THE TORAH], FOR EVERYTHING IS IN IT. LOOK DEEPLY INTO IT; GROW OLD AND GRAY OVER IT, AND DO NOT STIR FROM IT, FOR THERE IS NOTHING MORE EDIFYING FOR YOU THAN IT."

BEN HAY HAY SAID: "COMMENSURATE WITH THE PAINSTAKING EFFORT IS THE REWARD."

BEN HAY HAY — The commentaries[78] explain that Ben Hay Hay was a convert.[79] This is reflected in his teaching.

COMMENSURATE WITH THE PAINSTAKING EFFORT IS THE REWARD — It is an accepted principle of

---

78 . *Tosafos, Chagigah* 9b, *Machzor Vitri.*
79 . Or the descendant of converts. This is reflected in the name *Hay Hay*, for the Hebrew letter *hay* was added to the names of Avraham and Sarah as a sign of their Jewish identity.

The commentaries also explain that Ben Bag Bag was a convert or the son of converts. One of the proofs is that the Hebrew letters that spell Bag (ג and ב) are numerically equivalent to a *hay*.

faith[80] that G-d rewards man for the observance of His *mitzvos*. The *mishnah* is teaching that in calculating the nature of that reward, G-d looks not only at the task accomplished, but also at the effort invested. When a person labors and struggles to perform a *mitzvah*, G-d increases the reward he will receive.

More particularly, this refers to the effort a man invests in the fulfillment of a *mitzvah* when he is not obligated to do so, i.e., the observance of a *mitzvah behiddur*, in a beautiful and conscientious manner, or in the performance of *mili dechassidusa*, positive conduct that extends beyond the measure of the law.

Perhaps the most complete expression of this concept is the act of conversion.[81] A gentile is not at all obligated to accept the burden of Judaism; indeed, at first he should be discouraged from doing so.[82] Therefore, the painstaking effort he expends in the observance of *mitzvos* is surely worthy of reward.

(Likkutei Sichos, Vol. XXVII, p. 387ff)

כב הוּא הָיָה אוֹמֵר: בֶּן חָמֵשׁ שָׁנִים לְמִקְרָא, בֶּן עֶשֶׂר שָׁנִים לְמִשְׁנָה, בֶּן שְׁלֹשׁ עֶשְׂרֵה לְמִצְוֹת, בֶּן חֲמֵשׁ עֶשְׂרֵה לִגְמָרָא, בֶּן שְׁמוֹנֶה עֶשְׂרֵה לְחֻפָּה, בֶּן עֶשְׂרִים לִרְדּוֹף, בֶּן שְׁלֹשִׁים לְכֹחַ, בֶּן אַרְבָּעִים לְבִינָה, בֶּן חֲמִשִּׁים לְעֵצָה, בֶּן שִׁשִּׁים לְזִקְנָה, בֶּן שִׁבְעִים לְשֵׂיבָה, בֶּן שְׁמוֹנִים לִגְבוּרָה, בֶּן תִּשְׁעִים לָשׁוּחַ, בֶּן מֵאָה כְּאִלּוּ מֵת וְעָבַר וּבָטֵל מִן הָעוֹלָם.

---

80 . *Rambam, Commentary to the Mishnah*, Tractate *Sanhedrin*, Introduction to ch. 10, principle 11.

81 . In contrast, since a Jew is created "to serve [His] Creator," there is a dimension of obligation to every element of his divine service, even the observance of a *mitzvah behiddur*, or the performance of *mili dechassidusa*.

82 . *Yevamos* 47b.

22. HE USED TO SAY: "AT FIVE YEARS OF AGE, [ONE SHOULD APPROACH] THE STUDY OF SCRIPTURE; AT TEN THE STUDY OF *MISHNAH*; AT THIRTEEN THE *MITZVOS*, AT FIFTEEN THE STUDY OF *GEMARA*, AT EIGHTEEN MARRIAGE; AT TWENTY PURSUIT [OF A LIVELIHOOD]; AT THIRTY [ONE ATTAINS] FULL STRENGTH; AT FORTY UNDERSTANDING; AT FIFTY [THE POTENTIAL TO GIVE] COUNSEL; AT SIXTY OLD AGE; AT SEVENTY RIPE OLD AGE; AT EIGHTY [SPECIAL] STRENGTH; AT NINETY [THE BODY] IS STOOPED; AT ONE HUNDRED IT IS AS IF ONE WERE DEAD AND HAD DEPARTED AND CEASED CONNECTION WITH THE WORLD."

AT TWENTY... AT THIRTY — The *Kabbalah* explains that G-d brought all existence into being through the ten *Sefiros* (as reflected in the fact that there are ten utterances of creation). As such, each decade of a person's existence represents the blossoming of a new attribute and the attainment of another spiritual rung.

(Likkutei Sichos, Vol. II, p. 593)

AT NINETY [THE BODY] IS STOOPED — This is also a positive quality, referring to humility. The attainment of all the virtues mentioned previously should not lead one to pride. Instead, these positive qualities should encourage humility.

(Sichos Shabbos Parshas Nitzavim, 5737; Sichos Shabbos Parshas Eikev, 5740)

AT ONE HUNDRED IT IS AS IF ONE WERE DEAD — This represents a crowning stage in personal development. On the verse[83] "no man shall see Me and live," our Sages commented:[84] "While alive one does not see, but when dead one sees." At one hundred, a person can reach a level such that "it

---

83 . *Shmos* 33:20.
84 . *Sifri*, commenting on *Bamidbar* 12:8.

is as if he were dead," i.e., he can attain that degree of perception of G-dliness.

Similarly, the expression "had departed and ceased connection with the world" also has a positive connotation. It means the person has risen above all worldly matters.[85] His focus and concern are solely spiritual.

(Ibid.)

85 . *Or HaTorah, Chukas,* p. 817.

CHAPTER SIX

Chapter Six

א שָׁנוּ חֲכָמִים בִּלְשׁוֹן הַמִּשְׁנָה, בָּרוּךְ שֶׁבָּחַר בָּהֶם וּבְמִשְׁנָתָם. רַבִּי
מֵאִיר אוֹמֵר: כָּל הָעוֹסֵק בַּתּוֹרָה לִשְׁמָהּ זוֹכֶה לִדְבָרִים הַרְבֵּה, וְלֹא
עוֹד, אֶלָּא שֶׁכָּל הָעוֹלָם כֻּלּוֹ, כְּדַאי הוּא לוֹ. נִקְרָא רֵעַ, אָהוּב, אוֹהֵב
אֶת הַמָּקוֹם, אוֹהֵב אֶת הַבְּרִיּוֹת, מְשַׂמֵּחַ אֶת הַמָּקוֹם, מְשַׂמֵּחַ אֶת
הַבְּרִיּוֹת, וּמַלְבַּשְׁתּוֹ עֲנָוָה וְיִרְאָה. וּמַכְשַׁרְתּוֹ לִהְיוֹת צַדִּיק, חָסִיד,
יָשָׁר, וְנֶאֱמָן, וּמְרַחַקְתּוֹ מִן הַחֵטְא, וּמְקָרַבְתּוֹ לִידֵי זְכוּת, וְנֶהֱנִין
מִמֶּנּוּ עֵצָה וְתוּשִׁיָּה, בִּינָה וּגְבוּרָה, שֶׁנֶּאֱמַר: לִי עֵצָה וְתוּשִׁיָּה, אֲנִי
בִינָה, לִי גְבוּרָה, וְנוֹתֶנֶת לוֹ מַלְכוּת וּמֶמְשָׁלָה, וְחִקּוּר דִּין, וּמְגַלִּין לוֹ
רָזֵי תוֹרָה, וְנַעֲשֶׂה כְמַעְיָן הַמִּתְגַּבֵּר וּכְנָהָר שֶׁאֵינוֹ פוֹסֵק, וְהֹוֶה צָנוּעַ,
וְאֶרֶךְ רוּחַ, וּמוֹחֵל עַל עֶלְבּוֹנוֹ, וּמְגַדַּלְתּוֹ וּמְרוֹמַמְתּוֹ עַל כָּל
הַמַּעֲשִׂים.

1. OUR SAGES TAUGHT [THIS CHAPTER][1] IN THE LANGUAGE OF THE *MISHNAH;* BLESSED IS HE WHO CHOSE THEM AND THEIR TEACHING.

RABBI MEIR SAID: "WHOEVER OCCUPIES HIMSELF WITH [THE STUDY OF] TORAH FOR ITS OWN SAKE MERITS MANY THINGS; FURTHERMORE, HE IS WORTHY THAT THE WHOLE WORLD SHALL HAVE BEEN CREATED BECAUSE OF HIM. HE IS CALLED FRIEND, BELOVED; HE LOVES G-D, HE LOVES THE CREATED BEINGS; HE BRINGS JOY TO G-D, HE BRINGS JOY TO THE CREATED BEINGS. [THE TORAH] GARBS HIM WITH HUMILITY AND FEAR [OF G-D]; IT MAKES HIM FIT TO BE A *TZADDIK,* A *CHASSID,* UPRIGHT AND

---

1. See the Publisher's Foreword, which explains that this chapter is an addition, appended to the original tractate of *Avos* which is only five chapters.

FAITHFUL; IT KEEPS HIM FAR FROM SIN AND BRINGS
HIM NEAR TO MERITORIOUS DEEDS.

"OTHERS DERIVE FROM HIM THE BENEFIT OF
COUNSEL AND WISDOM, INSIGHT AND STRENGTH, AS
IT IS STATED:[2] 'COUNSEL AND WISDOM ARE MINE; I
AM UNDERSTANDING, STRENGTH IS MINE.' [THE
TORAH] BESTOWS UPON HIM ROYALTY, AUTHORITY,
AND DISCERNING JUDGMENT; THE SECRETS OF THE
TORAH ARE REVEALED TO HIM, AND HE BECOMES
LIKE A FOUNTAIN WHICH FLOWS WITH EVER-IN-
CREASING STRENGTH, AND LIKE A NEVER-CEASING
STREAM. HE BECOMES MODEST, PATIENT, AND
FORGIVING OF INSULT TO HIMSELF; AND [THE
TORAH] MAKES HIM GREAT AND EXALTS HIM ABOVE
ALL THINGS."

**THE SAGES TAUGHT [THIS CHAPTER] IN THE
LANGUAGE OF THE *MISHNAH* —** One might ask why the
study of *Pirkei Avos* was instituted in such a manner that the
chapter studied before the holiday of Shavuos includes *beraisos*
(teachings not included in the *Mishnah*) rather than *mishnayos*,
which are more authoritative.

It can be explained that the *Beraisa* reflects the manner in
which the Torah descends into the world at large, showing how
every new idea developed by an experienced sage was in fact
granted to Moshe at Sinai.[3] In this manner, it demonstrates the
dynamic allowing for the continuation of the chain beginning
when "Moshe received the Torah... and transmitted it."[4] For it
shows how the Torah can be internalized within a mortal mind,
and then transmitted to subsequent generations.

(Sefer HaSichos 5749, Vol. II, p. 481ff)

---

2 . *Mishlei* 8:14.
3 . See *Megillah* 19b; *Yerushalmi, Pe'ah* 1:4; *Likkutei Sichos*, Vol. XIX, p. 252 notes 20-
21.
4 . *Pirkei Avos* 1:1.

WHOEVER OCCUPIES HIMSELF — The Hebrew word עוסק, translated "occupies himself," relates to the Hebrew word for businessman, בעל עסק.[5] A person's occupation with the study of Torah must resemble a businessman's preoccupation with his commercial enterprise.[6] Just as a businessman's attention is never totally diverted from his business, the Torah should always be the focus of our attention.

WITH [THE STUDY OF] TORAH FOR ITS OWN SAKE — A person who devotes himself to the study of Torah for its own sake is not concerned with any of the material or spiritual benefits he might accrue. But what about a person who has not attained this level? Since it might be difficult to convince him to proceed on such a selfless path, the *beraisa* teaches us that through devotion to the study of Torah a person merits many things.

MERITS — These merits are merely the side benefits of Torah study; the true reward is the inner bond with G-d which it brings.

(Likkutei Sichos, Vol. XVII, p. 401ff)

MANY THINGS; FURTHERMORE... — The "many things" which a person merits are not merely the qualities which the *beraisa* enumerate.[7] The Torah is unlimited. And the "many things," the blessings and benefits it brings a person devoted to its study, are likewise boundless.

(Likkutei Sichos, Vol. VII, p. 370)

HE LOVES THE CREATED BEINGS — As mentioned in the notes to ch. 1, *mishnah* 12, the term "created beings" refers to individuals who have no redeeming virtue other than the

---

5. *Sefer HaMaamarim-Kuntreisim*, Vol. I, p. 516.
6. See *Bayis Chadash, Orach Chayim*, sec. 47.
7. See the gloss of the *Midrash Shmuel.*

fact that G-d created them. Why is a person able to show such boundless love and reach out to these people? Because of his selfless devotion to Torah study.

A person who has personal ambitions involves himself only with people who can help him realize those ambitions. A person who desires to be loved seeks out people who will love him. A person who has no thought for himself, and studies the Torah only because it is G-d's word, can open himself to all others, even to those individuals whose only redeeming virtue is that they are G-d's creations.

(Likkutei Sichos, Vol. XVII, p. 405-406)

HE BRINGS JOY TO THE CREATED BEINGS — This represents a higher level of behavior than the love mentioned previously. Even though a person may love another, the two remain distinct from each other. Happiness breaks down barriers,[8] and enables the two to establish a more complete bond.

Nevertheless, although joy represents a deeper bond than love, there is an advantage to love. Because love establishes a connection between two distinct entities, it enables a person to relate to a colleague within the latter's frame of reference. Because of the more complete bond established by joy, the person might feel that just as he himself does not indulge his own desires, so too, his colleague should learn to be content with little. Love, by contrast, causes one to appreciate what the other person desires and to extend oneself for him. Thus both qualities —- love and joy — are necessary to develop our relationships to the fullest.

(Sichos Shabbos Parshas Bamidbar, 5746)

[THE TORAH] GARBS HIM WITH HUMILITY... IT MAKES HIM FIT... IT KEEPS HIM FAR... AND BRINGS HIM NEAR... — The *beraisa* is emphasizing that Torah study alone cannot endow a person with these characteristics. On the

---

8. *Sefer HaMaamarim 5657*, p. 223ff.

contrary, they can be acquired only through effort and labor. Nevertheless, the study of Torah makes it far easier to attain such qualities.

OTHERS DERIVE FROM HIM THE BENEFIT OF COUNSEL — This refers to the ability to advise others in worldly matters. The study of Torah will develop a person's powers of understanding to the extent that he will appreciate the proper course of action in worldly matters as well. Thus on one hand, a person who devotes himself to Torah will be above all worldly pursuits. Simultaneously, however, he will find success for himself and others even on the worldly plane.

(Likkutei Sichos, Vol. XVII, p. 401ff)

ב אָמַר רַבִּי יְהוֹשֻׁעַ בֶּן לֵוִי, בְּכָל יוֹם וָיוֹם בַּת קוֹל יוֹצֵאת מֵהַר חוֹרֵב וּמַכְרֶזֶת וְאוֹמֶרֶת: אוֹי לָהֶם לַבְּרִיּוֹת מֵעֶלְבּוֹנָהּ שֶׁל תּוֹרָה, שֶׁכָּל מִי שֶׁאֵינוֹ עוֹסֵק בַּתּוֹרָה, נִקְרָא נָזוּף, שֶׁנֶּאֱמַר: נֶזֶם זָהָב בְּאַף חֲזִיר, אִשָּׁה יָפָה וְסָרַת טָעַם. וְאוֹמֵר: וְהַלֻּחֹת מַעֲשֵׂה אֱלֹהִי-ם הֵמָּה, וְהַמִּכְתָּב, מִכְתַּב אֱלֹהִי-ם הוּא, חָרוּת עַל הַלֻּחֹת, אַל תִּקְרָא חָרוּת אֶלָּא חֵרוּת, שֶׁאֵין לְךָ בֶּן חוֹרִין, אֶלָּא מִי שֶׁעוֹסֵק בְּתַלְמוּד תּוֹרָה, וְכָל מִי שֶׁעוֹסֵק בְּתַלְמוּד תּוֹרָה, הֲרֵי זֶה מִתְעַלֶּה, שֶׁנֶּאֱמַר: וּמִמַּתָּנָה נַחֲלִיאֵל, וּמִנַּחֲלִיאֵל בָּמוֹת.

2. RABBI YEHOSHUA BEN LEVI SAID: "EACH AND EVERY DAY A HEAVENLY VOICE GOES FORTH FROM MOUNT CHOREB, PROCLAIMING AND SAYING: 'WOE TO THE CREATED BEINGS BECAUSE OF [THEIR] AFFRONT TO THE TORAH!' FOR WHOEVER DOES NOT OCCUPY HIMSELF WITH TORAH IS CALLED CENSURED, AS IT IS STATED:[9] '[LIKE] A GOLDEN RING IN A

---

9. *Mishlei* 11:22.

SWINE'S SNOUT IS A BEAUTIFUL WOMAN WHO LACKS DISCRETION.'

AND IT IS FURTHER STATED:[10] 'THE TABLETS WERE THE WORK OF G-D, AND THE WRITING WAS THE WRITING OF G-D, *CHARUT* (ENGRAVED) ON THE TABLETS.' DO NOT READ *CHARUT* BUT *CHERUT* (FREEDOM), FOR THERE IS NO FREE MAN EXCEPT ONE WHO OCCUPIES HIMSELF WITH THE STUDY OF TORAH.

"AND ANYONE WHO OCCUPIES HIMSELF WITH THE STUDY OF TORAH BECOMES ELEVATED, AS IT IS STATED:[11] 'FROM MATTANAH [THE GIFT] TO NACHALIEL [THE HERITAGE OF G-D], AND FROM NACHALIEL TO BAMOS [HIGH PLACES].' "

EACH AND EVERY DAY A HEAVENLY VOICE GOES FORTH FROM MOUNT CHOREB — Our souls exist on several planes simultaneously. This Heavenly Voice reverberates, and is "heard" by our souls as they exist in the spiritual realms. And this causes our souls as they are enclothed within our bodies to be aroused to *teshuvah*.[12]

(Likkutei Sichos, Vol. IX, p. 25)

WOE TO THE CREATED BEINGS BECAUSE OF [THEIR] AFFRONT TO THE TORAH! — One might think that a more effective way of motivating people to study Torah would be to emphasize the positive qualities it possesses. But this call is addressed to "created beings"[13] — people who have no redeeming quality other than the fact that they are G-d's creations. Such people may be too crass and materially oriented to be able to appreciate the Torah's positive virtues.

---

10. *Shmos* 82:16.
11. *Bamidbar* 21:19. The *Beraisa* is offering a homiletic interpretation of the Hebrew names of these places.
12. See *Likkutei Torah, Seitze* 36d; *Ha'azinu* 71d.
13. See the notes to ch. 1, *mishnah* 12.

Nevertheless, all people possess a soul which is "an actual part of G-d from above,"[14] and thus share an inherent connection to the Torah. Hearing this stiff rebuke may stagger their crass tendencies and awaken their inner bond with the word of G-d.

(Likkutei Sichos, Vol. XV, p. 123)

WHOEVER DOES NOT OCCUPY HIMSELF WITH TORAH — Again, the word עוסק is used. Based on the explanation given above, this teaching can be interpreted as applying not only to a person who does not study Torah at all, but to one who does not study with the all-encompassing commitment that a businessman brings to his commercial interests.

(Likkutei Sichos, Vol. IV, p. 1228)

DO NOT READ *CHARUT* BUT *CHERUT* (FREEDOM), FOR THERE IS NO FREE MAN EXCEPT ONE WHO OCCUPIES HIMSELF WITH THE STUDY OF TORAH — Whenever our Sages offer an extended meaning for a word, they do not thereby nullify its simple interpretation.[15] Instead, the two reinforce each other. The freedom generated by Torah study results from the fact that the letters of the Torah are engraved.

The difference between letters engraved onto stone and letters written with ink is that engraved letters are part and parcel of the substance onto which they are written. When the Torah is engraved within an individual's personality, it makes a permanent impression on every dimension of his being. This liberates a person's conduct, enabling him to express G-dly truth in all aspects of his life.

(Sichos Shabbos Parshas Balak, 5745)

---

14. *Tanya*, ch. 2.
15. See *Halichos Eli*, sec. 3.

The Torah is called service. Thus when G-d promised Moshe that He would give the Jews the Torah, He said:[16] "When you bring the people out of Egypt, you will serve G-d on this mountain." But unlike human bondage, this servitude gives expression to the inner G-dly nature which every Jew possesses. Therefore it represents true freedom.

(Likkutei Sichos, Vol. XVII, p. 75)

FROM MATTANAH [THE GIFT] TO NACHALIEL [THE HERITAGE OF G-D], AND FROM NACHALIEL TO BAMOS [HIGH PLACES] — The Torah's ability to elevate a person to a higher and more refined plane of conduct (the "high places" mentioned in the verse) comes as a result of the concepts implied by the previous two locations.

The Torah is "the heritage of G-d" — an eternal Truth that could not be conceived by man alone. This unlimited Truth — a "gift" freely granted to us by G-d — enables us to rise above our individual nature and elevate our conduct.

(Sichos Shabbos Parshas Re'eh, 5740)

ג הַלּוֹמֵד מֵחֲבֵרוֹ: פֶּרֶק אֶחָד, אוֹ הֲלָכָה אַחַת, אוֹ פָּסוּק אֶחָד, אוֹ דִּבּוּר אֶחָד, אוֹ אֲפִילוּ אוֹת אַחַת, צָרִיךְ לִנְהָג בּוֹ כָּבוֹד, שֶׁכֵּן מָצִינוּ בְּדָוִד מֶלֶךְ יִשְׂרָאֵל, שֶׁלֹּא לָמַד מֵאֲחִיתֹפֶל אֶלָּא שְׁנֵי דְבָרִים בִּלְבָד, קְרָאוֹ רַבּוֹ אַלּוּפוֹ וּמְיֻדָּעוֹ, שֶׁנֶּאֱמַר: וְאַתָּה אֱנוֹשׁ כְּעֶרְכִּי, אַלּוּפִי וּמְיֻדָּעִי. וַהֲלֹא דְבָרִים קַל וָחֹמֶר, וּמַה דָּוִד מֶלֶךְ יִשְׂרָאֵל שֶׁלֹּא לָמַד מֵאֲחִיתֹפֶל אֶלָּא שְׁנֵי דְבָרִים בִּלְבָד, קְרָאוֹ רַבּוֹ אַלּוּפוֹ וּמְיֻדָּעוֹ, הַלּוֹמֵד מֵחֲבֵרוֹ, פֶּרֶק אֶחָד, אוֹ הֲלָכָה אַחַת, אוֹ פָּסוּק אֶחָד, אוֹ דִּבּוּר אֶחָד, אוֹ אֲפִילוּ אוֹת אֶחָת, עַל אַחַת כַּמָּה וְכַמָּה שֶׁצָּרִיךְ לִנְהָג בּוֹ כָּבוֹד. וְאֵין כָּבוֹד, אֶלָּא תוֹרָה, שֶׁנֶּאֱמַר: כָּבוֹד חֲכָמִים יִנְחָלוּ,

---

16. *Shmos* 3:12.

וּתְמִימִים יִנְחֲלוּ טוֹב. וְאֵין טוֹב אֶלָּא תוֹרָה, שֶׁנֶּאֱמַר: כִּי לֶקַח טוֹב
נָתַתִּי לָכֶם, תּוֹרָתִי אַל תַּעֲזֹבוּ.

3. HE WHO LEARNS FROM A COLLEAGUE A SINGLE CHAPTER, A SINGLE TORAH LAW, A SINGLE VERSE, A SINGLE STATEMENT, OR EVEN A SINGLE LETTER, MUST SHOW HIM HONOR.

FOR SO WE FIND CONCERNING DAVID, KING OF ISRAEL, WHO LEARNED FROM ACHITOPHEL ONLY TWO THINGS, YET HE CALLED HIM HIS TEACHER, HIS GUIDE, HIS MENTOR, AS IT IS STATED:[17] "YOU ARE A MAN EQUAL TO ME; YOU ARE MY GUIDE AND MY MENTOR."

SURELY AN OBVIOUS INFERENCE CAN BE DRAWN: IF DAVID, KING OF ISRAEL, WHO LEARNED FROM ACHITOPHEL ONLY TWO THINGS, CALLED HIM HIS TEACHER, HIS GUIDE, HIS MENTOR, ONE WHO LEARNS FROM HIS PEER A SINGLE CHAPTER, A SINGLE TORAH LAW, A SINGLE VERSE, A SINGLE STATEMENT, OR EVEN A SINGLE LETTER, HOW MUCH MORE OUGHT HE TO TREAT HIM WITH HONOR!

AND HONOR IS DUE ONLY FOR TORAH, AS IT IS STATED:[18] "THE WISE SHALL INHERIT HONOR," [AND IT IS STATED]:[19] "AND THE PERFECT SHALL INHERIT GOOD." AND [TRUE] GOOD IS ONLY TORAH, AS IT IS STATED:[20] "I HAVE GIVEN YOU A GOOD TEACHING; DO NOT FORSAKE MY TORAH."

HE WHO LEARNS FROM A COLLEAGUE... MUST SHOW HIM HONOR — *Pirkei Avos*[21] has already taught us to cherish the honor of our colleague as our own. Our *mishnah*,

---

17 . *Tehillim* 55:14.
18 . *Mishlei* 3:35.
19 . *Ibid.*, 28:10.
20 . *Ibid.*, 4:2.
21 . Above 2:10.

however, is teaching us an additional point, for as will be explained, it refers to a colleague whose conduct is not above reproof.

When a person's own conduct is flawed, it is natural that despite the natural justifications and rationalizations that stem from self-love, he would know his own failings and humbly look down at himself.

One may not view a colleague from whom one has learned Torah concepts in such a manner. Even when the other person's conduct is unworthy, he should be honored for the sake of the teachings which he communicated.

(Sichos Shabbos Parshas Bamidbar, 5733)

DAVID, KING OF ISRAEL, WHO LEARNED FROM ACHITOPHEL ONLY TWO THINGS — The Baal Shem Tov interpreted[22] the phrase, "only two things," as follows. Generally, when one studies Torah, every concept leads to others, for learning is a self-reinforcing cycle. When, however, one learns from a wicked person like Achitophel,[23] the information gained remains inert. Therefore, Achitophel's two teachings were solitary points of information; they did not have the potential to lead David to further knowledge.

One might ask: The ability of the Torah to bring about an ever-increasing flow of knowledge stems from its connection with G-d, since "the Torah and the Holy One, blessed be He, are one."[24] Human conduct, no matter how base, cannot detract from the eternal truth and wisdom of G-d's word. Why then were Achitophel's teachings not fruitful?

In resolution, it can be explained that the bond between G-d and the Torah is not always apparent. It is therefore possible, heaven forbid, for a person to study and even teach

---

22 . *Kesser Shem Tov,* sec. 22.
23 . *Sanhedrin* 106b.
24 . *Tanya,* ch. 4 and beginning of ch. 23, in the name of the *Zohar;* see *Zohar* II, 60a; *Likkutei Torah, Nitzavim* 46a.

Torah without regarding it as different from any other form of wisdom. When this happens, the growth potential within the Torah remains dormant. When, however, a person establishes a connection between the Torah and its G-dly source,[25] the infinite potential surfaces.

Achitophel, a wicked man, taught Torah in a self-contained manner. But David in his humility surrendered himself to the infinite dimension of G-dliness within Achitophel's dry teachings. This enabled David to breathe life into all he studied, even the two concepts which he learned from Achitophel.

(Sichos Motzoei Shabbos Parshas Bamidbar, 5739)

ד כָּךְ הִיא דַּרְכָּהּ שֶׁל תּוֹרָה, פַּת בְּמֶלַח תּאכֵל, וּמַיִם בִּמְשׂוּרָה
תִּשְׁתֶּה, וְעַל הָאָרֶץ תִּישָׁן, וְחַיֵּי צַעַר תִּחְיֶה, וּבַתּוֹרָה אַתָּה עָמֵל, אִם
אַתָּה עוֹשֶׂה כֵּן, אַשְׁרֶיךָ וְטוֹב לָךְ, אַשְׁרֶיךָ בָּעוֹלָם הַזֶּה, וְטוֹב לָךְ
לָעוֹלָם הַבָּא.

4. THIS IS THE WAY [TO ACQUIRE] TORAH: EAT BREAD WITH SALT, DRINK WATER IN SMALL MEASURE, SLEEP ON THE GROUND, LIVE A LIFE OF DEPRIVATION, AND TOIL IN THE TORAH. IF YOU DO THIS, "YOU SHALL BE HAPPY, AND IT SHALL BE WELL WITH YOU."[26] "YOU SHALL BE HAPPY" IN THIS WORLD; "AND IT SHALL BE WELL WITH YOU" IN THE WORLD TO COME.

*LIVE A LIFE OF DEPRIVATION, AND TOIL IN THE TORAH — Both poverty and wealth present challenges to divine service. The challenge of wealth, however, is more severe than the challenge of poverty.

---

25 . *Raya Mehemna, Zohar* III, 222b; *Likkutei Torah, Shelach* 47c, 51a.
26 . *Tehillim* 128:2.

The challenges presented by poverty are for the most part external; day-to-day life is simply more difficult, and it is harder to devote energy to divine service.

The challenges presented by wealth are largely internal. When a person is prosperous, there is a natural tendency for him to think, "My strength and the power of my hand achieved this bounty for me."[27] Such an approach runs in direct contradiction to the study of Torah. For the essence of our relationship with the Torah revolves around *kabbalas ol* — absolute acceptance of G-d's laws, even when they run contrary to one's own thinking. Any material success we may enjoy should be regarded as a reward given by G-d, and should not lead to pride.

Few of us today are beset by the challenges of extreme poverty. We do, however, confront the challenges of wealth. To overcome these challenges, we need self-control, and the reinforcement, humility and strength that one person can offer a friend.

(Likkutei Sichos, Vol. II, 643-644)

ה אַל תְּבַקֵּשׁ גְּדֻלָּה לְעַצְמְךָ, וְאַל תַּחְמוֹד כָּבוֹד, יוֹתֵר מִלִּמּוּדֶךָ עֲשֵׂה, וְאַל תִּתְאַוֶּה לְשֻׁלְחָנָם שֶׁל מְלָכִים, שֶׁשֻּׁלְחָנְךָ, גָּדוֹל מִשֻּׁלְחָנָם, וְכִתְרְךָ, גָּדוֹל מִכִּתְרָם, וְנֶאֱמָן הוּא בַּעַל מְלַאכְתֶּךָ שֶׁיְּשַׁלֶּם לְךָ שְׂכַר פְּעֻלָּתֶךָ.

5. DO NOT SEEK GREATNESS FOR YOURSELF, AND DO NOT DESIRE HONOR; LET YOUR DEEDS EXCEED YOUR LEARNING. DO NOT YEARN FOR THE TABLE OF KINGS, FOR YOUR TABLE IS GREATER THAN THEIRS, AND YOUR CROWN IS GREATER THAN THEIRS;

---

27 . *Devarim* 8:17.

AND YOUR EMPLOYER IS TRUSTWORTHY TO PAY YOU
REMUNERATION FOR YOUR DEEDS.

DO NOT SEEK GREATNESS FOR YOURSELF — As
reflected in the first teaching in this chapter and in many other
sources, Torah study may bring a person greatness, honor, and
position. He should nevertheless refrain from seeking these
things. If he is fit for them, they will be granted from heaven.

With regard to honor, the *beraisa* teaches that we should not
only avoid seeking it, it should hold no attraction for us at all,
as the teaching continues DO NOT DESIRE HONOR.

(Likkutei Sichos, Vol. IV, p. 1240)

YOUR EMPLOYER IS TRUSTWORTHY TO PAY YOU
REMUNERATION FOR YOUR DEEDS — A person might
think that since he has personal flaws, his Torah study is of no
value, as it is written:[28] "To the wicked, G-d said: 'What right
do you have to relate My statutes?'" In reassurance, the *beraisa*
teaches that G-d can be relied on to appreciate our positive
efforts. Ultimately, every individual will turn to G-d in *teshuvah*, and will receive reward for all his positive deeds.[29]

(Ibid.)

ו גְדוֹלָה תּוֹרָה יוֹתֵר מִן הַכְּהֻנָּה וּמִן הַמַּלְכוּת, שֶׁהַמַּלְכוּת, נִקְנֵית
בִּשְׁלֹשִׁים מַעֲלוֹת, וְהַכְּהֻנָּה בְּעֶשְׂרִים וְאַרְבַּע, וְהַתּוֹרָה נִקְנֵית
בְּאַרְבָּעִים וּשְׁמוֹנָה דְבָרִים. וְאֵלּוּ הֵן: בְּתַלְמוּד, בִּשְׁמִיעַת הָאֹזֶן,
בַּעֲרִיכַת שְׂפָתַיִם, בְּבִינַת הַלֵּב, בְּאֵימָה, בְּיִרְאָה, בַּעֲנָוָה, בְּשִׂמְחָה,
בְּטָהֳרָה, בְּשִׁמּוּשׁ חֲכָמִים, בְּדִבּוּק חֲבֵרִים, בְּפִלְפּוּל הַתַּלְמִידִים,
בְּיִשּׁוּב, בְּמִקְרָא, בְּמִשְׁנָה, בְּמִעוּט סְחוֹרָה, בְּמִעוּט דֶּרֶךְ אֶרֶץ,

---

28 . *Tehillim* 50:16.
29 . *Tanya*, end of ch. 39; *Hilchos Talmud Torah*, of the Alter Rebbe 4:3.

בְּמִעוּט תַּעֲנוּג, בְּמִעוּט שֵׁנָה, בְּמִעוּט שִׂיחָה, בְּמִעוּט שְׂחוֹק, בְּאֶרֶךְ
אַפַּיִם, בְּלֵב טוֹב, בֶּאֱמוּנַת חֲכָמִים, בְּקַבָּלַת הַיִּסּוּרִין, הַמַּכִּיר אֶת
מְקוֹמוֹ, וְהַשָּׂמֵחַ בְּחֶלְקוֹ, וְהָעוֹשֶׂה סְיָג לִדְבָרָיו, וְאֵינוֹ מַחֲזִיק טוֹבָה
לְעַצְמוֹ, אָהוּב, אוֹהֵב אֶת הַמָּקוֹם, אוֹהֵב אֶת הַבְּרִיּוֹת, אוֹהֵב אֶת
הַצְּדָקוֹת, אוֹהֵב אֶת הַמֵּישָׁרִים, אוֹהֵב אֶת הַתּוֹכָחוֹת, וּמִתְרַחֵק מִן
הַכָּבוֹד. וְלֹא מֵגִיס לִבּוֹ בְּתַלְמוּדוֹ, וְאֵינוֹ שָׂמֵחַ בְּהוֹרָאָה, נוֹשֵׂא בְעוֹל
עִם חֲבֵרוֹ, וּמַכְרִיעוֹ לְכַף זְכוּת, וּמַעֲמִידוֹ עַל הָאֱמֶת, וּמַעֲמִידוֹ עַל
הַשָּׁלוֹם, וּמִתְיַשֵּׁב לִבּוֹ בְּתַלְמוּדוֹ, שׁוֹאֵל וּמֵשִׁיב, שׁוֹמֵעַ וּמוֹסִיף,
הַלּוֹמֵד עַל מְנָת לְלַמֵּד, וְהַלּוֹמֵד עַל מְנָת לַעֲשׂוֹת, הַמַּחְכִּים אֶת רַבּוֹ,
וְהַמְכַוֵּן אֶת שְׁמוּעָתוֹ, וְהָאוֹמֵר דָּבָר בְּשֵׁם אוֹמְרוֹ, הָא לָמַדְתָּ: כָּל
הָאוֹמֵר דָּבָר בְּשֵׁם אוֹמְרוֹ, מֵבִיא גְאֻלָּה לָעוֹלָם, שֶׁנֶּאֱמַר: וַתֹּאמֶר
אֶסְתֵּר לַמֶּלֶךְ בְּשֵׁם מָרְדְּכָי.

6. TORAH IS GREATER THAN PRIESTHOOD OR ROYALTY. FOR ROYALTY IS ACQUIRED [TOGETHER] WITH 30 TENDENCIES, AND THE PRIESTHOOD WITH 24, BUT FOR ONE TO ACQUIRE TORAH, HE MUST HAVE THE FOLLOWING 48 TENDENCIES:

1) STUDY,
2) ATTENTIVE LISTENING,
3) VERBAL ARTICULATION,
4) AN UNDERSTANDING HEART,
5) DREAD AND AWE,   6) HUMILITY,
7) JOY,   8) PURITY,
9) SERVING THE SAGES,
10) CLOSE ASSOCIATION WITH COLLEAGUES,
11) SHARP DISCUSSION WITH STUDENTS,
12) SOBRIETY,
13) [KNOWLEDGE OF] SCRIPTURE [AND OF] *MISHNAH*,
14) A MINIMUM OF BUSINESS ACTIVITY,
15) A MINIMUM OF PREOCCUPATION WITH WORLDLY MATTERS,
16) A MINIMUM OF INDULGENCE IN [WORLDLY] PLEASURE,

17) A MINIMUM OF SLEEP,

18) A MINIMUM OF CONVERSATION,

19) A MINIMUM OF LAUGHTER,

20) PATIENCE, 21) A GOOD HEART,

22) FAITH IN THE SAGES,

23) ACCEPTANCE OF SUFFERING,

24) KNOWING HIS PLACE,

25) BEING HAPPY WITH HIS LOT,

26) MAKING A FENCE AROUND HIS WORDS,

27) REMAINS MODEST DESPITE HIS ACHIEVEMENTS,

28) BEING LOVED [BY OTHERS],

29) LOVING G-D,

30) LOVING [HIS] CREATED BEINGS,

31) LOVING THE WAYS OF RIGHTEOUSNESS,

32) LOVING JUSTICE, 33) LOVING REPROOF,

34) KEEPING FAR FROM HONOR,

35) NOT BEING ARROGANT WHILE STUDYING,

36) NOT TAKING PLEASURE IN HANDING DOWN *[HALACHIC]* DECISIONS,

37) BEARING THE BURDEN WITH HIS FELLOW,

38) JUDGING HIM FAVORABLY [GIVING HIM THE BENEFIT OF THE DOUBT],

39) ESTABLISHING HIM IN [THE PATH OF] TRUTH,

40) ESTABLISHING HIM IN [THE WAY OF] PEACE,

41) DELIBERATING IN HIS STUDY,

42) ASKING AND ANSWERING,

43) LISTENING AND ADDING [TO HIS ACQUIRED KNOWLEDGE],

44) LEARNING IN ORDER TO TEACH,

45) LEARNING IN ORDER TO PRACTICE,

46) INCREASING THE WISDOM OF HIS TEACHER,

47) PROPERLY UNDERSTANDING THE INTENT OF WHAT HE LEARNS, AND

48) QUOTING A CONCEPT IN THE NAME OF ITS AUTHOR.

INDEED, WE HAVE LEARNED: WHOEVER QUOTES A CONCEPT IN THE NAME OF ITS AUTHOR BRINGS

REDEMPTION TO THE WORLD, AS IT IS STATED:[30]
"AND ESTHER TOLD THE KING IN THE NAME OF
MORDECHAI."

ʹ **TORAH IS GREATER THAN PRIESTHOOD OR
ROYALTY** — This *beraisa* is somewhat problematic. Generally, emphasizing the advantages that one quality possesses
over another helps a person orient his priorities and seek the
quality that offers the greatest advantage. But it is impossible
for an ordinary person to acquire the qualities of priesthood or
royalty.[31] Why, then, is it necessary to emphasize that Torah
study possesses superior virtues?

The intent, however, is that within the realm of Torah
itself, there are qualities which represent priesthood (i.e., the
ability to summon up one's most refined potentials) and royalty
(the capacity to exercise control over one's deeds). Rather than
seek these virtues, a person should study Torah for its own
sake, *Torah lishmah*. One should devote himself to the Torah
for the sole purpose of attaining knowledge.

(Sichos Shabbos Parshas Bamidbar, 5724)

TENDENCIES — The *beraisa* uses the word "tendencies"
rather than "virtues" to emphasize that a person should not be
concerned with his own virtue or achievements. Instead, he
should humbly view the positive qualities he possesses merely
as mediums enabling him to carry out G-d's will.

(Likkutei Sichos, Vol. IX, p. 367)

**CLOSE ASSOCIATION WITH COLLEAGUES, SHARP
DISCUSSION WITH STUDENTS** — Appreciating another
person's perspective broadens and deepens one's own. It fol-

---

30 . *Esther* 2:22.
31 . For the priesthood was conveyed only to the descendants of Aharon, and royalty
     only to the descendants of David *(Rambam, Mishneh Torah, Hilchos Talmud Torah
     3:1).*

lows that the more colleagues and students with whom one associates, the greater the positive influence on one's growth.

(Likkutei Sichos, Vol. XXIV, p. 98)

QUOTING A CONCEPT IN THE NAME OF ITS AUTHOR — We find that Torah sages frequently relate concepts which they have heard from others without mentioning the name of the author. To cite an obvious example: Our Sages comment[32] that Rabbi Eliezer ben Horkenus never communicated a teaching unless he heard it from one of his masters. Nevertheless, we find many teachings from Rabbi Eliezer in which his sources are not mentioned.

Until a student is able to fully comprehend and internalize a teaching he received, he is required to quote it in the name of its author, for the concept still "belongs" to the teacher. Once he has grasped it completely, however, it is his own; he has acquired it by means of his comprehension, and it is now a product of his own thought.

(Likkutei Sichos, Vol. IV, p. 1178; Sichos Yud-Alef Nissan, 5733; Sichos Motzoei Shabbos Parshas Bamidbar, 5739; Sefer HaMaamarim-Meluket, Vol. II, p. 207)

WHOEVER QUOTES A CONCEPT IN THE NAME OF ITS AUTHOR BRINGS REDEMPTION TO THE WORLD — Associating a concept with its author enables one to associate the Author of the ten utterances of creation with His statements, i.e., one is better able to appreciate how G-d's speech is the life-force for creation. This awareness helps one bring the world to a state of Redemption — when the G-dly core of all existence will be openly revealed.

(Sichos Motzoei Shabbos Parshas Balak, 5738)

---

32 . *Sukkah* 27b.

ז גְּדוֹלָה תוֹרָה, שֶׁהִיא נוֹתֶנֶת חַיִּים לְעֹשֶׂיהָ בָּעוֹלָם הַזֶּה וּבָעוֹלָם
הַבָּא, שֶׁנֶּאֱמַר: כִּי חַיִּים הֵם לְמֹצְאֵיהֶם, וּלְכָל בְּשָׂרוֹ מַרְפֵּא. וְאוֹמֵר:
רִפְאוּת תְּהִי לְשָׁרֶּךָ, וְשִׁקּוּי לְעַצְמוֹתֶיךָ. וְאוֹמֵר: עֵץ חַיִּים הִיא
לַמַּחֲזִיקִים בָּהּ, וְתֹמְכֶיהָ מְאֻשָּׁר. וְאוֹמֵר: כִּי לְוְיַת חֵן הֵם לְרֹאשֶׁךָ,
וַעֲנָקִים לְגַרְגְּרֹתֶיךָ. וְאוֹמֵר: תִּתֵּן לְרֹאשְׁךָ לִוְיַת חֵן, עֲטֶרֶת תִּפְאֶרֶת
תְּמַגְּנֶךָ. וְאוֹמֵר: כִּי בִי יִרְבּוּ יָמֶיךָ, וְיוֹסִיפוּ לְךָ שְׁנוֹת חַיִּים. וְאוֹמֵר:
אֹרֶךְ יָמִים בִּימִינָהּ בִּשְׂמֹאולָהּ עשֶׁר וְכָבוֹד. וְאוֹמֵר: כִּי אֹרֶךְ יָמִים
וּשְׁנוֹת חַיִּים, וְשָׁלוֹם יוֹסִיפוּ לָךְ.

7. GREAT IS THE TORAH, FOR IT GIVES LIFE TO
THOSE WHO PRACTICE IT, BOTH IN THIS WORLD
AND IN THE WORLD TO COME, AS IT IS STATED:[33]
"FOR THEY [THE TEACHINGS OF THE TORAH] ARE
LIFE TO THE ONE WHO FINDS THEM, AND A HEALING
TO ALL HIS FLESH." AND IT SAYS:[34] "IT SHALL BE A
REMEDY TO YOUR BODY AND MARROW TO YOUR
BONES." AND IT IS STATED:[35] "IT IS A TREE OF LIFE
TO THOSE WHO HOLD FAST TO IT, AND THOSE WHO
SUPPORT IT ARE FORTUNATE."

AND IT [ALSO] SAYS:[36] "THEY ARE A GARLAND OF
GRACE FOR YOUR HEAD AND A NECKLACE FOR YOUR
NECK;" AND ALSO:[37] "IT WILL GIVE TO YOUR HEAD A
GARLAND OF GRACE; A CROWN OF GLORY WILL IT
BESTOW ON YOU;" AND FURTHER:[38] "INDEED,
THROUGH ME [THE TORAH] YOUR DAYS SHALL BE
INCREASED, AND YEARS OF LIFE SHALL BE ADDED TO
YOU;" AND AGAIN:[39] "LONG LIFE IS AT ITS RIGHT,
RICHES AND HONOR AT ITS LEFT," AND ALSO:[40]

---

33 . *Mishlei* 4:22.
34 . *Ibid.* 3:8.
35 . *Ibid.* 3:18.
36 . *Ibid.* 1:9.
37 . *Ibid.* 4:9.
38 . *Ibid.* 9:11.
39 . *Ibid.* 3:16
40 . *Ibid.* 3:2.

"LENGTH OF DAYS, YEARS OF LIFE, AND PEACE SHALL
THEY ADD TO YOU."

GREAT IS THE TORAH, FOR IT GIVES LIFE TO
THOSE WHO PRACTICE IT — "Those who practice it" refers to individuals who observe the *mitzvos*. By saying "great is
the Torah," the *beraisa* emphasizes that Torah study surpasses
observance of the *mitzvos*.

And it explains why: "for it gives life." It is possible that
even a person who is fastidious in observing *mitzvos* will do so
listlessly. Torah study inspires an understanding of the bond
with G-d that is established through the observance of *mitzvos*,
and thus infuses one's observance with energy and vitality.

(Sichos Shabbos Parshas Bamidbar, 5729)

BOTH IN THIS WORLD AND IN THE WORLD TO
COME — It is possible for a person to err, and think that since
the Torah is spiritual truth, its influence would be too ethereal
to affect our material world. Therefore the *beraisa* emphasizes
that the Torah grants life in this world.

Conversely, the *beraisa* indicates that the Torah also grants
life in the World to Come. This concept is seemingly obvious.
One might ask: why must the *beraisa* mention it?

In resolution, it can be explained that the *beraisa* is based
on the realization that the Torah imparts G-d's essence. One
might think that the revelation of this infinite G-dliness would
transcend even the World to Come and a person who studied
the Torah would be above that realm. The *beraisa* teaches that
instead, the Torah will grant life to those who merit a portion
in that realm, for in that era His infinity will permeate finite
experience.

(Sichos Shabbos Parshas Naso, 5741)

AS IT IS STATED — The *beraisa* quotes eight different prooftexts because the number eight is associated with the *sefirah* of *binah*, "understanding"; the eighth of the ten *sefiros* which structure the existence of the spiritual realms proceeding upward from the material to the infinite. *Binah* conveys the essential Divine power that permeates the entire chainlike progression of spiritual existence into the material realm. For on one hand, *binah* relates to the particular dimensions of a concept, thus recognizing the limitations of worldly existence. Nevertheless, the power of *Atik* (the spiritual realm in which G-d's Light is revealed without limitation or differentiation) is also expressed by *binah*.

(Ibid.)

ח רַבִּי שִׁמְעוֹן בֶּן יְהוּדָה מִשׁוּם רַבִּי שִׁמְעוֹן בֶּן יוֹחַאי אוֹמֵר: הַנּוֹי,
וְהַכֹּחַ, וְהָעשֶׁר, וְהַכָּבוֹד, וְהַחָכְמָה, וְהַזִּקְנָה, וְהַשֵּׂיבָה, וְהַבָּנִים, נָאֶה
לַצַּדִּיקִים וְנָאֶה לָעוֹלָם, שֶׁנֶּאֱמַר: עֲטֶרֶת תִּפְאֶרֶת שֵׂיבָה, בְּדֶרֶךְ צְדָקָה
תִּמָּצֵא. וְאוֹמֵר: תִּפְאֶרֶת בַּחוּרִים כֹּחָם, וַהֲדַר זְקֵנִים שֵׂיבָה. וְאוֹמֵר:
עֲטֶרֶת זְקֵנִים בְּנֵי בָנִים, וְתִפְאֶרֶת בָּנִים אֲבוֹתָם. וְאוֹמֵר: וְחָפְרָה
הַלְּבָנָה וּבוֹשָׁה הַחַמָּה, כִּי מָלַךְ יְ-י צְבָאוֹת בְּהַר צִיּוֹן וּבִירוּשָׁלַיִם,
וְנֶגֶד זְקֵנָיו כָּבוֹד. רַבִּי שִׁמְעוֹן בֶּן מְנַסְיָא אוֹמֵר: אֵלּוּ שֶׁבַע מִדּוֹת
שֶׁמָּנוּ חֲכָמִים לַצַּדִּיקִים, כֻּלָּם נִתְקַיְּמוּ בְּרַבִּי וּבְבָנָיו.

8. RABBI SHIMON BEN YEHUDAH SAID IN THE NAME OF RABBI SHIMON BEN YOCHAI: "BEAUTY, STRENGTH, WEALTH, HONOR, WISDOM, OLD AGE, THE GRACE OF WHITE HAIR, AND CHILDREN ARE PLEASING FOR THE RIGHTEOUS AND PLEASING FOR THE WORLD, AS IT IS STATED:[41] 'THE GRACE OF WHITE HAIR IS A CROWN OF GLORY; IT IS TO BE FOUND IN THE PATH OF RIGHTEOUSNESS;' AND IT SAYS:[42]

---

41. *Ibid.* 16:31.
42. *Ibid.* 20:29.

'THE GLORY OF YOUNG MEN IS THEIR STRENGTH,
AND THE BEAUTY OF THE ELDERLY IS THE GRACE OF
WHITE HAIR.' AND IT [ALSO] SAYS:[43]
'GRANDCHILDREN ARE THE CROWN OF THE AGED,
AND THE GLORY OF CHILDREN ARE THEIR FATHERS;'
AND ALSO:[44] 'THE MOON SHALL BE ABASHED AND THE
SUN PUT TO SHAME WHEN THE L-RD OF HOSTS WILL
REIGN ON MOUNT ZION AND IN JERUSALEM, AND
HONOR SHALL BE BEFORE HIS ELDERS.'"

RABBI SHIMON BEN MENASYA SAID: "THESE SEVEN
QUALITIES WHICH THE SAGES ENUMERATED [AS
PLEASING FOR] THE RIGHTEOUS WERE ALL REALIZED
IN REBBI [RABBI YEHUDAH HANASI] AND IN HIS
SONS."

BEAUTY — Beauty serves as a virtue only with regard to a person's relations with others; an attractive person influences others more easily. In a like manner, the other qualities mentioned affect primarily the interaction between a righteous man and his environment, and his efforts to sanctify G-d's name by living life in a manner which others will desire to emulate.[45]

Significantly, this teaching was authored by Rabbi Shimon ben Yochai. Although "Torah study was his occupation," and he sought no worldly calling, he recognized the importance of spreading appreciation of the Torah's wisdom throughout the world.

(Sichos Shabbos Parshas Bamidbar, 5740)

OLD AGE, THE GRACE OF WHITE HAIR — In Hebrew, the terms זקנה, translated as "old age," and שיבה, rendered as "the grace of white hair," are not synonymous. זקנה is

---

43 . *Ibid.* 17:6.
44 . *Yeshayahu* 24:23.
45 . See *Yoma* 86a, *Rambam, Mishneh Torah, Hilchos Yesodei HaTorah*, the conclusion of chapter 5.

associated with the Hebrew words זה שקנה חכמה, which mean "he who acquired wisdom."[46] This refers to knowledge gained from texts and teachers. שיבה refers to the serene, tranquil perspective granted only by the many experiences undergone in a long life.

(Ibid.)

CHILDREN — In an extended sense, the term "children" refers to one's students[47] — in many ways the ultimate influence on one's environment. For through students (who themselves become teachers), the truths one shares become ingrained both in the present and in the future.

(Ibid.)

THESE SEVEN QUALITIES... WERE ALL REALIZED — Certain of these qualities are contradictory in nature: e.g., physical strength and wisdom, for "the Torah drains a person's strength,"[48] or wisdom and wealth, as it is written,[49] "The wise will not have bread."

Nevertheless, these qualities all stem from the influence of the Torah, and the Torah is one with G-d. Since in His infinity He is capable of combining opposites, it is possible for these contrasting thrusts to be realized in a single righteous individual.

(Sichos Shabbos Parshas Balak, 5728)

Alternatively, it can be explained that these qualities present challenges to a person in his divine service. For example, beauty can stir a person's bodily appetites.[50] Wealth also presents obstacles, as reflected by the verse,[51] "Do not grant me

---

46 . *Kiddushin* 32b.
47 . *Sifri* (and *Rashi*) on *Devarim* 6:7.
48 . *Sanhedrin* 26b.
49 . *Koheles* 9:11.
50 . See *Nedarim* 9b.
51 . *Mishlei* 30:8.

position or wealth." And with regard to honor, our Sages taught:[52] "Envy, lust and honor drive a person from this world."

But despite the challenges, these qualities are granted to righteous men, and a righteous man may not forego them. For they are "pleasing to the world," facilitating the spread of goodness.

(Sichos Shabbos Parshas Nitzavim-Vayeilech, 5735)

IN REBBI [RABBI YEHUDAH HANASI] AND IN HIS SONS — One might think that these qualities could only be manifest in a person of exalted standing. Therefore the *beraisa:*

a) mentions Rebbi only as an example. Surely, there were righteous men before Rebbi who possessed these virtues. By mentioning Rebbi, the *beraisa* (which was compiled in his era), emphasizes that the manifestation of these traits could be realized in any — and every — generation.

b) mentions also Rebbi's sons, to include individuals who had not reached his level.

Moreover, the mention of Rebbe's sons also highlights how the teachings of the *beraisa* can relate to individuals in later generations. For, as mentioned above, one's students are also referred to as one's children. By studying Rebbi's work — the *Mishnah* which he compiled — each of us can become one of Rebbi's "children," and acquire the virtues mentioned in this teaching.

(Ibid., Sichos Motzoei Shabbos Parshas Nitzavim, 5738)

ט אָמַר רַבִּי יוֹסֵי בֶּן קִסְמָא: פַּעַם אַחַת הָיִיתִי מְהַלֵּךְ בַּדֶּרֶךְ, וּפָגַע בִּי אָדָם אֶחָד. וְנָתַן לִי שָׁלוֹם, וְהֶחֱזַרְתִּי לוֹ שָׁלוֹם, אָמַר לִי רַבִּי, מֵאֵיזֶה מָקוֹם אָתָּה, אָמַרְתִּי לוֹ מֵעִיר גְּדוֹלָה שֶׁל חֲכָמִים וְשֶׁל סוֹפְרִים אָנִי,

---

52 . *Pirkei Avos* 4:21.

אָמַר לִי: רַבִּי, רְצוֹנְךָ שֶׁתָּדוּר עִמָּנוּ בִּמְקוֹמֵנוּ, וַאֲנִי אֶתֵּן לָךְ אֶלֶף
אֲלָפִים דִּנְרֵי זָהָב וַאֲבָנִים טוֹבוֹת וּמַרְגָּלִיּוֹת, אָמַרְתִּי לוֹ: אִם אַתָּה
נוֹתֵן לִי כָּל כֶּסֶף וְזָהָב וַאֲבָנִים טוֹבוֹת וּמַרְגָּלִיּוֹת שֶׁבָּעוֹלָם, אֵינִי דָר
אֶלָּא בִּמְקוֹם תּוֹרָה, וְכֵן כָּתוּב בְּסֵפֶר תְּהִלִּים עַל יְדֵי דָוִד מֶלֶךְ
יִשְׂרָאֵל: טוֹב לִי תּוֹרַת פִּיךָ, מֵאַלְפֵי זָהָב וָכָסֶף. וְלֹא עוֹד, אֶלָּא
שֶׁבִּשְׁעַת פְּטִירָתוֹ שֶׁל אָדָם, אֵין מְלַוִּין לוֹ לְאָדָם לֹא כֶסֶף וְלֹא זָהָב
וְלֹא אֲבָנִים טוֹבוֹת וּמַרְגָּלִיּוֹת, אֶלָּא תּוֹרָה וּמַעֲשִׂים טוֹבִים בִּלְבָד,
שֶׁנֶּאֱמַר: בְּהִתְהַלֶּכְךָ תַּנְחֶה אֹתָךְ, בְּשָׁכְבְּךָ תִּשְׁמֹר עָלֶיךָ, וַהֲקִיצוֹתָ
הִיא תְשִׂיחֶךָ. בְּהִתְהַלֶּכְךָ תַּנְחֶה אֹתָךְ, בָּעוֹלָם הַזֶּה. בְּשָׁכְבְּךָ תִּשְׁמֹר
עָלֶיךָ, בַּקֶּבֶר. וַהֲקִיצוֹתָ הִיא תְשִׂיחֶךָ, לָעוֹלָם הַבָּא. וְאוֹמֵר: לִי הַכֶּסֶף
וְלִי הַזָּהָב נְאֻם י-י צְבָאוֹת.

9. RABBI YOSSE BEN KISMA SAID: "ONCE I WAS WALKING ON THE ROAD WHEN A CERTAIN MAN MET ME. HE GREETED ME, 'SHALOM,' AND I RETURNED HIS GREETING, 'SHALOM.'

"HE SAID TO ME, 'RABBI, FROM WHAT PLACE ARE YOU?'

"I SAID TO HIM, 'I AM FROM A GREAT CITY OF SCHOLARS AND SAGES.'

"HE SAID TO ME, 'RABBI, IF YOU WOULD BE WILLING TO LIVE WITH US IN OUR PLACE, I WOULD GIVE YOU A MILLION GOLDEN DINARS, PRECIOUS STONES AND PEARLS.'

"I REPLIED, 'EVEN IF YOU WERE TO GIVE ME ALL THE SILVER AND GOLD, PRECIOUS STONES, AND PEARLS IN THE WORLD, I WOULD DWELL NOWHERE BUT IN A PLACE OF TORAH.'"

AND SO IT IS WRITTEN IN THE BOOK OF *TEHILLIM* BY DAVID, KING OF ISRAEL:[53] "THE TORAH OF YOUR MOUTH IS MORE PRECIOUS TO ME THAN THOUSANDS OF GOLD AND SILVER [PIECES]." FURTHERMORE, AT A TIME OF A MAN'S PASSING FROM THIS WORLD,

---

53 . *Tehillim* 119:72.

NEITHER SILVER NOR GOLD NOR PRECIOUS STONES NOR PEARLS ACCOMPANY HIM, BUT ONLY TORAH [KNOWLEDGE] AND GOOD DEEDS, AS IT IS STATED:[54] "WHEN YOU WALK, IT [THE TORAH] SHALL GUIDE YOU; WHEN YOU LIE DOWN, IT SHALL WATCH OVER YOU; AND WHEN YOU AWAKE, IT SHALL SPEAK FOR YOU."

[THIS CAN BE INTERPRETED:] "WHEN YOU WALK, IT SHALL GUIDE YOU" IN THIS WORLD; "WHEN YOU LIE DOWN, IT SHALL WATCH OVER YOU" IN THE GRAVE; "AND WHEN YOU AWAKE, IT SHALL SPEAK FOR YOU" IN THE WORLD TO COME.

AND IT [ALSO] SAYS:[55] "MINE IS THE SILVER, AND MINE IS THE GOLD, SAYS THE L-RD OF HOSTS."

ONCE I WAS WALKING ON THE ROAD WHEN A CERTAIN MAN MET ME — The Hebrew word used for "met," פגע, also means "harmed." The entire encounter was harmful for Rabbi Yosse. As reflected by his answer, Rabbi Yosse's divine service centered on utter devotion to the study of Torah. Involvement with any other matter, even temporarily, would obstruct this thrust. For this reason,...

HE GREETED ME, "SHALOM," AND I RETURNED HIS GREETING, "SHALOM" — Although it is proper for a person to be the first to greet another,[56] Rabbi Yosse attempted to shy away from this encounter by not offering a greeting. He realized that this person would interfere with his concentration on Torah, and therefore tried to avoid him. Only after the other person greeted him did he return the salutation.

Alternatively, it can be explained that Rabbi Yosse was absorbed in reviewing his Torah studies, and did not at first

---

54 . *Mishlei* 6:22. V. *Rashi, loc. cit.*
55 . *Chaggai* 2:8.
56 . *Pirkei Avos* 4:15; *Berachos* 17a.

notice the presence of the other person. It was precisely this intense concentration which aroused the interest of the stranger, for it showed that Rabbi Yosse was a sage of sufficient caliber to lift the quality of Torah life in the stranger's community.

For this reason, he invited Rabbi Yosse to serve in his town, and promised him...

A MILLION GOLDEN DINARS, PRECIOUS STONES AND PEARLS — The offer was made so that Rabbi Yosse would not have to worry about his livelihood, and would be able to devote his attention entirely to elevating the spiritual level of the community. Alternatively, this wealth would enable Rabbi Yosse to give *tzedakah* generously.

Nevertheless, Rabbi Yosse refused the offer, replying...

EVEN IF YOU WERE TO GIVE ME ALL THE SILVER AND GOLD, PRECIOUS STONES AND PEARLS IN THE WORLD — Even if his circumstances allowed him to fulfill the *mitzvah* of *tzedakah* in the most complete way possible, and thus reach the pinnacle in the service of refining the world, Rabbi Yosse replied...

I WOULD DWELL NOWHERE BUT IN A PLACE OF TORAH — The wording he chose — "Even if you were to give me," and "I would dwell" — implies that the offer was not in itself improper, and might have been suitable for another individual. This approach to divine service was, however, inappropriate for Rabbi Yosse, for his efforts were to be directed solely to Torah study.

(Sichos Shabbos Parshas Bamidbar, 5734; Parshas Pinchas, 5741)

י חֲמִשָּׁה קִנְיָנִים קָנָה הַקָּדוֹשׁ בָּרוּךְ הוּא בְּעוֹלָמוֹ, וְאֵלוּ הֵן: תּוֹרָה,
קִנְיָן אֶחָד. שָׁמַיִם וָאָרֶץ, קִנְיָן אֶחָד. אַבְרָהָם קִנְיָן אֶחָד. יִשְׂרָאֵל קִנְיָן
אֶחָד. בֵּית הַמִּקְדָּשׁ, קִנְיָן אֶחָד. תּוֹרָה מִנַּיִן, דִּכְתִיב: י-י קָנָנִי רֵאשִׁית
דַּרְכּוֹ, קֶדֶם מִפְעָלָיו מֵאָז. שָׁמַיִם וָאָרֶץ מִנַּיִן, דִּכְתִיב: כֹּה אָמַר י-י
הַשָּׁמַיִם כִּסְאִי וְהָאָרֶץ הֲדֹם רַגְלָי, אֵי זֶה בַיִת אֲשֶׁר תִּבְנוּ לִי וְאֵיזֶה
מָקוֹם מְנוּחָתִי, וְאוֹמֵר: מָה רַבּוּ מַעֲשֶׂיךָ י-י, כֻּלָּם בְּחָכְמָה עָשִׂיתָ,
מָלְאָה הָאָרֶץ קִנְיָנֶךָ. אַבְרָהָם מִנַּיִן, דִּכְתִיב: וַיְבָרְכֵהוּ וַיֹּאמַר: בָּרוּךְ
אַבְרָם לְאֵ-ל עֶלְיוֹן, קֹנֵה שָׁמַיִם וָאָרֶץ. יִשְׂרָאֵל מִנַּיִן, דִּכְתִיב: עַד
יַעֲבֹר עַמְּךָ י-י, עַד יַעֲבֹר עַם זוּ קָנִיתָ. וְאוֹמֵר: לִקְדוֹשִׁים אֲשֶׁר בָּאָרֶץ
הֵמָּה, וְאַדִּירֵי כָּל חֶפְצִי בָם. בֵּית הַמִּקְדָּשׁ, מִנַּיִן, דִּכְתִיב: מָכוֹן
לְשִׁבְתְּךָ פָּעַלְתָּ י-י, מִקְדָּשׁ אֲדֹנָי כּוֹנְנוּ יָדֶיךָ. וְאוֹמֵר: וַיְבִיאֵם אֶל
גְּבוּל קָדְשׁוֹ, הַר זֶה קָנְתָה יְמִינוֹ.

10.

FIVE POSSESSIONS DID THE HOLY ONE,
BLESSED BE HE, MAKE HIS VERY OWN IN HIS
WORLD. THE TORAH IS ONE POSSESSION; HEAVEN
AND EARTH ARE ONE POSSESSION; AVRAHAM IS ONE
POSSESSION; THE NATION ISRAEL IS ONE POSSESSION;
THE *BEIS HAMIKDASH* IS ONE POSSESSION.

FROM WHERE DO WE KNOW THIS CONCERNING THE
TORAH? SINCE IT IS WRITTEN: "THE L-RD MADE ME
[THE TORAH] HIS POSSESSION PRIOR TO CREATION,
BEFORE HIS WORKS IN TIME OF YORE."[57]

FROM WHERE DO WE KNOW THIS CONCERNING
HEAVEN AND EARTH? SINCE IT IS WRITTEN:[58] "THUS
SAYS THE L-RD: 'THE HEAVEN IS MY THRONE, AND
THE EARTH IS MY FOOTSTOOL; WHAT HOUSE [THEN]
CAN YOU BUILD FOR ME AND WHERE IS THE PLACE OF
MY REST?'" AND IT [ALSO] SAYS:[59] "HOW MANIFOLD
ARE YOUR WORKS, O L-RD! YOU HAVE MADE THEM
ALL WITH WISDOM; THE EARTH IS FULL OF YOUR
POSSESSIONS."

---

57 . *Mishlei* 8:22.
58 . *Yeshayahu* 66:1.
59 . *Tehillim* 104:24.

FROM WHERE DO WE KNOW THIS CONCERNING AVRAHAM? SINCE IT IS WRITTEN:[60] "AND HE BLESSED HIM AND SAID: 'BLESSED BE AVRAHAM BY G-D MOST HIGH, POSSESSOR OF HEAVEN AND EARTH.'"

FROM WHERE DO WE KNOW THIS CONCERNING THE PEOPLE ISRAEL? SINCE IT IS WRITTEN:[61] "UNTIL YOUR PEOPLE PASS OVER, O L-RD, UNTIL THIS PEOPLE YOU HAVE ACQUIRED PASS OVER," AND IT [ALSO] SAYS:[62] "TO THE HOLY PEOPLE WHO ARE IN THE LAND, AND THE NOBLE ONES IN THEM, IS ALL MY DESIRE."

FROM WHERE DO WE KNOW THIS CONCERNING THE *BEIS HAMIKDASH*? SINCE IT IS WRITTEN:[63] "THE PLACE WHICH YOU, O L-RD, HAVE MADE FOR YOUR ABODE; THE SANCTUARY WHICH YOUR HANDS, O L-RD, HAVE ESTABLISHED," AND IT [ALSO] SAYS:[64] "AND HE BROUGHT THEM TO THE PLACE OF HIS HOLINESS, THE MOUNTAIN WHICH HIS RIGHT HAND HAS ACQUIRED."

FIVE — The framework of spiritual existence consists of four different realms. These are limited frameworks of existence which do not reveal G-d entirely. The number five points to an even higher domain, where infinite G-dly light is revealed without definition.[65] G-d desired to make all these realms...

---

60. *Bereishis* 14:19.
61. *Shmos* 15:126.
62. *Tehillim* 16:3.
63. *Shmos* 15:17.
64. *Tehillim* 78:54.
65. See *Or HaTorah, Bamidbar*, p. 210. [In other sources, the number five is understood as referring to a level which exists in complete connection to G-d's essence.]

HIS VERY OWN — to draw down His essential light within them, revealing how all existence is...

HIS WORLD — at one with Him. This concept is also indicated by the expression...

IS ONE POSSESSION — which is used in all five instances, i.e., all these five entities express G-d's oneness.

Although all five entities mentioned by the *beraisa* express G-d's oneness, in this context the Torah is the most fundamental. (And therefore this *beraisa* is included in the chapter which focuses on the greatness of Torah.) For the Torah is the medium which, though totally at one with G-d, extends itself into material reality, making it possible that this world can become a dwelling for Him.

(Sichos Shabbos Parshas Re'eh, 5737)

FIVE POSSESSIONS DID THE HOLY ONE, BLESSED BE HE, MAKE HIS VERY OWN — The Hebrew word קִנְיָן, translated as "possession" also implies the means of acquisition through which an entity is transferred from one person's ownership to another's. The five things mentioned are all mediums which enable G-d's ownership of all existence to become openly manifest. This concept is also emphasized by the expression "in His world," which highlights the ultimate intent — that it become clear that our world is His world, united with Him. This intent is also reflected in the expression used with regard to each of these five possessions — "one possession" — indicating that the purpose of each is to express G-d's oneness throughout the world.

(Ibid.)

SINCE IT IS WRITTEN: "UNTIL YOUR PEOPLE PASS OVER, O L-RD, UNTIL THIS PEOPLE YOU

ACQUIRED PASS OVER;" AND IT [ALSO] SAYS: "TO THE HOLY PEOPLE WHO ARE IN THE LAND, AND THE NOBLE ONES IN THEM, IS ALL MY DELIGHT" — The *beraisa* mentions two prooftexts with regard to the Jewish people. The first explicitly states that the Jews have been acquired by G-d, but describes the Jews when they lived in the desert and were being cared for overtly by G-d's miraculous providence.

Since, as explained above, the purpose of the *beraisa* is to highlight how each of these possessions establishes oneness in the world at large, a second prooftext is necessary. The latter verse, although it does not emphasize G-d's ownership of the Jews as clearly, describes them as they function "in the land" — within the natural order of day-to-day existence.

(Sichos Shabbos Parshas Balak, 5737)

יא כָּל מַה שֶּׁבָּרָא הַקָּדוֹשׁ בָּרוּךְ הוּא בְּעוֹלָמוֹ, לֹא בְרָאוֹ אֶלָּא לִכְבוֹדוֹ, שֶׁנֶּאֱמַר: כֹּל הַנִּקְרָא בִשְׁמִי וְלִכְבוֹדִי, בְּרָאתִיו יְצַרְתִּיו אַף עֲשִׂיתִיו. וְאוֹמֵר: יְ-י יִמְלֹךְ לְעֹלָם וָעֶד:

11. ALL THAT THE HOLY ONE, BLESSED BE HE, CREATED IN HIS WORLD, HE CREATED SOLELY FOR HIS GLORY, AS IT IS STATED:[66] "ALL THAT IS CALLED BY MY NAME — INDEED, IT IS FOR MY GLORY THAT I HAVE CREATED IT, FORMED IT, AND MADE IT;" AND IT SAYS:[67] "THE L-RD SHALL REIGN FOREVER AND EVER."

ALL... CREATED IN HIS WORLD — G-dliness is seldom openly revealed in our world. Nevertheless, this lack of

---

66 . *Yeshayahu* 43:7.
67 . *Shmos* 15:18.

manifestation does not change the reality. Everything, even those entities which appear totally secular in nature...

HE CREATED SOLELY FOR HIS GLORY — Moreover, to express G-dliness is not merely one of the purposes served by these entities; it is the *sole reason* for their existence.

Therefore a person should not shy away from worldly involvement. On the contrary, in whatever he does and wherever he finds himself, he should seek to find a means of honoring G-d. For example, new developments in technology and communications need not be ignored, or used only for commercial enterprise. The real purpose of their existence is that they be employed to express G-d's honor.

(Sichos Shabbos Parshas Nitzavim, 5728; Parshas Balak, 5741)

"ALL THAT IS CALLED BY MY NAME... I HAVE CREATED IT, FORMED IT, AND MADE IT" — This prooftext alludes to the four spiritual worlds: *Atzilus, Beriah, Yetzirah,* and *Asiyah.* "All that is called by My Name" refers to the world of *Atzilus,* for this is the realm of oneness, appropriately called by G-d's name. The phrases "I have created it, formed it, and made it" refer to the worlds of *Beriah, Yetzirah* and *Asiyah* as reflected by the Hebrew terms (בראתיו, יצרתיו, עשיתיו).

All existence, both spiritual and material, shares the same purpose: to express G-d's praise.

This teaching serves as an appropriate conclusion for *Pirkei Avos* — a work intended to teach *mili dechassidusa* — pious conduct beyond the measure of the law. When a person realizes that everything in this world and, as alluded to in the prooftext, also in the spiritual worlds, exists only to express G-d's praise, he will be more motivated to accept his role in this undertaking, and reflect G-d's honor through his pious conduct.

(Sichos Shabbos Parshas Nitzavim, 5728)

"THE L-RD SHALL REIGN FOREVER AND EVER" —
This phrase refers to the Era of the Redemption. This is the
ultimate goal of our pious conduct, to usher in the era in which
G-d's glory will be revealed in the most consummate manner.

(Sichos Shabbos Parshas Pinchas, 5744)

רַבִּי חֲנַנְיָה בֶּן עֲקַשְׁיָא אוֹמֵר, רָצָה הַקָּדוֹשׁ בָּרוּךְ הוּא לְזַכּוֹת אֶת
יִשְׂרָאֵל, לְפִיכָךְ הִרְבָּה לָהֶם תּוֹרָה וּמִצְוֹת, שֶׁנֶּאֱמַר: י-י חָפֵץ לְמַעַן
צִדְקוֹ יַגְדִּיל תּוֹרָה וְיַאְדִּיר:

R ABBI CHANANYA BEN AKASHYA SAID:[1] "THE
HOLY ONE, BLESSED BE HE, WISHED TO MAKE
THE PEOPLE OF ISRAEL MERITORIOUS; THEREFORE
HE GAVE THEM TORAH AND *MITZVOS* IN ABUNDANT
MEASURE, AS IT IS WRITTEN:[2] 'THE L-RD DESIRED,
FOR THE SAKE OF HIS [ISRAEL'S] RIGHTEOUSNESS, TO
MAKE THE TORAH GREAT AND GLORIOUS.'"

TO MAKE THE PEOPLE OF ISRAEL MERITORIOUS
— לזכות, translated as "to make meritorious," also means "to
refine." The goal of the Torah and its *mitzvos* is to refine the
Jewish people. This intention is manifest in *Pirkei Avos*, which
teaches us to lift our ethical conduct above the limits of human
wisdom and cultivate it according to G-d's desire.

(Likkutei Sichos, Vol. XVII, p. 416)

1. *Makkos* 23b.
2. *Yeshayahu* 42:21.

FOUNDERS OF CHASSIDISM & LEADERS OF CHABAD LUBAVITCH

Baal Shem Tov (בעל שם טוב; lit., "Master of the Good Name"): R. Yisrael ben R. Eliezer (1698-1760), founder of Chassidism.

The Maggid of Mezritch (lit., "the preacher of Mezritch"): R. Dov Ber (d. 1772), disciple of the Baal Shem Tov, and mentor of the Alter Rebbe.

The Alter Rebbe (דער אלטער רבי; lit., "the Old Rebbe"; Yid.): R. Shneur Zalman of Liadi (1745-1812), also known as "the Rav" and as *Baal HaTanya;* founder of the *Chabad*-Lubavitch trend within the chassidic movement; disciple of the Maggid of Mezritch, and father of the Mitteler Rebbe.

The Mitteler Rebbe (דער מיטעלער רבי; lit., "the Middle Rebbe"; Yid.): R. Dov Ber of Lubavitch (1773-1827), son and successor of the Alter Rebbe, and uncle and father-in-law of the *Tzemach Tzedek.*

The *Tzemach Tzedek* (צמח צדק): R. Menachem Mendel Schneersohn (1789-1866), the third Lubavitcher Rebbe; known by the title of his halachic responsa as "the *Tzemach Tzedek*"; nephew and son-in-law of the Mitteler Rebbe, and father of the Rebbe Maharash.

The Rebbe Maharash (מהר"ש; acronym for *Moreinu* ("our teacher") *HaRav Shmuel*): R. Shmuel Schneersohn of Lubavitch (1834-1882), the fourth Lubavitcher Rebbe; youngest son of the *Tzemach Tzedek*, and father of the Rebbe Rashab.

The Rebbe Rashab (רש"ב; acronym for Rabbi Shalom Ber): R. Shalom Dov Ber Schneersohn of Lubavitch (1860-1920), the fifth Lubavitcher Rebbe; second son of the Rebbe Maharash, and father of the Rebbe Rayatz.

The Rebbe Rayatz (ריי"צ; acronym for Rabbi Yosef Yitzchak), also known (in Yiddish) as *"der frierdiker* Rebbe" (i.e., "the Previous Rebbe"): R. Yosef Yitzchak Schneersohn (1880-1950), the sixth Lubavitcher Rebbe; only son of the Rebbe Rashab, and father-in-law of the Rebbe שליט"א.

The Rebbe *Shlita*: Rabbi Menachem Mendel Schneerson (b. 1902, שליט"א), the seventh Lubavitcher Rebbe; eldest son of the saintly Kabbalist, Rabbi Levi Yitzchak, *rav* of Yekaterinoslav; fifth in direct paternal line from the *Tzemach Tzedek;* son-in-law of the Rebbe Rayatz.

GLOSSARY

GLOSSARY

ahavas yisrael (lit., the love of Israel): the love for one's fellow Jews

achdus Yisrael (lit., the unity of Israel)

Amalek: The first nation to attack the Jewish people after the exodus from Egypt *(Shmos,* ch. 17*);* subsequently, as well, the arch-enemy of our people

Asiyah, the World of (lit., "the World of Action, or Making"): the lowest of the four spiritual worlds, the realm of spiritual existence which relates directly to our material world

atik, atik yomin (lit., "ancient days"): an elevated spiritual level that is in absolute oneness with G-d's essence

Atzilus, the World of (lit., "the World of Emanation"): the highest of the four spiritual worlds

baal teshuvah (lit. "master of return"; pl. *baalei teshuvah*): a person who turns to G-d in repentance

Beis HaMikdash: The Temple in Jerusalem

Beraisa, pl. *beraisos:* A body of teachings authored during the same period as the **Mishnah,* but not included in that text; when not capitalized, the term refers to a single teaching of this type

Beriah, the World of (lit., "the World of Creation"): the second (in descending order) of the four spiritual worlds

Binah (lit., "understanding"): the second of the Ten **Sefiros,* or divine emanations; the second stage of the intellectual process, the power that develops abstract conception, giving it breadth and depth

bittul: self-nullification, a commitment to G-d and divine service that transcends self-concern

chassid: a pious, kind-hearted person, whose commitment extends beyond the requirement of the law

chinuch: education

Eretz Yisrael (lit., the land of Israel)

Gan Eden (lit., the Garden of Eden): the place in which the narrative of Adam and Eve occurred, borrowed to refer to the spiritual realm of souls in the afterlife

Gemara: one of the portions of the Talmud; the elucidation of the *Mishnah,* and the discussion of related concepts by the Sages

halachah: the body of Jewish Law; alternatively a single law

Kabbalah (lit., "received tradition"): the Jewish mystical tradition

kabbalas ol (lit., "the acceptance of [G-d's] yoke"): an unswerving, selfless commitment to carrying out the will of G-d

Lashon HaKodesh (lit., "the Holy Tongue"): Biblical Hebrew

Mashiach: the Messiah

mashpia (lit., "source of influence"): one who plays an active role in the spiritual development of a person or his environment

Men of the Great Assembly: The body of 120 Sages convened by Ezra at the beginning of the Second Temple Era which canonized the Bible, structured the prayer service, and presided over the renewal of Jewish practice in *Eretz Yisrael* after the return from the Babylonian exile

mezuzah (pl., *mezuzos*): the parchment scroll affixed to the doorpost, and containing the first two paragraphs of *Shema (Devarim* 6:-9 and 11:13-21*)*

Midrash: the classical collection of the Sages' homiletical teachings on the Bible

mikveh: a ritual bath

mili dechassidusa: pious conduct beyond the measure of the law

Mishlei: The Book of Proverbs

Mishnah: the first compilation of the Oral Law authored by Rabbi Yehudah HaNasi (approx. 150 C.E.); the germinal statements of law elucidated by the *Gemara,* together with which they constitute the *Talmud;* when not capitalized, a single statement of law from this work

mitzvah (lit., "commandment; pl., *mitzvos*): one of the 613 Commandments; in a larger sense, any religious obligation

Nasi: (a) in Talmudic times, the head of the *Sanhedrin,* the highest Jewish court; (b) in later generations, the civil and/or spiritual head of the Jewish community at large

Pirkei Avos: The Ethics of Our Fathers; the Talmudic tractate which focuses on ethics

pnimiyus HaTorah (lit., "the inner dimension of [the Torah]"): the mystical dimension of Torah study

pushkah: charity box

Rebbe (lit., "my teacher [or master]"): saintly Torah leader who serves as spiritual guide to a following of chassidim

sefirah, pl. *Sefiros:* the Kabbalistic term for the attributes of G-dliness which serve as a medium between His infinite light and our limited framework of reference

Shabbos: the Sabbath

Shema: the fundamental Jewish prayer which we are obligated to recite each day, in the evening and in the morning

siddur: a prayer book

Talmud: the basic compendium of Jewish law, thought, and Biblical commentary, comprising **Mishnah* and **Gemara;* when unspecified refers to the *Talmud Bavli,* the edition developed in Babylonia, and edited at end of the fifth century C.E.; the *Talmud Yerushalmi* is the edition compiled in **Eretz Yisrael* at end of the fourth century C.E.

Tanach: The Bible

Tanya: the classic text of *Chabad* chassidic thought authored by the Alter Rebbe

tefillin: small, black leather boxes each containing four Biblical passages which the Torah commands adult males to wear daily

teshuvah (lit., "return [to G-d]"): repentance

tzaddik: righteous man

tzedakah: charity

World to Come: a) the afterlife; b) the Era of the Resurrection of the Dead

yetzer hora: the evil inclination

Yetzirah, the World of (lit., "the World of Formation"): the third (in descending order) of the four spiritual worlds

yiras shomayim: the fear of Heaven

Zohar (lit., "radiance"): the title of the classic mystical work embodying the teachings of the *Kabbalah

———

לזכות

הוו״ח הרה״ת ר׳ **משה אהרן צבי בן מרים** שיחי׳
וזוגתו מרת **העניא רבקה רות** בת **צפורה** שתחי׳
ובנם **שלום אליעזר** שיחי׳
וייס
שערמאן אוקס, קאליפורניא

שהקב״ה ימלא כל משאלות לבבם לטובה בגו״ר

♦

Dedicated by

Rabbi Moshe and Ruty שיחיו Weiss

Sherman Oaks, California

May the Almighty fulfill their hearts' desires
both materially and spiritually